P9-AZX-327

Remembering Poets

Also by Donald Hall

Poetry

Exiles and Marriages
The Dark Houses
A Roof of Tiger Lilies
The Alligator Bride
The Yellow Room
The Town of Hill
A Blue Wing Tilts at the Edge of the Sea

Prose

String Too Short to Be Saved
Henry Moore
Writing Well
Dock Ellis: In the Country of Baseball
Goatfoot Milkfoot Twinbird

REMEMBERING POETS

Reminiscences and Opinions

Dylan Thomas, Robert Frost, T. S. Eliot, Ezra Pound

by Donald Hall

HARPER & ROW, PUBLISHERS
New York, Hagerstown, San Francisco, London

Portions of this work originally appeared in *Commentary*.

Copyright acknowledgments appear on page 253.

 For information address Harper & Row, Publishers, Inc., 10 East 53rd Street, New York, N.Y. 10022. Published simultaneously in Canada by Fitzhenry & Whiteside Limited, Toronto.

FIRST EDITION

Designed by Gloria Adelson

Library of Congress Cataloging in Publication Data

Hall, Donald, 1928–
Remembering poets.
Includes index.
1. Hall, Donald, 1928– —Friends and associates.
2. Poets, American—20th century—Biography.
I. Title.
PS3515.A3152Z526 818′.03 76-47266
ISBN 0-06-011723-0

78 79 80 81 82 10 9 8 7 6 5 4 3 2 1

To Charles Christensen

Contents

We Poets in our youth begin in gladness;
But thereof come in the end despondency and madness.

—William Wordsworth,
"Resolution and Independence"

We work in the dark—we do what we can—we give what we have. Our doubt is our passion and our passion is our task. The rest is the madness of art.

—Henry James, "The Middle Years"

Introduction

There is a minor tradition in literature, or at the edges of literature, that occasionally finds room for a book like this one. The tradition derives from curiosity about people we admire. I do not speak of literary biography, a scholar's task. I speak of the *genre* of literary gossip, reminiscences by friends and acquaintances of authors. In the last hundred years, in both England and America, the reading public has shown continual appetite for such books; a neighbor of E. A. Robinson's published *Next Door to a Poet;* William Dean Howells recollected *Literary Friends and Acquaintances;* Charles J. Woodberry assembled *Talks with Ralph Waldo Emerson;* Mark A. de Wolfe Howe edited *Memories of a Hostess,* drawn chiefly from the diaries of Mrs. James T. Fields.

An early example of the *genre* is a small triumph of literature—William Hazlitt's essay, "My First Acquaintance with Poets." A piece of autobiography, it begins, "My father was a Dissenting minister at Wem, in Shropshire, and in the year 1798. . . ." Hazlitt turned twenty that year; he reminisces twenty-five years later about Coleridge's face:

> His forehead was broad and high, light as if built of ivory, with large projecting eyebrows, and his eyes rolling beneath them, like a sea with darkened luster. . . . His mouth was gross, voluptuous, open,

eloquent; his chin good-humored and round; but his nose, the rudder of his face, the index of the will, was small, feeble, nothing—like what he has done.

I love Hazlitt for his willingness to judge, for his lack of timidity—and for his prose; he continues his excursion into Coleridge's nautical face—"as if Columbus had launched his adventurous course for the New World in a scallop, without oars or compass."

Later, he describes a three weeks' visit to Coleridge during which Mr. Wordsworth put in an appearance. I find it wonderful to make the acquaintance of Wordsworth without white whiskers, wearing something besides the blue-bound covers of the Oxford Standard Authors: "He was quaintly dressed . . . in a brown fustian jacket and striped pantaloons." And:

There was a severe, worn pressure of thought around his temples, a fire in his eye, . . . an intense high narrow forehead, a Roman nose, cheeks furrowed by strong purpose and feeling, and a convulsive inclination to laughter about the mouth, a good deal at variance with the solemn, stately expression of the rest of his face.

Most, I like to hear Wordsworth's voice:

He sat down and talked very naturally and freely, with a mixture of clear, gushing accents in his voice, a deep guttural intonation, and a strong tincture of the northern *burr,* like crust on wine.

Coleridge and Wordsworth wrote poems, which are words in books, and which are not men; but Hazlitt lets me know that poems are written by people with small noses or Roman ones, voices that never stop talking or voices with northern *burrs.* If we love the poem, it is natural to be curious about the poet. Hazlitt felt curiosity, love—and later felt betrayed by these men as they grew older; I am grateful that he wrote his feelings and his recollections out.

When Ezra Pound wrote his memoir of Gaudier-Brzeska—the extraordinary sculptor, killed in the Great War at the age of twenty-three—he apologized:

In reading over what I have written, I find it full of conceit, or at least full of pronouns in the first person, and yet what do we, any of us, know of our friends and acquaintances save that on such and such a day we saw them, and that they did or said this, that or the other, to which words and acts we give witness.

If Pound felt apologetic about the letter "I" in connection with his dead young friend, then I should feel worse, to intrude my name on great poets whom I knew so little. Yet I am shameless, or nearly. This book records a portion of my education. Whether my own poems look worthy in retrospect is irrelevant: I grew up as a poet, for better or worse, among other poets. I took most of my poetic education from brothers and sisters. I took least from father-teachers; although they were intelligent and critical, it was dangerous to take help from them. But the grandfathers! One can accept the jewels of Asia from old hands.

Yet from none of these men, in conversation, did I learn a critical thing. It would have been improbable that they could tell me anything useful about my poems, if they had read them. Instead, they gave me the gift of their existence. Three of them were models of persistence in art, of endurance and courage; the fourth was a virtual suicide, a counterexample. Endurance is as admirable as energy.

Many poets have taken courage from grandfathers. Some have acknowledged the laying-on of hands. Robert Graves recalls how Swinburne met the infant Graves in a cradle, as if some magic moved from the diminutive elder to the poet in swaddling clothes. Of the poets here, Pound knew the grandfathers best. His attentions to the neglected old are legend, like his organized visit to Wilfrid Scawen Blunt. He wrote letters of homage to Thomas Hardy, whom he never met. And when Henry James died—Pound said in 1960, speaking of 1916—"one felt there was no one to ask about anything. Up to then one felt someone knew."

Many people have helped me with this book. Jane Kenyon helped me sort out my sentences. Grace McGorrian and Paula

Sharp explained a poem to me. John Peck talked with me about Pound. Harry Levin gave me permission to repeat an anecdote, and over many years—as my teacher and tutor—has taught me ten thousand things. I thank my former wife, Kirby Hall, for making suggestions about portions of this manuscript, and remembering things I had forgotten. Pam Croome, who once lived there, reminded me of details about the Boat House. The Houghton Library at Harvard allowed me access to papers I had donated. George Plimpton commissioned two interviews. James Laughlin has read my words on Pound, and has helped me by making corrections, and by arguing with assumptions. Donald Davie helped me avoid errors in connection with Pound and Eliot; Jac Tharpe and William Sutton helped in the same way with Frost, and Ralph Maud with Thomas. Lewis Hyde's essay on alcoholism in the *American Poetry Review* has contributed to my understanding, not only in connection with Dylan Thomas. I am always indebted to conversations with Robert and Carol Bly. Frances McCullough's enthusiasm encouraged me, and her criticism, together with Richard Ford's, helped me with my final revisions. Dorothy Foster and Sharon Giannotta and Lois Fierro typed manuscript with compassion and finesse.

I owe a different sort of debt to authors of various books. None of these poets has yet been subject of an adequate biography. Constantine Fitzgibbon's *The Life of Dylan Thomas* comes closest.* Several people have begun the story of Pound's life, and I am indebted to Noel Stock and to David Heymann. In the matter of Frost I am grateful to have his letters, and to have the memoir so gracefully written by Kathleen Morrison. I am less grateful for the biography by Lawrance Thompson, completed after his death by R. H. Winnick. Thompson is handicapped by resentment of someone larger than himself. He is not the first literary biographer who learned when young to bow and scrape before his subject, then took ven-

*Paul Ferris's biography of Thomas had not appeared when I wrote my pages about Thomas.

geance by "exposing" the writer after his death. The results are depressing. Nor is it enlightening to watch herdish book reviewers as they rush to deplore the cruelty and selfishness of Robert Frost, learned out of blunt-witted Thompson.

When Eliot died, he specified that there be no biography. Two old acquaintances thereupon wrote bad books about him; I understand that Mrs. Eliot now plans to commission an authorized biography. Eliot was lucky enough, in his own lifetime, to be subject of a critical book by Hugh Kenner, *The Invisible Poet.* Kenner is the best critic of modern literature. He is not a biographer, but neither is he paralyzed by fear of biographical heresy. In his critical writings appear anecdotes about his subjects, when behavior gives insight into the kind of men they were. Thus the invisible poet puts in an appearance, making fastidious choice of a cheese in his London club.

Although Ezra Pound lacks a thorough biography, he has been luckiest in his critics. There is first of all Kenner's magnum opus *The Pound Era,* in which Kenner writes about Eliot as well as Pound, and about Joyce and Wyndham Lewis and William Carlos Williams and other citizens of the era. Anecdote helps to fix Pound's tone and rhythm on the page. Donald Davie has written two excellent books on Ezra Pound. There are a dozen other books that have given me notions for which I am grateful—Michael Reck's, Mary de Rachewiltz's, Christine Brooke-Rose's, Harry Meacham's, George Decker's, Julien Cornell's, and others. Finally, Louis Simpson's *Three on the Tower*—adding Williams to Eliot and Pound—is a delight for being written in prose, as well as for shrewdness and intelligence.

Donald Hall

Wilmot, New Hampshire
April 1977

DYLAN THOMAS AND PUBLIC SUICIDE

1. Harvard

Everyone knew Dylan Thomas. I knew him only the way everyone did—in pubs, late in his short life, drinking, laughing, telling stories. He was the most gregarious man in the world, and took pleasure in talking with strangers, who were treated as friends if he liked them at all. His *real* friends—people from Swansea, or the first years in London, or wartime years—watched him perform with strangers and called him "Instant Dylan." I suppose that his gregariousness was another refuge from pain, the anesthesia of promiscuous acquaintance, like drink's anesthesia that slid toward death; what's more, I suppose that Dylan knew it all—laughter and death and public suicide.

I met him on March 1, 1950. I was a junior in college, and for some months had known that Dylan Thomas would come to read his poems. The fad or fashion for Thomas had not begun—this was his first reading tour of the United States—but I had heard about the quality of his reading. (Caedmon had not yet recorded him.) I had known his poetry for several years, first in an Oscar Williams anthology, then in a *Selected Writings* which New Directions brought out, edited by Jack Sweeney, who ran the Poetry Room at Harvard. I loved his poems. I hoped I might meet him. A few weeks before he was due to come, F. O. Matthiessen—literary critic and professor at Harvard—called us at the *Advocate,* the undergraduate literary magazine, to ask if we would like to throw a party for Thomas after the reading. It was kind of Matthiessen to offer to share the poet with undergraduates; at most colleges, the faculty eats the poet all by itself.

Thomas read in New Lecture Hall, at four o'clock. First he read poems by other poets: Hardy, W. H. Davies, Henry Reed, Yeats. We were spellbound—an audience determined not to be spellbound. Behind the lectern stood a small unsmiling figure, huge belly, pudgy face, nose like the bulb on a Klaxon horn, chinless, red-faced, pop-eyed, curly-haired, with an expression at once frightened and insolent. Out of this silly body rolled a voice like Jehovah's, or Ocean's, or Firmament's. R's rolled, vowels rose and fell—he had a range like Yma Sumac's—consonants thudded and crashed and leapt to their feet again. When he read Hardy I was astonished. I had never read Hardy's best poems. He spoke "The Naming of Parts" by Henry Reed, and the same author's parody of T. S. Eliot, "Chard Whitlow." When he read the Reed/Eliot, he parodied Eliot's accent, which he defined as Church-of-English, producing a Thomas/Reed/Eliot three-decker. He read several Yeats poems I loved; Yeats had been my favorite poet for two years, but early in 1950 the Yeats *Collected Poems* was still a 1933 edition; the posthumous *Last Poems* remained locked in the rare book room. Therefore, when Thomas read "News for the Delphic Oracle" it was news to us; when he read "Lapis Lazuli" it introduced us to the poem. The magnificent voice held the syllables out in the air:

> Their eyes mid many wrinkles, their eyes,
> Their ancient, glittering eyes, are gay.

I hovered five inches above my uncomfortable chair in New Lecture Hall, stunned by the beauty of poem and reading. Although I was later to meet him under different guises, I remember the first Dylan Thomas I saw: a small and disheveled figure bodying forth great poetry in great performance, an act of homage to poetry, an act of love for the magnificence of words.

When he had finished reading other poets he made a deprecating remark, which seemed perfunctory but was not, and read several of his own poems, ending with "Poem in October" spoken with force and sweetness. We applauded mightily. The little man on the platform nodded, nervous, and lit up a cigarette. I approached him, along with Sweeney and Matthiessen, to pick him up and take him to the *Advocate.* As I came near, I saw a janitor walk over to him, where he stood below the stage talking to students, and snarl at him, "Put out that cigarette. Can't you read?" He had already seemed diminished, but now he shrank like Alice; he pretended to stomp out the cigarette, looked sullen, but did not.

We drove the short distance to the *Advocate.* Someone mentioned his reading of "News for the Delphic Oracle" and he told us a story. His voice rose, mellifluous and unnatural, filling the small car like a blast from Aeolus; as I would understand later, he was intolerably uncomfortable, surrounded by academic politeness and deference. The story was about someone visiting Yeats in Ireland, not long before Yeats's death, when the old poet was making "News for the Delphic Oracle." The poem ends, ". . . nymphs and satyrs / Copulate in the foam." Yeats showed Dylan's friend the poem in a draft ending, "nymphs and satyrs / Fuck in the foam." Then he told us, "And I think it's a fine thing that Yeats changed it. Otherwise, it would only be known as a poem with the word 'fuck' in it. We're not intelligent enough for that." Yet all the while he told the story, I knew that he was telling it for effect. Harvard was not ready for "fuck" in 1950.

In a moment I heard the great voice open itself up again, like a bag of tricks: "Will there be anything to drink at this party?"

Matthiessen answered: "Why, yes. The boys usually have only martinis, but I'm sure they can get you some beer." Thomas had drunk beer all day.

"Oh, no," said Thomas. "Now that I've done my work, I can get down to the serious stuff." How well he said it. His accent parodied upper-class speech, but he made it obvious that he was *acting*. After a moment's delicate pause, he added in a whine—now doing a character long-suffering from deprivation—"Scotch will do for me."

We sent out for some Scotch, and it did for him. He roared and raved, he teetered and tottered. He would approach a young man, say, "There's a long street where I live, fucked every woman on it, fucked their mothers too," and then weave on, often to a young woman whom he would pretend to desire. Sometimes he was funny. Most of the time he wasn't. After a while I was annoyed; Dylan Thomas was an ass playing The Poet. I saw pretense; I saw premeditation, trying to look spontaneous; I saw nastiness: it was not from love of women that he suggested bed.

Everyone knows these stories—Dylan the Drunken Boor, Dylan the Roaring Boy. I will add only one to the world's store; it was typical—mildly funny, mildly cruel. There was at the party a young woman I will call Rachel. Rachel was eighteen years old, a Radcliffe freshman. Rachel had changed clothes in her boyfriend's room, because she wanted to wear her best dress unwrinkled to the party. Her best dress was low cut. Dylan approached her, as she stood next to her boyfriend, peered down her dress, put his hands on her waist, and rocked from side to side. Embarrassed, eighteen years old, naïve, Rachel asked him when he was going back to England. "Now," he boomed. "Immediately," he crooned. *"Now."*

"When did you get here?" she asked.

"This afternoon," he said. As he spoke or sang, he swung back and forth with her, and gazed into her eyes. "I will write sensual poems to you," he went on. "They will begin—" and he made a low, throaty whistle. "They will be the only poems in the language that begin—" and he gave the whistle again.

Blushing deeply, Rachel struggled to speak, telling him that she had liked his reading very, very much.

In low and velvet tones, looking deep into her blinking eyes, Dylan intoned, "Did you *wear*—that *dress*—to my reading?" Then he bent forward to make it obvious to everyone—spectators followed him around—that he looked down her dress; he exaggerated like a burlesque comedian. His rhetorical question brought Rachel nearly to tears. As she stumbled to answer his question, loath to confess the compromising truth, Dylan interrupted her to intone his curtain line, delivered with the sonority of a provincial Prospero, "I would rather—suckle those paps—than go back—to my old wife—in Wales." As the long diphthong of "Wales" slid into the final *z*, Dylan forgot his passion for Rachel, turned on his heel, and looked for someone new.

I went home and wrote about Dylan in a journal I kept; I did not like him. The next week or two I kept hearing more stories—how he had rolled on the floor at Matty's later in the evening, his shirt open and his belly showing; how Charlee Wilbur and Betty Eberhart had put him to bed, early the following morning, in the Faculty Club where he had a room; how he had drunk his way to Mt. Holyoke the next day, and what he said to the woman there who asked him about modern poetry.

2. London

Two years later, when I was studying at Oxford, I went to London to find Dylan Thomas. Two years had diminished my annoyance; I loved his poems more than ever, and in my own work I tried to achieve those sensuous textures. Besides, I was doing what I was told: the Oxford University Poetry Society, of which I was secretary, wanted Thomas to read his poems. We sold membership cards for fifty cents, out of which we bought sherry and dinner for visiting poets, and paid their train fares to Oxford. That's all we paid, and poets came from all over England to read for nothing at Oxford; generally, they charged us First Class. The secretary of OUPS did all the work, made arrangements with poets, reservations for dinner and hotel room, and held a sherry party in his own rooms. It was not onerous, and one was rewarded by becoming president of OUPS the following term.

From someone I heard that Dylan and Caitlin had left Wales for London, and were living in Camden Town not far from the Regents Park Zoo. Dylan was doing BBC work, I was told—as actor, as poet, as talker—and it was convenient to live in town. I wrote him letters at an address supplied. No answer. I decided to take a train up to London and look for him. So I arrived at Paddington at nine o'clock one morning and took the tube to Camden Town. I found the road I had written to; I found the number; I knocked on the door and was directed elsewhere: Yes, they had been living "out back" for a while, but now they had moved a few blocks away. I continued my search, and a few blocks away I found an African at the new address I had been given, who knew nothing of people named Thomas. I tried at the corner sweet shop; the old woman shook her head. I ran after the postman; there was no Dylan Thomas on his route.

By ten-thirty in the morning, I had exhausted my leads. I wondered if I could call Louis MacNeice at the BBC; I had met him briefly at my college. Shy about calling MacNeice, I decided to postpone the question with a pint of bitter. The hour of ten-thirty opened the pubs and made postponement attractive. Near the tube was a great nineteenth-century gin palace, which I entered when the landlord opened the doors. I stood near the porcelain beer engines, studying my Bass, when I felt a minor commotion at the level of my shoulder. I looked down and caught Dylan's face looking up—he was "above medium height, for Wales," as he liked to put it—and in my surprise I blurted out his name. To my greater surprise he recognized me, enough to remember where he had seen me before. "Oh, God," he said, "you were at the *Advocate.* You must hate me."

We spent the day drinking together, all over London. After the first flush of alcoholic guilt, Dylan settled down to quiet drinking and talking. I began to see the everyday Dylan, sober at first, then mildly drunk, gregarious, funny, generous, political, opinionated, and warm. The night before, Dylan and Caitlin had gone to the Swedish film of Strindberg's *Miss Julie,* a devastating movie which I had seen the summer before—a nightmare of misogyny, or gynophobia, in which a young woman uses sexual power over her valet, a social inferior and sexual enemy. Dylan and Caitlin had been disturbed by the film, as well they might have been, and had walked around

London half the night, unable to quiet down to sleep. This morning he needed a drink. Clearly he intended to have a pint or two and go back home to work. He never did. John Davenport dropped in, we went to the *vernissage* of an exhibition, we went to the Mandrake Club—and one thing led to another. On that particular lost day, in Dylan's life of lost days, I was the hanger-on who provided the excuse to keep on drinking.

In the pub that morning we talked politics and money. Dylan was an anarchist that morning—and frequently, so far as he was political; he was anarchist by nature. At Harvard, he told me, he had "liked everybody" except for Archibald MacLeish, because MacLeish had been in government. (I remembered MacLeish telling me of an encounter with Dylan late at night after the reading. MacLeish had asked him, "We all know what you've done with the first thirty-five years of your life. What will you do with the next thirty-five years of your life?" Dylan drew himself up and boomed, "I will write poems, fuck women, and annoy my friends.") He spoke of F. O. Matthiessen's party, when he had rolled on the floor, and I mentioned that it was just a month later—April Fool's day, 1950—that Matty had jumped from the window of a Boston hotel. "Oh, God," said Dylan, "was I *that* bad?"

And Dylan talked money, the lack of it; tax men were after him, and books were unfinished. Worry about money worked its way through his speech like a thread in tweed. We talked poetry-gossip, and poetry-business. He agreed instantly to come to the Poetry Society in May, and we settled on a date. (No help to money problems there.) He talked about American poets he had met on his tour. Mostly he was funny about them, and put down their work, but his dismissals were strangely unmalicious; he was a hard and serious judge. I remember his distaste for Kenneth Patchen, whom he dismissed as fake-tough. He dredged up lines of Patchen which fit the description, which he carried around with him like a cartoon to laugh at: "Cold stars watch us, chum / Cold stars, and the whores." The pauses around "chum" made the lines precious. As Dylan quoted them all day long, his accent became tougher and tougher, moving through James Cagney and George Raft to John Garfield.

Friends of Dylan came into the pub, had a pint, and left. By this time I was his "American friend, Don." I allowed myself to believe him; it was easy; his laughter when I joked was genuine, and his amusement at Oxford stories. This was not the cruel show-off I had met at Harvard. Laughing and friendly, he put me up to chug-a-lugging pints, one after the other, telling me that at *my* age, *he* could. . . . (That day in 1952, Dylan was thirty-seven; I was twenty-three.) With the aid of numerous pints, I relaxed totally. I don't remember that we ate lunch. Toward closing time in midafternoon, John Davenport came in—good friend of Dylan's, drinker, one of those brilliant men who whirl around literary London *just about* to write something great, and never do. Davenport had invitations to the *vernissage* of a Dali exhibition, the show in which Dali revealed his new piety by painting Virgins with holes through their stomachs. Neither Davenport nor Dylan nor I—I was volunteering my opinions by this time—admired Dali, but for some reason we decided to go.

The *vernissage* was crowded, stuffy, smoky, filled with people calling "Dylan!"—and he knew them all, and he grinned out of his fond friendly absurd face, and in ten minutes we pulled ourselves out to the street and looked for another taxi. I didn't know where we were going; I didn't care; I was lurching around London with Dylan Thomas, my *friend* Dylan Thomas, drunk as a lark and happy as a lord. Opening the door of the taxi, I heard the cry of "Dylan!" again. A young man with long blond hair flopping ran toward us down the street, and exchanged a word with Dylan, who introduced his American friend Don from Oxford to Ken Tynan just down from Oxford, and Tynan ran off, we entered the taxi, and Dylan directed the driver to the Mandrake. Then he told me where we were going. Licensing laws had sponsored the growth of *clubs* throughout England, nominally social clubs exempt from laws governing pubs, really nothing but off-hour drinking places, which thrived during the hours pubs were closed. The Mandrake was a legal blind pig, patronized especially by BBC people and artistic sorts. When we entered the establishment subdued "Dylan!" 's arose from men and women at the bar, and soon Dylan stood at some distance from the bar, a glass in each hand, contriving a semicircle of listeners, as he monologued and everyone bought him drinks. I remember Dylan's long rendition of an American movie, which he made up as he went along, a gangster movie in which he played all the parts, doing a sampler of American accents, each of them accurate and hilarious.

But I don't remember a great deal. When it turned six we migrated to a pub. Dylan met a Communist friend accompanied by a young woman with long hair and long legs. I watched them speak in low voices, drawn aside. Then Dylan beckoned me off, saying we had to go somewhere, and walked me a few blocks; then he told me he had to meet someone, an appointment. I was dumped; I think I knew it; I think I didn't care, for I knew I was out of my mind.

As the day approached when Dylan would read at Oxford, I wrote him about arrangements at his London address. No answer. I had been afraid that he might forget a date set in a pub. I wrote again. I telegraphed. A few hours before he was supposed to read, I thought to telephone Wales. Yes, he was there, Caitlin said; no, he would not be in Oxford that evening; no, he could not come to the phone; no, she would not ask him.

I posted a notice, on the door of the lecture hall, that Dylan Thomas had been forced to postpone his reading.

3. Wales

That summer I returned to the United States, married, and returned for the final Oxford year. Now I was president of the Poetry Society, with a secretary named George MacBeth carrying my burdens. I determined to see that Dylan would read poetry during my term as president. I wrote him in Wales, and proposed that if he could read at Oxford in October, at the beginning of term, we would drive to Laugharne in our wedding-present car and fetch him back to the reading. I presented the notion as a convenience to him; of course it was an adventure for me, and a convenience as well: if I drove him myself, I would be sure that he got there; if I counted on him to catch a train for Oxford, I would never be sure until I saw his figure step down from First Class.

On blue stationery, in a small and delicate hand, he wrote to apologize for missing the previous engagement—he had no memory of it—and to agree to the date I suggested.

We drove from Oxford to Wales, and to Dylan's village. Laugharne was the place we had heard of: cottages and ruined castle, small stone houses, tidy and miniature, as if a toy train might hoot through at any moment. From an old man on the street I asked directions to the Boat House, where Dylan and Caitlin lived. I learned where to park the car in order to walk there; one did not drive to the Boat House. We parked the Morris Minor—my wife Kirby pretty in her muskrat coat, twenty years old—and walked together along a dirt cliff over Carmarthen Bay, seagulls swooping and honking above us. Unknowing, we passed Dylan's workshed as we walked—Dylan inside it writing *Under Milk Wood*—and came suddenly upon the Boat House, which dropped to our right down to water level and the bay. A gate opened to a path which swooped down to the front door of the house built from water to cliff top, the house made of stone washed in a pale pink. It had been the ferryman's house, and the backyard at bay level was the boatyard, complete with a disused landing stage and a used outhouse. (There was no running water in the Boat House.) The kitchen was one story up from water level, and next to it a dining room with one wall of cliff rock. At the third level—where you entered if you walked from Laugharne as we did—was a tiny hallway, a bedroom, and a sitting room, with a veranda outside the sitting room overlooking the bay. A staircase led to two children's bedrooms on a fourth story. It was a house as awkward and as beautiful as I have ever seen.

Caitlin greeted us, looking tired and pretty, fierce, struggling with a head cold. When she led us to the bedroom she took sarcastic notice of Kirby's muskrat coat; then she asked, "How long have you been married?" About six weeks, Kirby told her, and when Caitlin heard the length of time, she snorted, "I suppose that accounts for the rosy glow." Caitlin had small reason to love her husband's admirers; people married to anyone famous learn quickly to loathe the followers, and Caitlin had more injury to complain of than most. When Dylan went up to London—where he would entrain from Oxford, day after tomorrow, to perform for the BBC—he would disappear when he had done his work. Some hangers-on would buy him drinks and be audience to the perpetual performance; women hangers-on would take him home to bed. To vomit with Dylan, or to sleep with him, brought glory.

After Dylan had not turned up for a few days, Caitlin would carry herself to London, check through the familiar clubs and pubs and girls, and take Dylan home with her. Then he would undergo a hangover like withdrawal from heroin. Both Dylan and Caitlin described these hangovers, Dylan with attempted humor—for it turned out that when I had called the spring before, he had been enduring a bad one. Not only could he not come to the telephone, the distant ringing of the phone was agony to him. And his eyes could not admit a flick of light from the curtained windows, or they rasped in agony. His stomach burned and he could keep nothing on it, not milk nor medicine. These hangovers lasted four days, or five. When he went to the United States everything was worse. He stayed longer, threw away more money, and she could not fetch him home. In addition, he tended to "fall in love" with someone when he visited the United States. If Caitlin was sarcastic to the smiling American twenty-year-old bride, it is small wonder.

We put our bags in their bedroom. Dylan and Caitlin would sleep on a sofa in the living room that night. Dylan was still working, Caitlin told us, but it was almost six o'clock. He quit work when the pubs opened. In a few moments the familiar figure waddled down the lane and turned in at the Boat House gate. He looked as bloated as ever—Dylan resembled those little fish that blow themselves up with air, by way of protection, and his chin was as weak as a fish's, and his strong eyes stared like a mackerel's cold on a marble slab—but there was something unfamiliar about him also, to me who had seen him in America and in London. After a moment's shyness, he was cheerful and gay, without the help of a pint of bitter. This was the healthy and happy Dylan of Laugharne, who had just worked four hours straight on his play. He looked at his watch, and said it was time to walk to town. The pubs would be open by the time we got there.

Caitlin stayed behind to make the risotto we would have for dinner when we returned. When she had put the two young children to bed—their eldest Llewellyn was away at school—she would join us in town.

We left behind us the pink-washed stone of the Boat House and walked slowly along the lane back to town. Dylan told us about his day—this day in particular, and his ideal day of work in Wales. He had written two lines today, for *Under Milk Wood,* and two lines a day was what he had learned to expect of himself. Dylan would use many sheets of scratch paper, digging out his two lines, and when he had made them he would add them to the ongoing manuscript of the work. Most writers make whole drafts, and make them over and over again, but Dylan's first whole draft was generally his last—if you did not count as drafts the scratch sheets he filled as he went along. Today it was not a poem he was making, but a play; yet he wrote it much the way he made a poem. He still called the play Llareggub, the title under which it first appeared, and it delighted him to have invented the Welsh-sounding town's name which was "bugger all" spelled backwards.

Typically in Wales, as he told it, Dylan would arise about nine o'clock, eat a huge breakfast—he was an eater, when he was not drunk, and his belly was not only beer—and then read for a spell in the outhouse. At ten or ten-thirty he would walk into town for his mail, drink a couple of morning pints, have a gossip, do the crossword with his dying father who lived in a Laugharne cottage, and saunter back to the Boat House for a large lunch. From two to six he wrote in his shack, which had begun life as somebody's bicycle shed. Evenings from six to ten he lived the pub life, chatting, drinking in a desultory fashion, coming down from an afternoon of work. After the pub closed came dinner, and bed, and another day.

We walked under the curlew's cry. As we passed his workshed he invited us to look inside. He worked at the front end of the tiny structure, by windows that gave him the bay and St. John's Hill. On the walls were pictures of writers he had cut from the newspapers—W. H. Auden, Thomas Hardy, Walt Whitman, Marianne Moore, Edith Sitwell. The floor was a wilderness of papers, books, cigarette packages, magazines, and beer bottles.

Then we walked among the stone cottages of Laugharne, and stopped first at Brown's Hotel, a pub kept by Mrs. Ivy Williams, who was immediately introduced to "my American friends Kirby and Don." Conversation was slow. Men and women dropped in, and paused to chat. We drank our pints. With his second, Dylan added a small whiskey on the side. After an hour, we moved to Laugharne's other pub, the Cross Hands, where Dylan found friends already gathered, and made introductions again. The circle of cronies planned a pub crawl through the Welsh countryside, Dylan not ringleader but co-conspirator. The puzzle of the night was whom to recruit as driver, to count on for sobriety. A platoon of names produced no one reliable. Conversation was otherwise general, the American strangers included. I drank my pint slowly. Caitlin joined us carrying a can of milk, on the theory that whiskey mixed with milk would cure her cold. She was as easy as Dylan in this company. After another hour we went back to Brown's Hotel, which had filled, the people different and the same. Before closing time, we paid one more visit to the other pub, and Dylan and I filled pockets with bottles of beer for the return to the Boat House.

Caitlin's risotto was thick with onions and tomatoes. Dylan ate four enormous helpings. Now we talked about poetry again, especially such matters as the fees paid by magazines. I remember Caitlin telling Kirby how she relied on Dylan to keep her warm at night; he was like a bloody gas fire, she said. Then she went off to bed, tired, and Kirby followed her, Caitlin making Dylan promise to come upstairs soon, or she would freeze to death.

Dylan opened the bottles we had brought back from the pub, and we sat at the table talking. Feeling tender and close and grateful, I told him that he was a great poet. I meant it, and I had been saving it to tell him. He shook his head; he said that he was not; he was at best a minor poet. There were three good poems, he said; the rest was trash. He was not being flippant; he was melancholy. He *forgave* me for being stupid—he expected no more—but he would not agree with my stupidity. I asked him which three. He told me "Poem in October," "Poem on His Birthday," and "This Bread I Break." I didn't remember the last one. "Oh, it's an early, Hardy-ish piece of mine," he said.

I tried to argue with him about his poems, unwilling to hear him disparage himself. I felt as if it were my own self-esteem that he attacked. I told him that "Do Not Go Gentle," his villanelle, was a favorite of mine. He shook his head again. "Why don't you like it?" I said.

"Because I didn't write it," he said.

I understood him, when he said it. "You mean Yeats," I said.

He nodded his head. The language came from Yeats, he said. I told him I liked the newest poem of his I had seen, "Lament." He said that it began all right, but ended badly; he had been bored with the poem, he said, and had hurried the end. I began to understand: he disparaged himself only in service to standards that demanded greatness. This was the boy who would show Keats his heels. Still, I wanted him to take the disparagement back. I argued. He took none of my comfort. When I put forward the notion that writing with his intensity must be painful, he waved the idea away. Writing poetry was easy, he said; not exactly *easy*—it was very *slow*—but poetry was always there, always available. Poetry was a dark river flowing *down there* somewhere; he could send down the bucket anytime he wanted, and come up with poetry. Two lines a day.

But anyway, he shrugged the subject away, he wouldn't write poetry much the rest of his life.

I asked him why.

He would write prose instead; there was more money in it.

All night at the pubs, and in our walking back and forth, Dylan had talked about money. He didn't want to do another American tour, he said, and Caitlin surely didn't want him to—but he needed the money. He didn't want to go up to London this week, to read for a BBC school program; he wanted to work on his play instead—but he needed the money. And when he talked about writing prose for money, it is pathetic to realize that he was talking about earning fifty dollars for a short story, instead of twenty-five dollars for a poem. He could have done as well ferrying people across Carmarthen Bay. In a few minutes several complacent securities, fixed in my head like stars in the old astrology, crashed forever inside me. Even if when you grew up you turned out to be Dylan Thomas, life could be neither simple nor easy nor happy.

Then I heard a voice crying "Dylan!"—Caitlin's fierce voice—"for *Christ's* sake come up here!" He finished what he was saying. "Dylan! Dylan!" He stood and emptied his bottle and climbed the stairs to sleep beside his cold wife.

When we walked down to the kitchen the next morning, Caitlin was making porridge. Her daughter Aeronwy, nine years old, was asking Caitlin to comb her hair. Three-year-old Colm wandered about underfoot, a small Dylan with piled golden curls, with an expression of innocence and madness; rumpled and angelic, like the Dylan painted by Augustus John. The real Dylan remained upstairs. I made conversation to which Caitlin grunted replies. She was still combing Aeron's hair, and turning to stir the porridge one-handed, when Dylan's voice—being mellifluous this morning—called downstairs, "Caitlin, where is my tie?"

"I don't know, Dylan," she called back.

After thirty seconds' pause—Colm was dragging on Caitlin's skirt—Dylan's voice called with a greater urgency, "Caitlin, where *is* my *tie?*"

She shouted back instantly, "Dylan, I cannot help you now."

He repeated his question a third time: "CAITLIN, WHERE IS MY TIE?"

She was as quick, shrieking, "Dylan, I *cannot* help you now.

I'm making breakfast and combing Aeron's hair! Find it yourself!"

After ten seconds, the organ tones upstairs rolled out a sentence that filled the pink-washed Boat House with melody: "Fuck you, then, you cruel bitch!" The commas around "then" were visible, printed on the shuddering air; in the word "cruel," Dylan rolled the *r* and trilled the *l*. It was beautiful. Kirby and I tried to look as if we had not noticed. Caitlin, Aeronwy, and Colm looked as if they hadn't.

4. Oxford

We started for Oxford at nine-thirty, which was a good thing, because the reading was at half past eight that night. We stopped in Laugharne while Dylan, ever the good son, said goodbye to his mother and father. We stopped for petrol once, and people at the pumps were making noises I could not decipher; Dylan confirmed that it was Welsh, and that he couldn't understand a word. In the first hour we drove steadily, but at ten-thirty the pubs opened, and in the next four hours I suppose we spent about forty-five minutes driving. At one pub Dylan challenged me to a game of darts; he let me *almost* win, then swept me off the board with his delicate, practiced wrist. In another pub we played shove ha'penny; same thing. The publicans greeted Dylan fondly, at least for the first hour or two; reminiscence flowed. At noon Dylan led us to a glittering pub in a city we drove through—I can't remember the city—and we ate sausages and Scotch eggs and potato salad with half-raw potatoes.

At two-thirty we were able to drive again. Most of the afternoon in the car we improvised on the American game which awards points for hitting pedestrians, high scores for degree of difficulty—like zapping a pole vaulter carrying his pole—or for degrees of cruelty. Dylan had never encountered this scheme. He loved to *develop* jokes, carrying them on for hours and hours. His ultimate invention he scored for twenty points, and I remember it well: "a crippled nine-year-old blind orphan nun, leading a three-legged kitten on a string." Then he added, "It's worth three more points if she's pregnant."

It was a near thing, getting to Oxford. At about four-thirty, Dylan led us out of our way to park beside a closed pub where he knew the landlord *well,* and was *certain* that the landlord would open up for us. It never occurred to me to argue with Dylan, or to disobey him; he gave no orders, but his charm was so engaging, his bosom friendship so overwhelming, that you did what he asked. We knocked and knocked. Fortunately, the landlord never opened up.

We arrived in Oxford at six-fifteen and drove directly to New College, where the sherry party began at six. When Dylan heard where we were taking him, he told us that he hated sherry, and hated sherry *parties* worse than sherry. Was there a pub we could go to? There was a tiny local near New College called The Turf, which you could find only by assiduous search. We drank beer again in the minuscule public bar, a coal fire burning in October. Meanwhile, back at the sherry party, forty-seven leading Oxford poets were convinced that we would never arrive. The three of us showed up precisely at seven, time to go to Oxford's Café de Paris for supper.

After a superb reading, we took Dylan back to our flat on Banbury Road, and brought with us half a dozen Oxford poets. I had laid in a supply of beer, and Dylan sat in a corner chair drinking and talking quietly. He took a fancy to one young woman, but he did not give her the *Advocate* treatment; she was flattered more than she was embarrassed, and his fancy though passing was true enough. When people made motions as if to leave, Dylan felt called upon to provide a curtain. From his chair in the corner he improvised a story. It was clear that he made it up as he went along. He spoke slowly, mimicking, telling about a keeper in the London Zoo who fell in love with a warthog. I'm not sure that Dylan knew what a warthog looked like, but he knew warts and he knew hogs, and warthog was good enough for him. The keeper Dylan invented—he knew him from a pub, he said, when he lived near the zoo—had a wife, but preferred the warthog, and grumbled in bed at night at his bad luck in sleeping companions. Then the warthog took sick, and Dylan made stories out of the keeper's anxiety, his increasing resentment of his healthy wife, and his devices for curing the ailing beast. At the end of the story the keeper bought a large fish, and artfully rotted it in his warm kitchen at home, until it reached a level of putrefaction which revived and restored the exhilarated warthog of the London Zoo.

Oxford poets took off on their bicycles, and Dylan and I drank the last bottle of Tolly. I was complaining about some Sunday paper critic who used phrases like "death-wish." Out of brutal innocence I added, "What a dumb idea anyway. Who wants to die?"

Dylan looked up at me. "Oh, I do," he said.

"Why?" I said. I thought of what I had heard in Laugharne the night before.

"Just for the change," he said.

In the morning he looked rested, bright-cheeked, with an orange-red shirt and a blue bow tie with white polka dots. He wore gloves as usual, with a jacket but no top coat, and we set off after breakfast for the depot, and arrived early and drank horrid British Railways coffee. Then he touched me for two pounds and went off to London—to the BBC and the Mandrake and somebody's bed, Caitlin's rescue, and a five-day hangover, and death in a year's time.

5. Public Suicide

In a year's time I was living in California. The one connection between Oxford and Stanford should have been Dylan Thomas, who was flying West after doing *Under Milk Wood* in New York. Then one noon a friend's postcard told us that Dylan lay dying in New York. The afternoon paper reported his death. Astonished, we lived with private grief. But all year I met the public grief; gradually the public grieving, which was mythic and impersonal, took private grief away. At Stanford that year, and in San Francisco, I met people who talked in familiar terms of Dye-lan and Kate-lin, and told outrageous stories. A graduate student from Berkeley, who visited Stanford, made much of the fact that she had "had an affair" with Dylan when he had visited her college two years earlier. When she had written Dylan in Wales, Caitlin answered her; she liked to show Caitlin's letter to people. Slowly and with some shame, I realized that, like everyone else, I had not known him at all.

Everywhere were *stories,* The Merry Tales of Master Dylan: how drunk Dylan grabbed matronly breasts; how drunk Dylan, in charge of infant Llewelyn, mislaid him in the long grass in his portable crib, where he slept the night through; how drunk Dylan, at an *Advocate* party in 1950, rode a Radcliffe girl to the floor and copulated in public. Which was of course a lie. The Merry Tales was largely a book of lies—many of them Dylan's lies—which began in Wales, moved to London, came to America with his college readings, increased with his popularity before his death, and multiplied many times after his death, growing like a corpse's hair in the grave. The anecdotes accounted for most of the popularity. Of course many people admired his readings; and some people admired his poems; but the Merry Tales made him fashionable, and added his *Collected Poems* to suburban bookshelves. In November of 1953 there was only one more thing he could have done, to increase his popularity, and he did it.

Celebrities, asked to name their favorite poet, spoke of a dead Welshman they had never read. Producers commissioned a crude, exploitative play to be called *Dylan. Under Milk Wood,* written for BBC radio and a few pounds, played to standing-room crowds in New York. In Hibbing, Minnesota, Bob Zimmerman rejected his last name for the name of a dead poet, martyred for his art; nobody would mispronounce "Dylan" again. A poet on the West Coast wrote an elegy accusing "you" of killing Dylan Thomas, "You killed him! You killed him. / In your God Damned Brooks Brothers suit, / You son of a bitch." Everywhere, people told us what he died for, who killed him, and politicized a dead drunk.

Because the "dead" derived from the "drunk," Dylan's death was a slow, twenty-four-year suicide. When you persist in anything likely to kill you, you are on your way to being a suicide—drugs and drink as much as crazy driving. The Dylan stories celebrated his drunkenness, therefore his self-destruction. Suicide has always had its admirers, but there are moments in history when it acquires general *chic.* Goethe's *Sorrows of Young Werther* made suicide fashionable in Europe for a decade. In the West, suicide has grown increasingly popular since the beginning of the Cold War, and literary suicides have led the way. After Dylan's death Sylvia Plath's suicide created a female Young Werther. Anne Sexton's suicide a decade after Plath's was as predictable as Haley's Comet; but not so rare. And they differed: Sexton's suicide was public, Plath's private—though Plath imagined a public for it. I suggest that there is something called public suicide, whether the coroner's report indicates self-murder or not; Dylan Thomas, like Jack Kerouac and Brendan Behan, was a public suicide in his alcoholism. John Berryman and Ernest Hemingway were public suicides in their drinking, who put the final touch to themselves by more violent means.

Sylvia Plath's favorite poet for a time in college was Dylan Thomas. She wrote poems that recounted her early suicide attempt, and threatened another. "Like the cat," she wrote with sad inaccuracy, "I have nine times to die." Perhaps that is public enough, but she did not experience in her lifetime a public that stood below the building where she perched on the ledge, and cheered her on to jump. She only imagined that a crowd watched her performance of death and resurrection:

> What a million filaments.
> The peanut-crunching crowd
> Shoves in to see
>
> Then unwrap me hand and foot—
> The big striptease.
> Gentlemen, ladies,
>
> These are my hands,
> My knees.
> . . . .
>
> Dying
> Is an art, like everything else.
> I do it exceptionally well.

Her irony, and the bitterness of her sarcasm at her expense, amount to self-criticism; they are efforts she directed at herself to dissuade the impulse toward self-destruction. But many posthumous admirers show no such restraint; they applaud her suicide, find her a martyr to sensitivity or a martyr to male chauvinism, romanticize her murder of the poet she was—and of the greater poet she might have become. I do not make light of the suffering, horrible and vivid in her last poems, which she snuffed out with gas from the oven. I hate the glorification of her death.

Many other poets have enacted their self-murders to the present applause of crowds. Anne Sexton's flirtation with death was public and chronic, encouraged by poetry-groupies and death-groupies across the country. Her booking agent once guaranteed a lecture committee that Sexton would weep on the platform. Barkers at the sideshow of literature, consumers of suffering—teachers and students, would-be poets, critics, morbid observers—applauded her tears and goaded her to surpass herself, to call her own bluff; death-collectors, they too found in themselves an urge to destroy themselves, but they *muted it;* they evaded or avoided confrontation with their own darkness. Instead, the peanut-crunching fans paid Anne Sexton seven hundred and fifty dollars to wail their miseries for them.

Denise Levertov is a tough survivor, who refuses the striptease that killed Sexton and Plath. After Sexton's suicide, Levertov wrote:

> . . . My own sadness at the death of a fellow poet is compounded by the sense of how likely it is that Anne Sexton's tragedy will not be without influence in the tragedies of other lives.
>
> She herself was, obviously, too intensely troubled to be fully aware of her influence or to take on its responsibility. Therefore it seems to me that we who are alive must make clear, as she could not, the distinction between creativity and self-destruction. The tendency to confuse the two has claimed too many victims. Anne Sexton herself seems to have suffered deeply from this confusion, and I surmise that her friendship with Sylvia Plath had in it an element of identification which added powerfully to her malaise. Across the country, at different colleges, I have heard many stories of attempted—and sometimes successful—suicides by young students who love the poetry of Plath and who suppose that somehow, in order to become

poets themselves, they had to act out in their own lives the events of hers.

Innumerable young poets have drunk themselves into stupidity and cirrhosis because they admired John Berryman or Dylan Thomas and came to think they must think like them to write like them.

In Lewis Hyde's analysis of alcoholism in Berryman's poetry, printed in the *American Poetry Review,* he writes about a *Life* article:

> . . . there are the typical photographs of the poet with the wind in his beard and a glass in his hand. . . . Like Hemingway, they got him to play the fool and the salesman the last ten years of his life.
>
> I am not saying that the critics could have cured Berryman of his disease. But . . . in the future it would be nice if it were a little harder for the poet to come to town drunk and have everyone think that it's great fun. . . .

Let the final sentence be engraved in bronze over the desks of lecture agents, program chairmen—and poets.

The poet who survives is the poet to celebrate. The human being who confronts darkness and defeats it is the most admirable human being. For all his outrageous vanity, Robert Frost is admirable, who looked into his desert places, who confronted his desire to enter the oblivion of the snowy woods, and who drove on.

Philoctetes needed the wound, to make the bow strong and accurate. The analogy to artistic creation has been observed. No one who loves literature can deny that disease can give birth to great poems. And suffering is not merely pandemic among artists, after all, but among humanity; life without suffering is life unlived, the challenge refused. Because the artist must censor nothing, perhaps artists must endure suffering without anesthetic. Surely, some will succumb and administer to themselves the permanent anesthetic of death. But not all succumb. There are counterexamples, like Frost and Eliot, like Yeats and Emily Dickinson and Henry James, who suffered but kept on, who survived.

On the other hand, in the old story Philoctetes was not surrounded by a throng cheering for the wound and ignoring the bow. If everyone must suffer, not everyone is applauded for suffering—the more tears the more cheers. In our culture an artist's self-destructiveness is counted admirable, praiseworthy, a guarantee of sincerity. There seems to be an assumption, widely held and all but declared, that it is *natural* to want to destroy yourself; that health is bourgeois or conventional; that if we did what we really wanted, if we lived like an animal by instinct, we would be drunk all the time or addicted to heroin or at least suicidal. The assumption continues: the poet, because the poet is a free spirit, immune to civilization's inhibitions and prohibitions, does the *natural* thing and kills herself. Or himself.

But the assumption expresses only middle-class culture's self-hatred. Death and destruction are enemies to art, to consciousness, and to the growth of consciousness. Gas and sleeping pills kill poets; drink and drugs kill poets more slowly, but on the way to killing the poet they kill the poems. Dylan Thomas was a minor poet, rather than a major one, because he was a drunk, because the death in him was too strong for the life. And he was surrounded by people who applauded the death, and cared nothing for the life. It was his weakness—deplorable, understandable—that he played to this audience, the consumers of vicarious death who applauded him when he boasted of drinking eighteen whiskeys in a row at the White Horse before he collapsed into a coma; who cheered diabetic Brendan Behan entertaining the Dublin barflies and the barflies of death; who clapped for John Berryman, drunk at his poetry readings, blacked out and murderous, waving goodbye to his world as he jumped from a Minneapolis bridge. Perhaps if he had lived in a society which valued life over death, the

Dylan Thomas who loved poetry and made it—the vital maker—would have been sponsored and energized; perhaps he would not have entered the dark wood.

And perhaps he would have anyway; his suicide began in private, twenty-four years before he completed it in public.

6. Twenty-four Years

The year he died, I studied microfilm of Dylan's worksheets for "Ballad of the Long-Legged Bait." It was clear that he wrote the way he said he wrote, scratching out hundreds of alternatives until he got his line right, or his quatrain, then adding it whole and finished to the ongoing draft of the poem. When he had told me he wrote this way, I had been astonished; it seemed to imply that his mind commanded the poem before the poem started. I could not write that way; I make whole draft after whole draft, the poem starting vague in my mind, only clarified by pen on paper, by revision and rearrangement. As I studied his worksheets, and returned to study his other poems, I understood gradually that I had been mistaken. No more than I did Dylan have a worked-out notion of the poem in advance. He was not writing poems; he was writing *poetry*. He started with a general scene or idea which supplied coherence to the poem—rural place or pantheistic thought—and then he improvised the poem as he improvised an American movie or a joke about a warthog, only more slowly and more grandly. Out of the sounds of words, out of amusement, out of love for spectacle and bombast, out of *talent* he made up his poems—two lines a day.

Dylan was the maddest of word-mad young poets. All poets

start from loving words, and loving to play with them. Then they learn to love poetry as well, or the Muse herself, and make poems from this love of poetry—hoping to add new stars to the heavens. But the great poets as they turn older look past the Muse—who is objectified taste, composed of all great poems of the past—to pursue vision, to discover motions of spirit and of human consciousness, which it is art's task to enlarge. Sometimes a poet developed past the love of words will lose poetry altogether, will disavow language in favor of vision—and write endless boring theological sonnets like Wordsworth's. Often the best poems happen when lines cross; the poet writes in pursuit of the spirit, while words still roar with years of obsession and love. The luckiest poet is like Yeats; from the time he could say that he sought "an image not a book," he kept words and vision together.

Poetry, Dylan said, was a dark river flowing inside him, to which he could lower the bucket daily. The river had beautiful words in it, but free of the river the words lacked structure. Of the three poems he was willing to acknowledge, that night at the Boat House, the earliest is most a *poem,* written like so many early Thomas poems with repetitive syntax in a riddling diction.

> This bread I break was once the oat,
> This wine upon a foreign tree
> Plunged in its fruit;
> Man in the day or wind at night
> Laid the crops low, broke the grape's joy.
>
> Once in this wind the summer blood
> Knocked in the flesh that decked the vine,
> Once in this bread
> The oat was merry in the wind;
> Man broke the sun, pulled the wind down.
>
> This flesh you break, this blood you let
> Make desolation in the vein,

Were oat and grape
Born of the sensual root and sap;
My wine you drink, my bread you snap.

"This Bread I Break" does resemble Thomas Hardy, especially a Hardy poem called "Transformations":

Portion of this yew
Is a man my grandsire knew,
Bosomed here at its foot:
This branch may be his wife,
A ruddy human life
Now turned to a green shoot.

These grasses must be made
Of her who often prayed,
Last century, for repose;
And the fair girl long ago
Whom I often tried to know
May be entering this rose.

So, they are not underground,
But as nerves and veins abound
In the growths of upper air,
And they feel the sun and rain,
And the energy again
That made them what they were!

The Hardy is less dazzling, but I think it is a better poem. There is nothing in Dylan's poem so touching as "May be entering this rose," where human particles walk through the door of a house, or the portals of a church. The voice of an old man speaks, it is located, one senses the poet's *feeling* about impending death and molecular survival; his emotions concern something outside the poem itself, or its words. In Dylan's handsome stanzas, the words watch themselves in the mirror, and the words love what they see.

"Poem in October" or "Poem on His Birthday" are not poems but poetry, each of them a long and gorgeous rendition of weather and landscape, bird and water. They are determinedly joyful and optimistic, as only a doomed man would make them. But

> Pale rain over the dwindling harbour
> And over the sea wet church the size of a snail
> With its horns through mist and the castle. . . .

could replace

> I hear the bouncing hills
> Grow larked and greener at berry brown
> Fall and the dew larks sing. . . .

and except for the form and shape and a change in the weather—no one would be wiser. Throughout the *Collected Poems,* we find poems with interchangeable lines. Of course form and shape make the poems beautiful, honey in the mouth, minor monuments of English literature—but they are *minor* exactly because form and shape do not alone make great poems. When Thomas refuses to mourn the death by fire of the child in London, we do not experience the child's death; we hear noble words arranged by rumors of pantheism. When we cut through the glorious vegetation of "Fern Hill," we see that the soil and rock underneath are commonplace: it was pleasant for a city child to come to the country on his summer vacation; then he grew up.

Dylan never put his poetry in service to anything outside himself except the Muse. He served the Muse; he wrote pure poetry. But what is pure poetry *pure of?*—it is pure of thought and pure of feeling; pure of vision; pure of enlarged consciousness; its only emotion is love for words.

The alcoholic, Lewis Hyde says, cannot go outside himself, lacks compassion and empathy, loses spirit by drowning under spirits. But why does a man choose this death? I have argued that his culture applauded his dying; but he undertook to die before his culture knew he was there. Why in particular was it necessary or inevitable for Dylan Thomas to take on himself the suffering and death of alcoholism? Of course drinking was not pure suffering; it began by relieving pain. In the early stages of drink, not yet drunk, Thomas *enjoyed* the relaxed pub life; and at Brown's Hotel and the Cross Hands in Laugharne, four hours at night after four hours of writing, his relaxed and gregarious pleasure was only the smallest death. But he was hardly a stupid man, and he knew that the pleasure led only to pain; nothing outside himself had power to overcome the craving for alcohol, pain, and death. Laugharne pubs led to London, New York, the *Advocate,* and the ten thousand bars—hangovers, vomiting, blackouts, the horrible visions of delirium tremens.

Dylan chose the suffering not as the release of natural instincts but as punishment for the sin of writing poems. Such an assertion must sound as romantic as suicide-worship, if not quite so destructive. The notion of poetic sin takes outward form in popular clichés that associate poets with forbidden sexuality, with absinthe and orgies, with romantic alienation. Dylan's behavior (at the *Advocate* party, for instance) danced to the tune of these commonplaces; beneath them, however, we can glimpse something genuine: in the Conclusion to this book, I will argue that poetry attempts psychic revolution, not to overthrow reason, but to add old or irrational elements to the light of consciousness by means of language, which is the instrument of consciousness. Poetry says, with Freud, "Where id was, let there ego be." To make poems is to add metaphors of the forbidden child to words of the rational adult, making a third thing, which enlarges human consciousness; Plato called this enlargement insanity, and represented a western consensus when he prohibited poets from his Republic. Inside everyone lives a fearful Platonic Censor, who shudders at the thought of enlargement, and forbids it. To make poems is to violate Platonic standards of civilization; the poet grows up in civilization, subject to its prohibitions; the Plato inside him banishes—and punishes—Orpheus and Dionysus.

Thomas was brought up by his mother in a Welsh church of

Devil and sin. When he became a poet he joined the Devil's party. Therefore, to poetry he added other wickedness available to a young man in Wales in his day: he smoked cigarettes, he talked lewdly about women and later added behavior to talk (doubtless in adolescence he thought masturbation a unique vice)—and he drank. Throughout his life Dylan praised wickedness, and laughed at piety or respectability—and was terrified of Satan, of vampires and black magic and goblins. When Dylan saw Aleister Crowley in London—the Satanist black magician who called himself the Great Beast—Dylan was terrified, and would not remain in the same room. *Dylan knew that he was damned.* He was damned because he agreed to be damned, early in life, as if he had sold his soul to the Devil. Through much of his life, he spoke of his days as numbered, finite, his early death already determined. In London during his last year he spoke of his death as imminent. In his last week in New York he told people around him that he would soon die. He told John Brinnin that in his alcoholic visions he had seen the gates of Hell.

Dylan became a poet young. At fifteen he wrote lines and fragments of poetry as brilliant as he would ever write. He progressed rapidly and wrote prolifically. *Eighteen Poems* appeared when he was twenty, and by that age he had drafted at least half the work in his *Collected Poems.* From then on, the dying took over. In the last wretched decade of his life, he made about a poem a year. In the despair that overtook him, he no longer even read poetry, unless it was pushed on him; he had lost poetry, given up on it in his anguish, and the poems that remained to him were mostly poems he had loved when he was young, which he still spoke magnificently at readings. When he read books—when he was neither gossiping nor drinking nor writing, nor too drunk to see the page—he read junk; Mickey Spillane, trashy magazines and newspapers, *anything* to blunt and deaden consciousness.

He lived twenty-four years after he began to be a poet. Twenty-four years of poetry, dwindling rapidly in the last decade. The Devil is known to sell his services for various terms; one of the traditional terms is twenty-four years. For his twenty-fourth birthday, Dylan wrote the poem:

> Twenty-four years remind the tears of my eyes.
> (Bury the dead for fear that they walk to the grave in labour.)
> In the groin of the natural doorway I crouched like a tailor
> Sewing a shroud for a journey
> By the light of the meat-eating sun.
> Dressed to die, the sensual strut begun,
> With my red veins full of money,
> In the final direction of the elementary town
> I advance for as long as forever is.

In his last weeks, when he was not raving or vomiting, he strove to revise *Under Milk Wood.* He wrote near the edge of oblivion which would close his living eyes to horror. In old stories about the Devil, he gives us what we ask for, and it is our ruin. Dylan wanted *poetry,* and he got it, but he asked for nothing more; and he never found the enlarging, enhancing wisdom that is poetry's real wickedness and real salvation.

VANITY, FAME, LOVE, AND ROBERT FROST

1. Frost's Reputation

When I grew up—in the suburbs, at suburban schools—I heard adults mention one living poet, and only one. Professors might prefer Eliot; young poets might imitate Auden—but for the American public Robert Frost was the Great Living Poet. His *Complete Poems,* like Longfellow's the century before, wedged among popular novels on affluent bookshelves. Everyone knew him, and everyone loved him: with the aid of *Life,* we recognized Frost's character: rustic, witty, avuncular, *benign.* Now, a decade and a half after his death, his reputation has changed totally, and a consensus agrees that the old commonplaces were fraudulent. Reviewing a biography in the *New York Times Book Review,* an outraged critic confirms that "Frost was a liar . . . Frost was cold. . . ." The same culture that applauded Frost as a simple farmer now reviles him as a simple monster. But he was not simple.

He was vain, he was cruel, he was rivalrous with all other men: but he could also be generous and warm—when he could satisfy himself that his motives were dubious. He was a man possessed by guilt, by knowledge that he was "bad," by craving for love, by the necessity to reject love—and by desire for fame which no amount of celebrity could satisfy.

I met Frost when I was sixteen; I saw him last a few months

before he died. Over the years, he changed for me, from a monument to a public fraud to something more human and complicated than either praise or blame could deal with. When I look back now, with knowledge of the life he lived, I look at old scenes with new eyes.

To him—I learned over the years—his family background seemed precarious, dangerous; and his adult life cursed with tragedy, for which he took responsibility. His father was a sometime drunk, dead at an early age; his mother endured a bad marriage, was widowed young, and failed as a schoolteacher when she returned to her native Massachusetts; yet she was a fond mother, kind to her children—and she wrote poems. Her son felt dangerously close to her, and followed that fondness into devotion to one young woman, Elinor White, whom he courted extravagantly, romantically, and doggedly. Apparently losing her, he considered suicide; at least, he later dropped hints to friends that he had considered suicide. When Elinor and Robert finally married, they settled in Derry, New Hampshire, and lived in poverty, enduring an extraordinary series of family misfortunes: their firstborn child, a son named Elliott, died of *cholera infantum* at the age of three; in later years, warning or bragging about his "badness," Frost said that the doctor who attended Elliott blamed him for the death, for not having called a doctor sooner. The next child was Lesley, daughter and eldest survivor, celebrator and denouncer of her father. Then there was Irma, mad in middle life and institutionalized; Frost's only sister had been insane, he himself frequently fearful of madness; he blamed himself and his genes for his daughter's insanity. Then came Carroll, son, who killed himself at the age of thirty-eight. Youngest was Marjorie, dead after childbirth at twenty-nine.

When I speak of poverty in Derry, I speak of something rural, not so desperate as the poverty of cities. The family lived in natural beauty, among country pleasures. But the Frosts were almost destitute, owning only a few chickens and a garden, nothing else. In the Derry years, only an ego as obdurate as granite could remain firm; for years, without encouragement from editors or critics, Frost worked at writing his poems—*instead* of weeding vegetables or tending his chickens or teaching school to support his family.

Finally he took a job at a school, and gathered thereby a small income. Then he sold the farm, and with the capital took off with his family for England until the money ran out. There, by a stroke of luck, he found a publisher—and started the journey to fame. But by the time he returned to the United States—to find magazines at last open to his poems, universities ready to hire him—he was almost forty years old, and his children nearly grown up. In retrospect, he realized that they had grown up insecure, anxious, poor. In retrospect, it seemed to him that out of selfish ambition he had starved and mistreated his family, that from his family's suffering came madness, suicide, and early death.

His family agreed with him. A thousand stories affirm that Elinor Frost never wholly forgave him the deprivation suffered. He asked her forgiveness as she lay dying, and she would not grant it. Shortly after her mother's death, Lesley told him in bitterness that he should never have married; at the very least, he should never have had children. Frost felt guilty every minute he lived, and sought forgiveness everywhere, and accepted none of it. "When I am too full of joy," he told another poet, "I think how little good my health did anyone near me." *He knew he was a bad man.* Writing a close friend, he said he "wondered about my past whether it had not been too cruel to those I dragged with me. . . ." And this was before he watched his son slide into suicide—watched, and *argued* with Carroll, *argued* with his own son not to kill himself, and lost. Of course he found reason to blame himself for the suicide, as he did for everything else. In his guilt, his ego showed its old omnipotence, but he felt true anguish also, nearly to the point of madness. And when he thought he was dying in Florida, in 1962, he told a friend that in his delirium he saw the vengeful face of one of his children, staring at him, finger pointing, "accusing, accusing." He told his friend, with a laugh unpleasant to hear, that the vision had terrified him back into life.

2. Vain Granite

In August of 1945, when I was sixteen, I went to Bread Loaf Writers' Conference at the old wooden Inn outside Middlebury in Vermont. Frost had been connected with the Writers' Conference from the beginning, and he was my main reason for going. The year before, I had spent my first year at prep school, and I had met an English teacher who knew Robert Frost *personally,* quoted him in conversation, and told me about Bread Loaf. Aspirant writers could spend two weeks there in the summer, being read and criticized by professionals; there, you could catch a glimpse of Robert Frost.

At fourteen I had decided to become a poet, and I had worked on poems two or three hours a day after school. I collected rejection slips from *The New Yorker* and *Atlantic,* and when I was sixteen I began to publish in little magazines—very little magazines, like *Trails, Matrix,* and *Experiment.* I was exhilarated; surely book publication and undying fame would follow as the night the day. Going to Bread Loaf would accelerate matters.

My teacher's conversation not only made me want to go to Bread Loaf; it restored Robert Frost to me. My mother had read him to me when I was small. Then, just as I began to write poetry myself, when I was thirteen, an eighth-grade teacher praised Frost to our class in terms which forced me to despise him: he was a lovable codger with a heart of gold. Becoming a poet, I knew that poets were dangerous figures despised by ordinary society. For a while I dismissed Robert Frost as a poet that English teachers and parents promoted. Now I read him again, with my new teacher's help, and recovered him. I remember finding the poem "To Earthward," which became my favorite poem that year. I recited it to anyone who would listen. There was one stanza in particular I said for the saying's sake:

I had the swirl and ache
From sprays of honeysuckle
That when they're gathered shake
Dew on the knuckle.

The *shape* of this single sentence—deployed so artfully over four tight, rhymed lines—delighted me, the rhyme itself satisfying, almost amusing, and the rhythm an eloquent swoop of syntax. I loved especially the way the third line shaped itself like a saucer, a whole clause separating the first and last words, which are themselves another clause.

By the time "To Earthward" finishes, however, it's a harsh journey. It starts, "Love at the lips was touch / As sweet as I could bear," but the poem is about aging, and about losing with age the ability to *feel*—except the ability to feel pain. Frost ends by saying that he looks for pain in order to feel; and then he says that he looks forward to death—or he almost says it:

When stiff and sore and scarred
I take away my hand
From leaning on it hard
In grass and sand,

The hurt is not enough:
I long for weight and strength
To feel the earth as rough
To all my length.

I loved the pitch and roll of these sentences, and the rhymes—but I loved also the danger of the lines, the brave approach to forbidden feelings. I could not name the forbidden feelings at sixteen—but I felt them *there,* and they made the lines honest and powerful. With the help of some friends—and thirty years of aging—I know more about the poem now. When Frost longs for a "weight" to press down on him from above—the way his body pressed his hand down—the weight could be six feet of dirt, and the body still sentient although dead; but the weight could also come from sexual assault, an imagined rape by an Amazon, or by a man, with Frost turned into a woman. A poem that begins "Love at the lips" ends with rape and suicide; because if you *long for* "strength" to achieve this painful pressure, it must be strength of will to undertake the pain. This Robert Frost—masochistic, androgynous, suicidal—was not my eighth-grade teacher's Frost, nor a Bread Loaf Writers' Conference Frost, nor Frost's Frost either. But it was, in fact, a *real,* ambivalent human being: trust the poem not the poet.

The first night at Bread Loaf we heard a speech of welcome by the director, Theodore Morrison. All of us gathered in a large lecture hall. I sat next to a row of French doors. As Morrison talked—the history and the purpose of Bread Loaf, what to expect—my eyes wandered over the gathered people, wondering which of these people were writers I knew about. I was keeping my eyes out for Frost, in particular, hoping that he might attend the opening lecture, hoping for a glance at a man who made great poems. Looking casually to my right, through the glass doors, I saw him. He was walking with two friends, Frost a little ahead, his mouth moving humorously as he talked. The ground outside sank away, and Frost, approaching the lecture hall uphill, appeared to be rising out of the ground. His face was strong and blocky, his white hair thick and rough. He looked like granite, some old carved stone like menhirs in Ireland which I saw in the *National Geographic*. But he was gifted to walk and to speak. Through the window I saw his mouth move with speech, and the faces of his companions broke into laughter.

But I had no mind, at sixteen, for his companions. I had seen the great poet, the maker of "To Earthward," and "After Apple-Picking." He was palpable, human, in the flesh. I felt light in head and body. Merely seeing this man, merely laying startled eyes upon him, allowed me to feel enlarged. My dreams for my own life, for my own aging into stone, took reality in the stern flesh of Robert Frost, who rose out of a hill in Vermont.

Frost attended some of the poetry workshops, conducted outdoors by Louis Untermeyer after lunch. When Frost came, we learned to tremble. Whatever poem was up for discussion that day, Frost was liable to be cutting, sarcastic, dismissive. The day when Untermeyer chose to read and discuss my poems was a day Frost didn't come. I was relieved. One day Frost took over the workshop all by himself. He chose a young woman's poem to read aloud, and asked for comments. A few people said a few fatuous things; only the brave or the stupid would lay themselves open to Frost's wit. He dismissed the fatuities with a cast of his forearm. Then he said, "Who *wrote* this poem?," his voice heavy with disgust. The young woman—I remember that she was small, attractive in a Cambridge manner, married to a Harvard graduate student—acknowledged authorship, looking deliberately stalwart. *"No,"* said Frost, "I mean, who *really* wrote it?" There was silence, bewilderment. After a long pause, while Frost held to the sides of the podium with evident anger, and stared at the audience as if he dared anyone to speak, the woman spoke again. "I wrote it," she said, "and I don't know what you're talking about."

"You didn't write it," Frost said, and waved the typed page in the air. "You know who wrote it?"—his voice pronounced

the name with the heaviest sarcasm he could summon, and he could summon sarcasm as well as anyone: "*T. S. Eliot!*"

That afternoon at the workshop, I gulped at Frost's asperity, but I accepted the notion that it was warranted. And it *was* warranted—I will argue, now—if we take poetry more seriously than we take social smoothness. The poem *was* "written by T. S. Eliot," on a bad day; and if anyone imitates another author, and shows it to other poets—well, she gets what's coming to her. If we devote our lives to poetry, and take our lives seriously, we must praise and denounce with equal ferocity. People who follow the notion that praise is requisite—"Boost Don't Knock"—should sell cars. To be a poet, as Frost was wont to say, you've got to have a snout for punishment.

But there was another side to his harshness: if the young woman had imitated Robert Frost instead of T. S. Eliot, Robert Frost would not have been so angry. He would have been scornful, but he would not have been angry. Frost was angry because most of the professionals in the modern poetry business—teachers or critics or reviewers—preferred Eliot over Frost. In his competitive ambition, Frost was outraged. For him—as he liked to say—there was room for only one at the top of the steeple—and he demanded to be the one. He was jealous of all other poets.

And not only of poets.

One day, I sat on the porch talking with him. I sat with a young woman from Bryn Mawr and her mother, both good looking. Frost rocked and spoke laconically yet wittily, proud and strong, delighted to hold this audience. We sat in the breeze, late afternoon, late summer, three of us looking at one of us, waiting for the words he would utter, and I was aware—as at times of love, of triumph, and of catastrophe—of the moment as I lived it. He asked me about my school, and about where I would go to college. Then Frost, who had gone to Lawrence High School and fitfully to Dartmouth and Harvard, disparaged higher education. At the time I felt uncomfortable, and did not know why: he was one-upping me; he could not help but make himself out to be better than any male around him, even if the male was sixteen.

3. Public Frost

I talked with Frost a few times during my four years at Harvard. He lived in Cambridge fall and spring. Around Harvard, Frost was cagey. America's foundation is possibly not so much freedom of religion as freedom of competition; or possibly the religion of competition: Harvard is its Vatican City. The only Americans more competitive than Harvard undergraduates are Harvard faculty members. When I saw Frost at Harvard, it was among undergraduates and faculty, and he kept his elbows close to his sides, and he saw to it that he sat in a corner of the room, with his flanks covered. This was a sophisticated Robert Frost, suspicious, combative, happy, blessedly far from the benign farmer, capable of verses, one met in the news magazines. The great competitor appeared to enjoy the schoolyard of competition. If he made a slip it would never be forgotten. He made no slips.

Here sits Robert Frost in a corner, his eyes scanning the room for approaching enemies. Undergraduates ask questions about Yeats, Eliot, Pound. The corpses of Yeats, Eliot, and Pound litter the floor of the housemaster's living room. Someone mentions Robert Lowell's name. Frost says he guesses Lowell is pretty good. Of course he's a *convert,* he says, he lays the word out like a frog in a biology lab. Frost remembers a story. Because he smiles when he remembers it, his audience understands that it is a malicious story. Frost tells us that Allen Tate's a convert too; once he saw Tate at a party standing next to a Jesuit, and he walked over to them; he asked the Jesuit, "Are you a *convert?*" "No," says the Jesuit; "Well, neither am I," says Frost, and walks away. Telling his story he grins, and when he finishes he laughs a slow long laugh, happy and mean. We laugh also. Tate's and Lowell's bodies join the heap on the carpet.

Three years after graduation I spent a year at Stanford on a writing fellowship. When I heard that Frost would read his poems there, I was delighted. But the reading was horrid. It took place in a huge auditorium, packed full. Some faculty attended and some students, but most of the audience appeared to be Robert Frost's peculiar audience, who would not have attended a poetry reading by Wallace Stevens or William Carlos Williams, but would have crossed flooded rivers and burning forests to hear Robert Frost. Many were people who celebrated Frost for what he was not—and for them, he pretended to be what he was not. Finding himself with this audience, he cooed and chuckled, he trotted out his country sayings, and he performed his tricks: speaking one poem, he interrupted himself in the middle, smiled a "mischievous grin" at his audience, and cackled, "Now, *that*'s a good line." And Frost put down "the professors," those fancy intellectuals who read all those hidden meanings into a simple old fellow's poems. Everybody laughed, everybody roared in delight. Almost everybody. I felt angry at his betrayal of himself and of poetry; he pretended to be the poet my grade-school teacher had praised. He *performed* in order to be *loved.* He played Mortimer Snerd for these people; he played the combination of Edgar Bergen and Mortimer Snerd, making himself his own dummy.

Yet I went to Wallace Stegner's cocktail party afterward.

Stegner was an old friend of Frost's from Bread Loaf, and he lived in a modern house fashioned neatly into the dry grass of California hills, great glass panels looking west toward sunsets. In the living room with its low soft furniture, blond wood and glass, Robert Frost sat in a deep chair with a martini in his hand. But this was not the creature of an hour before—kindly and folksy, cuddly and chuckly; this Robert Frost held the stem of his martini glass neatly between thumb and forefinger, drank a few, held his liquor, and denounced other poets. I remember that he spoke of Yvor Winters—who taught at Stanford, and who had written unfavorably of Frost—as "clever," using the word as they use it at Oxford, as permanent dismissal: shallow, callow, meretricious, pretentious.

I had seen two versions of Frost: one a performer who manipulated an audience by lying to it, the other a malicious literary figure attacking his enemies. Neither version seemed connected to the poet who had made great poems. I went home and read "Home Burial" again, that early narrative, better than "The Death of the Hired Man," sensitive to all measure of feeling. The wife has lost a child, and stands always at a special place on the stair, from which she can see his grave. The practical husband says that the living have got to go on living. But the wife finds it irreconcilable that life should simply go on, when her baby has died.

> . . . The nearest friends can go
> With anyone to death, comes so far short
> They might as well not try to go at all.
> No, from the time when one is sick to death,
> One is alone, and he dies more alone.
> Friends make pretense of following to the grave,
> But before one is in it, their minds are turned
> And making the best of their way back to life
> And living people, and things they understand.
> But the world's evil. I won't have grief so
> If I can change it. . . .

Frost was inconsolable, over the losses of death. I think or "Out, Out—" where the boy loses his arm to a saw, and then dies of shock. "And they,"—the poem ends, outraged—"since they / Were not the one dead, turned to their affairs."

So what was this man doing—I asked myself—being a buffoon on the platform, and a literary hit-man at a cocktail party, when he had written such poems?

The question was part silliness. The man on the platform, and the man at the cocktail party, was vain and vulnerable, needed adulation, needed victory; he was a man not a monument. Because he had written great poems, I demanded greatness at all times and in all matters. "And I am not a demigod," said Pound in a late Canto. The old poet has created—over decades of work, rejection, suffering, failure, and success—a *body* of work; not an edifice, not a monument, not an institution. If he is a great poet, then that body is an alternate to his own; it is permanent, and it contains the best of him. The poet in his own skin will never equal his poems.

Still, the question bears asking another way: what purposes did it serve Frost to mount and present—that day at Stanford, and on many other days—a public character so far from his own? The deception, I think, served large purposes. The best of his poems represented his feeling with honesty and accuracy—and with terror. Robert Frost lived in terror of madness and suicide. (If a child dies, and you cannot go on—what is it that you plan to *do?*) When he wrote the poems that told the terror, and that summoned intelligence to control the terror, he must have suffered in the telling. When he retold his poems at poetry readings, or answered questions about them, he lied and lied and lied—in order not to repeat that ordeal over and over again. So his performance was the opposite of Anne Sexton's, and equally disturbing. She exploited her own suffering for a morbid audience; he denied all suffering for a sentimental audience.

There was, I think, another reason as well: the need for love and applause was a need for forgiveness. I will speak of this notion later.

When I was back at Harvard as a Junior Fellow I helped Robert Pack and Louis Simpson edit *The New Poets of England and America.* I wrote Frost to ask if he would write an introduction for us; I did not think he would. For some months he did not answer. I wrote a second time; still no reply. At the publisher's impatient request, we tried someone else, and a few days later I had a letter from Robert Frost:

September 18, 1956

Dear Don Hall:

There would be no excuse in the world for my not writing you juniors a preface to your poetry unless it were the poor one that I try to keep a rule of not writing prefaces. But rules aren't meant to be kept. They're meant to break on impulse when you have any impulse left in you; before the evil days when fun ceases. So if you will let me see some of the poems to take off from I'm your cheerful victim. I'll be down in Cambridge in a week or two now where I can see you to talk the matter over. I've been hoping to see you anyway.

Mind you I'm roused up to do this con amore and I'm not so lazy that I can't do it.

Ever yours
Robert Frost

I was surprised, and pleased for the book. I sent Frost some poems. I did not see him. Although his letter invited me to pay a visit, I waited for him to telephone, as if he should prove his invitation's sincerity by pursuing me with a lasso. After another wait, the brief and elegant introduction arrived. It was called "Maturity No Object," and did little dances among notions of poetry and growing older. The prose was typical in its eloquent tortuousness, epigram softened by idiom. Frost was concerned that almost all American poets were students or teachers and in his preface dealt with his doubts by promenading them without calling them doubts. And oh, he could make a sentence; he could make a pun, and turn his heel on it for a transition.

In fact the poet and scholar have so much in common and live together so naturally that it is easy to make too much of a mystery about where they part company. Their material seems the same—perhaps differs a little in being differently come by and differently held in play. Thoroughness is the danger of the scholar, dredging to the dregs. He works on assignment and self-assignment with some sense of the value of what he is getting when he is getting it. He is perhaps too avid of knowledge. The poet's instinct is to shun or shed more knowledge than he can swing or sing. His most available knowledge is acquired unconsciously. Something warns him dogged determination however profound can only result in doggerel. His danger is rhyming trivia. His depth is the lightsome blue depth of the air.

It's the work of an older man. As I read it now, and I come close to fifty, it talks to me more than it used to talk.

Now the book was ready, and I sent the introduction to New York. But I did something else—or I failed to do something else. I did not write Frost to tell him that we had received the introduction, that we admired it, that we were grateful. I was still too young or too cloddish to understand that Frost of all people would be waiting to hear our approval. Really, *anyone* would be waiting—but perhaps especially an artist in his seventies making connections with artists in their twenties. I could not conceive that "Robert Frost" could care for my opinion. I could not grant him that humanity. Institutions do not have feelings, do not need bolstering. In a week or two, an aggrieved Kathleen Morrison telephoned to wonder what was happening. I am sure she had heard certain grumblings.

When Frost wrote the Introduction to our anthology, I know that he served himself. He wanted to stay in touch with the young; although he would be jealous of any of us caught mounting the steeple, he wanted us to like him, to praise him. At the same time, perched where he was, it was generous of him to write for us at all, and he wrote well. Whatever the motives he acknowledged to himself, his motives were complicated; I believe that he would acknowledge only the selfish ones. When caught in the act of virtue, he would proclaim it vice. And about the time he wrote the Introduction, he began to involve himself in another act of generosity. Or rather, Archibald MacLeish saw to it that he became involved.

Everyone knows that Ezra Pound was locked up in Washington from 1945 to 1958, as a result of treason charges. Almost everyone knows that Frost had a hand in the release. This magnanimity fit Frost's old reputation for benignity, but does not square with Frost's new, posthumous reputation for nastiness. But Frost's character wore at least three faces. He could appear simple and sweet to the masses, twenty years ago, while in private and to his literary acquaintances he avowed that he was selfish and cynical. The third and least obvious Frost was secretly magnanimous, while accusing himself of being a saint for the Devil's reasons. To get Frost to do something good, you had to convince him that he could do it for a wicked reason.

Archibald MacLeish was leader among a circle of people who worked to free Ezra Pound. Perhaps MacLeish was the most effective of all the group, because his dedication was accompanied by political sophistication, by friends in Washington and in government. Still, the push to release Pound needed a stronger public force. Only Robert Frost was visible enough and respectable enough to push Congress.

The first and essential move was to persuade Frost to act. Now, Frost never *liked* Pound. He owed Pound a debt of gratitude, which may account for initial dislike; they are rarely generous people who can forgive anyone for helping them get started. Pound had nothing to do with Frost's original publication, but as soon as Pound read Frost's poems, he promoted them with Poundian zeal, reviewing them, recommending them, and bullying the American public about this neglected writer. Frost didn't like the bullying part, disliked Pound's ridicule of America for Philistinism, and was fearful that American editors and critics would associate him with Pound's rhetoric. There were obvious disparities between the two men. Frost was older, from New England, quiet, and private. Pound was young, noisy, flamboyant—it was the period when Pound wore trousers fabricated of green billiard table cloth—and Frost would not have taken to him under any circumstances. Then for forty years Pound was champion of modernism and free verse, while Frost wrote sonnets and took every occasion to ridicule verse without meter. "I'd just as soon play tennis without a net," Frost said one million times. While Pound, in his remarkable detachment, could praise Frost because Frost was excellent, even when Frost's excellence ran contrary to Pound's theories and advocacies—Frost was more like the common run of humanity, and could not forgive the difference.

Finally, Frost was a patriot. Pound considered *himself* a patriot, for that matter, and found it ironic that *he* should be called a traitor. But Frost shared the more conventional opinion that to broadcast for an enemy, in time of war, and to ask American troops to lay down their arms, sounded like giving aid and comfort to an enemy. Frost was a patriot of an old fashion which it may be difficult for a reader to understand, if the reader has grown up after the Second World War—through Korea and Vietnam, through Greece and Chile, through assassinations and revelations of crookedness in high places. Frost came from the world of the *Republic,* when Fourth of July orators denounced the British Empire—and all other empires, ignoring our own adventures in Cuba, Panama, and the Philippines—and praised the independence and separation of this continent from the crowned heads of Europe and their wars. When the United States went to war, you *knew* that it was a righteous war, and you knew who would win. When Chinese troops overran the Americans in Korea, in the Yalu Valley, and Marines and regular army made the most massive retreat in American history, Robert Frost wept for three days. When Frost returned from a USIA trip with

Faulkner, and Faulkner had been drunk on foreign soil, he denounced Faulkner as "a disgrace to the colors."

So when MacLeish decided to convince Frost to help release Pound from St. Elizabeth's, where he languished rather than stand trial for treason, it appeared a formidable charge. But MacLeish knew his man. I asked MacLeish how he planned to persuade Frost to intervene. Oh, he said, he would just tell Robert that Ezra was getting *too much attention,* locked up down there; if we get him out, people won't notice him so much.

So Frost talked to the Attorney General on a couple of occasions, he called on some legislators, he talked with Sherman Adams, and his opinions were accepted in the newspapers as benign and fair-minded. MacLeish started the campaign, but once he was committed to help, Frost worked hard, making special trips to Washington, trying with his charm to influence the influential. Gradually Washington's attitudes toward Pound altered and the Justice Department was able to release him in 1958. Four years later, when I saw Frost next, I asked him how he had happened to work for Pound's release. He looked cunning, amused, and pleased with himself as he told me that Ezra was getting *too much attention,* being locked up down there; we got him out, now people don't notice him so much. . . .

4. Remember Me

At the inauguration of President Kennedy, in 1960, Robert Frost read his old and fine poem about the sense of nationhood, "The Gift Outright," altering the tense of one verb, predicting great things by means of the future tense. He knew the poem by heart. Harsh sunlight kept him from reading aloud some chatty lines he had written for the occasion. For the first time in our history, a poet had taken part in an inauguration; and for the first time in our history, tens of millions of Americans heard a great American poet read a poem.

Frost was eighty-six, with only two more years to live. The inauguration changed his life, at the end of it. He became *famous,* like a president or an athlete. When he flew to Russia, and talked with Nikita Khrushchev, two books were written about that quick trip. When he went off to England for honorary degrees, and returned to his walkways of fifty years before, the return was well photographed and reported on; his life became a series of media events.

He loved it.

I was teaching at Michigan, where Frost had been poet in residence briefly in the early twenties. He had planned to stay in Ann Arbor back then, but the university president who invited him died, and the new president asked Frost an indelicate question: as I understand it, the new president asked him just exactly what he *did* around here. This insult gave Frost in his pride an excuse to pack up and return to New England, where he wanted to live anyway.

In 1962 the Student Union wanted Robert Frost to return to Ann Arbor and read his poems. He agreed to come, wanting to return to Ann Arbor on the tour he was making of places crucial to his life, the great goodbyes of an energetic ancient, goodbyes cherished and then repeated, the old man always retaining some confidence that he would, somehow, really be back *yet again.* The Union asked me to introduce him. I agreed, but I was nervous about it, half expecting him to say something rude about me, maybe one of his lines about professors.

He would read on April 2, a Monday night. Student Union officers met him on Sunday at the airport, and took him to Inglis House, an elegant estate willed to the university and used as a guest house. Then a small group of us—undergraduate officers of the Union and his old Ann Arbor friend Erich Walter and I—sat around with Frost for an hour, chatting while he drank a 7-Up. Walter talked old Ann Arbor times with him. I told Frost I had seen Pound two years before, and that Pound regretted what the newspapers had quoted him as saying—that Frost had taken long enough, to help him get out of St. Elizabeth's—and Frost said, well, he should regret it.

Then he went on about Pound. He had seen a lot of people *about* Pound, he told us, but he never saw *Pound;* he didn't want to see him, because of all the crazy things he heard Pound quoted as saying; he didn't want to see him in that shape. Then he told us that he had never really liked Pound anyway, though he had things to be grateful for. In fact, he said, Pound was one of the reasons he moved from Beaconsfield, near London, down to a farm in Gloucester. He left Beaconsfield in order to avoid seeing Pound, at the same time not wanting to offend him; if he had stayed in Beaconsfield he would have had to refuse invitations all the time. Why did he dislike Pound? He found Pound *affected,* always looking for something new, trying to be new, trying to find what hadn't been done yet and doing it. Then he went on to say that he found Yeats affected too, and didn't like him either. He told how Yeats had once observed to George Russell, "I think we must absolve the stars." And old Robert Frost—sitting in Inglis House surrounded by admirers, eighty-eight years old, in 1962 remembering fifty years back—roused himself to anger over the ancient blarney of William Butler Yeats.

"Bunk!" he roared in his best American. "Bunk!"

Monday, the day of his reading, began with a press conference at eleven. We picked Frost up at Inglis House, and took him to the Regents' Room in the administration building. A man from the university television studio showed Frost a drawing of himself made by a local artist for use in a television series. He signed the picture as requested, but grumbled: he didn't like the picture, it thickened his face and made him look too stolid; also, the artist had swept his hair romantically down over his forehead. "I don't wear my hair that way," he said. "They're trying to make me look like Sandburg." Then he remembered a story to tell on Carl Sandburg, and as he told it, his own malice cheered him up, and his grumpiness vanished. I heard him tell the story twice later in the day, when he found some new faces to tell the story to:

When Frost was in Ann Arbor—the year he lived out on Pontiac—he brought Sandburg to read his poems at the university. Before the reading, Frost, who was living alone, cooked Sandburg a lamb chop. As dinner was ready to serve, Sandburg went upstairs to the bathroom, and didn't come downstairs for an hour and a half. Frost was furious, the dinner was ruined. "What were you *doing* there?" he asked Sandburg. "I had to do my hair," Sandburg said, "for the boys." Or that's what Frost *said* Sandburg said.

At the press conference, Frost sat at the head of a long table, the television lights bright in his eyes and three cameras cranking. I sat beside him, my job to bellow repetition of questions into his ear, on account of his deafness. Frost was funny and lively, repeating things he had said before, happy, the center of everything. Then he signed some books for people, and we went back to Inglis House for lunch. Now he talked politics. We should have settled the Cuban problem a long time ago, he said, but he didn't tell us how. And he ridiculed welfare, which he had been doing for thirty years. And he told about an argument he had with Justice Black. Frost met Black at Frost's eighty-eighth birthday party, just a few days before, and Frost had immediately launched into a hymn of praise for the Supreme Court, one of the greatest institutions the world had ever known—he told us he said—and above partisanship. Black disputed the point, perhaps out of modesty. Frost's praise, Black said, was sentimental; Black avowed that *he* was not removed from partisanship; he was a labor man and he had always been a labor man. As Frost told the story, he became angry; he told us that he told Black the court should put "patriotism above party."

After lunch someone drove us back to my house. In my living room he signed books for me—"from his old friend Robert Frost with high regard"; "remembering old Bread Loaf days"—and told me stories. Talking about the Kennedys brought up Teddy's cheating on an examination at Harvard. Then he said that he never cheated in school, he *wouldn't* have done such a thing; but his virtue, he hastened to assure me, was by-product of a vice: he would not cheat because he was proud. He looked at me shrewdly—aware of giving himself away, delightedly giving himself away—and said that when he had gone to Lawrence High School he had been good at Latin; that he would come to school and hide in the bushes until the bell rang, then dash inside.

When he had told me so much he stopped, and watched me to see if I got the point. I did. He hid in the bushes with his

Latin homework done by hand and finished. He would take no help on his homework—and he would give none either.

He wanted to see some classrooms, he said. We parked and walked through Mason and Angell halls. Passing one lecture hall, I mentioned that I taught a class in it. "How much do they make you teach?" he asked.

I liked my schedule. I taught the same number of classes as anyone else, but they were jammed together into two afternoons; morning has always been my best time for work. "Tuesday and Thursday afternoons," I said. "One to four."

His face changed; we might have been rivals for team captain, or for a girl, or for a last piece of chicken tetrazzini. Smug and powerful, he said, "They didn't make me teach that much."

He grew tired, after half an hour, and I took him back to Inglis House. He asked me what I had written lately, and said he wasn't always sure what people were up to. I told him my latest book was prose, a memoir about my summers on the New Hampshire place where my grandfather farmed. He asked if he could see it; maybe he could read in it before his afternoon nap. After we left him at Inglis House, I went home and picked up a copy and took it back to the housekeeper for him. I was anxious that he like it. It was a book of love for my grandparents, and the other old people of the country, and for the culture they had known when they were young—culture of Lyceum and political debate, fairs, and baseball games that pitted married men against single men, of high schools that required Latin and offered Greek, of two-hour sermons and Christian Endeavor and the Willing Workers Circle of the Kings Daughters. It was a book of love for the dead and the dying, and of bitterness over loss.

When we picked him up that night, Frost wanted to know how tickets had gone, and when he discovered that Hill Auditorium was sold out, his pleasure expanded to fill the limousine which the Union had rented for the occasion. Four thousand seats; standing room only. His pleasure in a crowd found its counterpart if ever he lacked a crowd. Someone who ran a series of poetry readings in a large city has told me about Frost's "madness of old age"—though I suspect that old age only made manifest what had earlier been lightly disguised. When Frost read in a series, she told me, she could allow no empty seats visible from the platform. If there were empty seats, the old poet would be inconsolable, would rage and fume, would invoke conspiracy and intrigue. In desperation, when she had a small audience for him, she and her assistants dredged additional bodies from offices nearby—free tickets, *please* come, just sit there. . . .

Inside, we walked to a green room behind the stage so that Frost could rest for a moment. He told me he had been reading my book; it was good, he told me, and his eyes took on that amusement which let me know he had a wisecrack. "You talk about the *decay* of New England," he said; of course he wouldn't like that part so much, although he was a poet of deserted villages and abandoned farms. "It's a *compost heap,*" he said.

When I left him backstage, to go out to introduce him, he said, "You know I can't hear you. You can abuse me all you like." Of course it was a joke; of course it expressed that same distrust which *I* felt. When he shuffled onstage, to immense and prolonged applause, I stayed long enough to hook the lavaliere microphone around his neck. Then I went backstage, and watched the reading for a while on the television monitors; then I snuck out front and stood against the wall to watch him read for the last time. Bread Loaf, Stanford, Ann Arbor. It was the best of the three. He was triumphant, utterly happy, as he returned to a scene of his struggling middle age. In his triumph, he read with energy and conviction, stopping to make jokes on occasion, but not jokes to humiliate poetry, or the professors who looked for hidden meanings. And I, who had been afraid that he would belittle me, heard him speak of me with affection. He said he wanted to come to Ann Arbor, despite his recent illness, for a number of reasons, and one of them was to see a young poet he had helped to bring up. He left with the audience the impression that he had supervised my writing from the age of sixteen. He referred to me as a son. He started to mention *String Too Short to Be Saved,* but he couldn't remember the title, so he changed the subject. Then he said that New England was in decay, all right; it was a compost heap from which had come five presidents and Donald Hall and himself, so it wasn't so bad.

After reading for an hour he looked as tired as he looked pleased, and he slowed himself down and stopped. I climbed onto the stage and undid his microphone. The audience applauded and stood up. He waved me off and holding the microphone in his hand said one more poem. Then he followed me from the stage—the audience standing and applauding again, determined to stand and applaud forever—and when we stood in the dark corridor behind the stage, he said, "It's a pity not to let them have more when they are like that. Why don't you go out and ask them if they want any more?" There was no stopping him. I told him that the question was unnecessary, that if he felt strong enough he should go out and do another.

After the second encore I led him back to the green room again—exhausted, gray-looking, but his eyes bright with triumph. Ten minutes restored him, and he was ready to return to Inglis House for scrambled eggs and 7-Up. When we opened the green room door, we found hundreds of students crowded into the backstage corridors, waiting for sight of the old poet. The white hair behind me drew cheers, and there was movement through the crowd as people pushed to see him. Hands held out copies of books for signing, autograph books, scraps of paper. We moved toward the car, Jim Seff and I running interference. Behind us Frost was saying thank you, thank you, and refusing to sign anything. Looking ahead,

I could see that the doors were open and the limousine waiting. Hundreds more people milled outside around the car. He had dreamed his entire life of moments like this, and when the dreams came true *they were every bit as good as he had expected them to be.* At the same time, there was something in Frost that needed to reject the adulation when it took concrete form. In front of me as I struggled through the crowd I saw two girls; one of them looked shy, and held a piece of paper; the other, her bold friend, was urging her, "Go ahead. Give it to him." So the shy one handed Frost a drawing she had made of him during the reading; the old poet squinted and shoved it back at her, still shuffling forward, growling, "What do I want with that?"

When we reached the car, he turned back to the crowd for a moment, before negotiating his way into the back seat, raised his arms above his shoulders like Eisenhower giving the victory sign, and said in a loud, tremulous voice, "Remember me."

"We will," said voices around us and in back of us and in front of us. "We will."

Wedged into the back seat, Frost spoke slowly as the car moved cautiously out into the crowd, turning into the street. Oh, it was wonderful—to come back in this way, to have this kind of *tribute.* And it was so strange, he said, because even as late as when he was forty-five years old, he had never expected real recognition. He only hoped, he only felt *able* to hope that he might make a couple of little poems that would stick. Stick in an anthology somewhere.

I listened to him, moved, and feeling closer to him than I had ever felt or dared to feel. Many times I had found myself amused or aghast at a poet's vanity—since I first discovered it at Bread Loaf—Frost's or my own or another's. But "vanity" was a word used for the light side of a heavy thing. "Fame is the spur," said Milton, in lines that faintly embarrass a good many people, "that last infirmity of noble minds." The notion of fame embarrasses us because we confuse it with *mere* vanity, like preening before a mirror. Or we confuse it with celebrity, as if Milton had been confessing his desire to become Johnny Carson. Fame is a word for the love that everyone wants, impersonal love, love from strangers for what we are, what we do or make. People write poems when they are ten so that their mothers will love them; when they are sixteen so that their peers will love them; when they are thirty (and eighty-eight) so that the Muse will love them, and ages to come, and *all* men and women, universally, forever and ever, as long as the language exists and maybe longer. Although Frost had become a contemporary celebrity, and although Hill Auditorium resembled Johnny Carson's audience more than Milton's, Frost's response to applause came from his deep and vast ambition to be a great poet, to be immortal, to write poems that would *stick.* His ambition was never merely to be a celebrated poet—that is *mere* vanity; it was larger and more serious than that, for he knew that to write great poems he had to make perfect works of art, which embodied wisdom and knowledge beyond the perfection of art. In pursuit of such ambition you may become pitiless and harsh to those around you. Like Orpheus you kill your wife a second time, by turning around to see if she enjoys your singing; then perhaps you deserve to be torn apart by the Thracean ladies, or by the Furies.

Or you think you deserve it; the poet sees to his own punishment. I was watching Frost's face in the faint light of the back seat, and suddenly his face turned dark. "But it's sad too," he said. He spoke of "sadness," which is a faint and crepuscular word, but his face looked more like "despair" or "agony." "It has a sad side, too," he said. For a while he said nothing; I did not know what he meant. "We were so poor," he said. I remembered the years at Derry, the deaths of children, suicide, madness.

So he was a guilty man, and guilty over the wrongs he felt he had done to people he loved—the same guilt that Ezra Pound lived with. Therefore, perhaps he courted love, *any* love, even the kind he took from his Stanford audience, to assuage his conviction that he was *bad.* The need for love and applause was a need for forgiveness. And when he received the love he asked for, he knew it was worthless; he rejected it, and asked for more.

I left him at Inglis House, to eat his supper with undergraduates. He asked if he would see me the next day, and I told him that I hadn't planned on it. He asked if I could visit him in Vermont next summer and I told him I could.

The next morning I had an errand in Detroit, so I wasn't there when he telephoned. He wanted me to come over and talk with him, he told Kirby. He had been reading *String* when he went to bed, he told her, and he wanted to talk to me some more about it. He asked if I could come over in the afternoon before he left for the airport; no, she said, I was teaching then, but she'd ask me to telephone him when I got back for lunch. Then she told him that she liked his reading the night before. The compliment allowed him to ask a question that had been troubling him: he had brought *two* different black suits with him, he told her, and while he was out on the platform last night he had realized that he was wearing the pants from one suit and the coat from the other; could she tell? could she notice? Did she think anyone noticed? She could tell him without hypocrisy that she had noticed nothing, and he seemed relieved; well, he said, he guessed they were pretty much the same color.

When I called him up we made it definite about Vermont next summer. "I want to see a lot more of you," he said, and referred to me again in metaphor as his son. All of this visit, he had remarked how tall I had grown. "I hardly recognized you," he said, "when we first met. I didn't remember you were so tall." On the way to the press conference he had said, "You're getting taller every time I look at you." When I was sixteen at Bread Loaf I had my full height; it was as if Frost had to invent a new, larger man to explain his interest. Then on the telephone he returned to *String Too Short to Be Saved.*

"So much more happened to you than ever happened to me," he said, about a book in which little happened. Then he said something I carry with me. "You can do anything in poetry you want to do," he said; I took it, correctly, that he meant to say that I hadn't yet done a great deal.

5. Last Versions

In June, on our way from New Hampshire back to Michigan, we stopped at Frost's cabin on the Homer Noble Farm at Ripton in Vermont, near Bread Loaf.

We were to come at midmorning. First we called at the old farmhouse, where Kathleen and Ted Morrison spent their summers, about two hundred yards downhill from Frost's cabin. Mrs. Morrison telephoned uphill to the cabin, and told us that Robert would be ready for us in fifteen or twenty minutes. I felt annoyed—ungenerous; suspicious—as if someone with power kept me waiting in order to assert power. We passed the time of day with Mrs. Morrison—who must have spent so many hours like this, as doorkeeper or receptionist—until the phone rang and we were directed toward the cabin. It was a cool, sharp day, little sparks of rain in our eyes, a quick wind, as Kirby and I struggled uphill with our children. The log cabin appeared before us, not beautiful but comfortable, and the old man opened the door, smiling and handsome and vigorous. Behind him a fierce fire of birch logs blazed in the living room fireplace. He had kept us waiting—he told us when he let us in—because it was such a raw and rainy day; he wanted to have a good fire going.

We visited for two hours, five of us, and the children were

attentive and quiet. Frost monologued most of the time, out of his deafness. He wore a white shirt, dark trousers, and canvas shoes with thick rubber soles which comforted his feet. The flap of his belt—the loose part that sticks out past the buckle—incompletely fitted into the leather loop that was supposed to restrain it; this incompleteness bothered Philippa, who spent much of the two hours attempting to straighten the belt through the loop and smooth it flat. Frost accepted her ministry without complaint. Late in the visit, Philippa made her only show of boredom. "Do you have a TV?" she asked him. There was no set visible in the cabin. Frost would accept adulation from anyone. He looked down on the three-year-old, smiling from his deaf tower, and acknowledged: "You've seen me on TV?"

He rambled on, friendly and impersonal. He had turned down an invitation from Robert and Ethel Kennedy that day; they had asked him to a dinner dance, and he told us about it, bragging and making fun of himself. "I never been to a dinner dance," he said. "That's not my sort of thing, a dinner dance. They throw each other in the pool. I would have been ashamed. Not for them, for myself." And he told about Ethel showing him around the grounds, which were "affluent," he said. "We live like Republicans," Ethel told him, "and act like Democrats." Then maybe Frost felt he had gone far enough, showing fondness for the Kennedys. Just the other day, he told us, a Philadelphia newspaper had asked him to write a short patriotic essay, two hundred and fifty or three hundred words, on how the country had changed after Kennedy's election. The notion made Frost impatient. "That's *bunk,*" he said. "It's not the administration. It was always there."

So his talk went, in June of 1962, with this strange and happy audience. And all the time, as I sat listening and relaxed, I was aware that I would almost certainly never see him again, aware that this eighty-eight-year-old complexity, that I had seen walk out of the ground when I was sixteen, that I had admired, despised, feared, and loved—would go into the ground forever, before I could see him again. I could almost look ahead to a morning next winter, when we turned on the radio at breakfast and heard that Robert Frost had died in Peter Bent Brigham Hospital in Boston. And I could feel the loss as I would not have felt it a year earlier. I would feel—after so many years of fear and defense—that I had lost a model of survival, endurance: a model you need not so much at sixteen as at thirty-five.

That morning in the cabin Frost was vigorous and many-sided, determined to survive, complex and energetic. He talked about other poets; while we had visited New Hampshire, Frost had returned to Ann Arbor—*yet again*—to receive an honorary degree along with Theodore Roethke. Frost had known Roethke before, and spoke of him tolerantly, but criticized him—of all things—for being so competitive with other poets. Perhaps it was Roethke's *style* which bothered Frost; Roethke made his competitiveness obvious with a boyish enthusiasm. (A few months after Frost's death I saw Roethke in Seattle—not long before Roethke died, as it happened. He met me as I came into a house for a party, pulled me aside, dragged yards of galley out of the pockets of his jacket, and sat me down to read *The Far Field,* saying, "I've got a book coming out that's going to drive Wilbur and Lowell *into the shadows.*" This announcement was made without malice toward Wilbur or Lowell.) Frost asked me as well if I knew a poet from the Midwest, a man I'll call Harry Dutcher, who was writing a book on him. Frost had met him and liked him a lot. Was Harry Dutcher a good poet? I said he was, and tried to say what *kind* of a good poet he was. Frost listened intently, and I felt that I could follow a trail of feelings across his face. I could see Frost the schemer, wanting Dutcher to write a favorable book, anxious that I should carry Frost's flattery back to Dutcher. But on the other hand, I felt I could tell that his liking for Dutcher was genuine. And when Frost asked me the quality of Dutcher's poems, he wanted to hear two distinct answers: one Robert Frost wanted to hear that Dutcher was good, because Frost liked him; another wanted to hear that Dutcher was bad, and be rid of a potential steepleclimber.

As we chatted, I looked around his room, at the lapboard he used for writing, at the books he was reading, notes sticking out of them—Robinson's edition of Chaucer was there, and a volume of Horace. And I remember him attacking the idea that there was an American language. That notion was silly, he said; at least the notion that American and English poets were writing their poems in a different language was silly. Then with his usual ambivalence he contradicted himself: he said he wrote the way he talked, and it was an American way; he preferred the way he talked to the way Englishmen talked. "You went over there, too," he told me. I had spent three years in England, and would return a year later. "I'm glad you didn't stay over there and turn into an Englishman." I don't know if Frost knew that I had thought about it; he sounded as if he knew. Then he said something astonishing, that reflected his new amiability. "I like Eliot, and I like Pound . . ."—of course these clauses necessarily led into "but"—"I like Eliot and I like Pound," he told us, "but they left us behind. They should have stayed over here." He meant what he said; still, the old mind needed to flip again: "Of course, I heard an Englishman say, 'What's there to stay for?' "—and he laughed a brief, mellow laugh.

It was late in the morning. He walked to the door and looked out at the sun beginning to shine through the damp air. "It's done rainin', ain't it?" he said. It was time to go. We shook hands all around, and talked about when we would see each other again. With eighty-eight years on one of us, we agreed to make this Vermont summer visit an annual occasion, and to stay longer next time.

We said these things as Frost walked us to our car. As we started off I watched him in the rear-view mirror, and saw him suddenly run after us. I stopped, and he caught up with us; he leaned in the window on the driver's side, and reminded me to give his good wishes to Harry Dutcher when I saw him; he repeated that he hoped he was a good poet. We said goodbye again and I started up. This time I didn't look in the mirror, but slowed down because of a hole in the driveway, when I realized that Robert Frost had run after us again—eighty-eight years old, with sore feet, jogging after the car—because his face suddenly appeared at my window. He had thought of one more thing; I would please *not* tell Harry that Frost had hoped he was a good poet, because that would reveal that Frost had not read his work.

NOTES ON T. S. ELIOT

"Mr. Hall"—began the letter, which I received as a junior in college—"I wish that you would date your letters." It was my first letter from T. S. Eliot, and I have dated every letter, note, rejection slip, postcard, and coupon I have written since. It is hard to credit the authority Eliot's name commanded in 1949; much less his signature. Had the letter begun, "Mr. Hall, I wish you would commit arson upon the person of an elderly gentleman residing in your vicinity," or had it merely requested that I appear cross-gaitered, I would have set out to burn down a nearby old man, or to purchase gaiters. No one since has embodied, or seemed to embody, such authority—not Robert Lowell, not Allen Ginsberg, not Gary Snyder, not Robert Bly. Perhaps none of them would wish the power that Eliot possessed or seemed to possess. It doesn't matter; no one can assume the center of that stage, as Eliot did: there is no longer such a stage.

In retrospect I sense that the appearance of authority was Eliot's joke played on pomposity: on literary journalists in England, and on professors in the United States. Although Eliot was eminently serious, and serious about the role of the man of letters, for him the role must have carried its comedy. This comedy was lost on almost everyone; and it was essential to the comedy that it go unnoticed.

The Harvard Advocate is the literary magazine of Harvard College. Poets the *Advocate* published as undergraduates include T. S. Eliot, Wallace Stevens, and E. E. Cummings. In my day—I was class of '51—the *Advocate* published Adrienne Rich, Robert Bly, Peter Davison, Kenneth Koch, Frank O'Hara, L. E. Sissman, and John Ashbery. Many of us were editors; Adrienne was not, because at that time the *Advocate* was stag.

Back in 1938, the *Advocate* printed a special T. S. Eliot issue, full of essays and memoirs concerning the *Advocate*'s most famous alumnus, and reprinting his undergraduate poems. The issue was greatly successful, and doubtless pulled the magazine out of one of its financial canyons. Ten years later, in the fall of 1948, we trembled on the lip of the same canyon, and again seemed ready to plunge and destroy ourselves. Once or twice a week, all year, we would receive a letter from someone wanting to buy a copy of the 1938 Eliot issue, which had gone out of print ten years past. From time to time, someone would bring up the idea of another Eliot issue, to raise money. The suggestion went no further, until one night, as we gathered to paste up an issue, we discovered that we were six pages short. This fecklessness was not without precedent. The people who ran the magazine were *literary* sorts, far beyond efficiency or other narrow concerns. We worked hard, but we worked hard to keep standards high, which is to say that we worked hard at rejecting things. When there was an argument, the negative could be counted on to win. When in doubt, reject.

The *Advocate* of Eliot's day, in his memory, was as nasty as the *Advocate* of mine. "Everyone threw his poems into a basket," he remembered later in life, "and then they held a round robin to see who could say the most sarcastic things about the other man's work." One of the best contemporary poets had even less luck with the *Advocate.* When Robert Lowell was a freshman at Harvard, he tried out for the editorial board, which twice a year held competitions for new members. As he remembered it later, the *Advocate* encouraged him to show up and tack the carpet (we accomplished our redecorating by means of these competitions; I had painted woodwork in February of 1948) and then told him not to bother to return. Lowell transferred to Kenyon College, studied with John Crowe Ransom, roomed with Peter Taylor, befriended Randall Jarrell, and with *Lord Weary's Castle* became in 1946 the best of the young poets—a sequence of events not lost upon subsequent *Advocate* editors.

So we discovered in October or November of 1948 that negative judgment had cooperated with bad arithmetic to give us six blank pages. The issue was scheduled, with a printer who wanted no more antic chaos. If we delayed the issue, we would lose sales, which were already small. For a while, we considered leaving the pages blank, as testimonial to High Standards. This proposal had its charm, but perhaps would not have pleased the trustees—brokers and lawyers and other hard-headed sorts—to whom we would soon perforce appeal. The literary editor of the moment—he always carried the title "Pegasus"—came up with the suggestion which carried the day: we should reprint Eliot's poems, and thus make sure that we sold the issue out; we would even be able to pay off a few debts. It seemed at the time like an excellent idea. Because these were the days before Xerox, we had to type the poems out, in order to deliver copy to the printer in the morning. No one could find a copy of the old Eliot issue, but we had bound volumes from the first decade of the century, with Eliot's fragile little poems laid out in columns.

I forgot to mention that the refrigerator was full of beer that night, and we had been at it. Pegasus picked two of the drunkest editors to type up Eliot's poems, while the rest of us finished pasting galleys. Then we discovered that a blank page remained, even after we reprinted Eliot's poems. Someone suggested that we dedicate the issue to Mr. Eliot himself, in honor of his sixtieth birthday, which had been the subject of celebrations and publications earlier in the year. The typists delivered the copy, we fabricated a dedicatory note, and next morning delivered a sloppy bundle to the printer. When we picked up a thousand copies, a week or two later, we were initially pleased; the Eliot Supplement looked almost deliberate. Then we read over the dedication to Eliot, on the first page. Our printer, though a pleasant and tolerant man, had the drawback of being enterprising. When he read that we were dedicating the issue to T. S. Eliot in honor of his sixtieth birthday, he decided that we had made a simple error in typing. After all, no Harvard undergraduate was likely to be sixty years old. Opening the issue, we discovered that we were congratulating T. S. Eliot on turning sixteen.

The issue sold out quickly. Within weeks, we began to receive requests for the issue from academics and librarians anxious to acquire T. S. Eliot's undergraduate poems. Soon we had collected a hundred letters, many of them including checks. One of us knew a pamphlet printer, and volunteered to have a thousand copies of the Eliot poems printed up as a small pamphlet which we could sell at a profit. It seemed sound business. Within a week or two we found ourselves wallowing in boxes of T. S. Eliot's juvenalia.

None of us, at any point, had considered consulting Mr. Eliot. None of us, I think, had read the poems over, either. This was not so strange as it may seem. Eliot was so dominant a figure, so central to everyone concerned with modern literature, that we had read and studied his undergraduate poems long before. I'm sure that all of us on the *Advocate* had read Eliot's poems in our first week as editors, reading them *in the original,* in the old bound volumes on the wall. Our teachers had read them in the old Eliot issue, and for years had handed them around to be read like John Donne in manuscript. Therefore, none of us bothered to look at the new issue. If we had looked at it, we might have discovered the misspellings, omitted words, transposed stanzas, and general incompetence.

Not having noticed it, or considered Mr. Eliot's rights or feelings, we cheerfully sold the pamphlet for a dollar, distributing it in local bookstores and by mail order. Bagfuls of mail orders arrived at our offices. We cashed checks, paid off outstanding debts, and spent long hours addressing envelopes. I remember the day a polite letter arrived from a librarian at Yale, ordering six copies and enclosing a check for six dollars. Letters came from all over the country, from England, from Germany. We set about editing another issue of the *Advocate,* defending high standards as ever, secure in the annuity supplied by reprinting our earlier editor.

One day my tutor handed me a copy of our Eliot pamphlet, and suggested that I take a look at it. It was annotated in pencil, in a small and precise hand which took continual note of misspellings, omitted words, transposed stanzas, and general incompetence. A prominent artistic Harvard alumnus had sent my tutor the annotated pamphlet, with a note suggesting that perhaps the boys ought to be advised about their errors, and about the use these errors were being put to. For the prominent artistic Harvard alumnus, along with a few other alumni, had received his annotated Eliot pamphlet from the Yale University librarian to whom I had mailed six copies a few weeks before. I believe that this librarian concerned himself with acquiring manuscripts.

One of the alumni gifted with our botched and pirated pamphlet was Mr. Eliot himself. His letter dropped down on us like a wolf on the fold. Among other styles, Mr. Eliot had mastered the invective of English wrath. He was able to express rage with a steely, syntactic vastness that surpassed our limited American experience. We were withered by the letter, as fig trees are withered by Messiahs; therefore, we admired the letter greatly, treasured it—someone stole it, I think—and we tucked the crippled pamphlets away in a closet, whence they disappeared like confiscated wine from Italian government warehouses, as each editor departed with seven or ten souvenirs.

Eliot's letter was appropriately angry, of course. We had perpetrated enormities: reprinting poems without asking permission, not considering his rights or privileges, and in addition botching every poem we stole. But Eliot threatened no lawsuits, no vengeance. With something as amorphous and changeable as a college magazine, mind you, it is difficult to take action or to seek revenge. By the time you discover the committed outrage, the editors responsible have left college. When Eliot's letter arrived at our building, the old Pegasus was living in an eight-dollar-a-week room in Manhattan, writing Shakespearian sonnets and working as a scab house-painter. I was the new Pegasus, and to me it fell to answer Mr. Eliot's letter: to explain, apologize, alibi, and pass the buck.

As it happened, I had also to bring up another, related subject. I would have been writing Mr. Eliot anyway, if a Yale librarian had not supplied him with reason for writing first. Twayne Publishers had asked me to edit an anthology from the bound volumes of the *Advocate,* collecting the juvenilia of famous men. Besides Stevens, Cummings, and Eliot, Harvard undergraduates who had appeared in our pages, over the years, included Theodore Roosevelt, Franklin Roosevelt, Leonard Bernstein, John Reed, Malcolm Cowley, John Dos Passos, Norman Mailer, Howard Nemerov, Conrad Aiken, Robert Benchley, Van Wyck Brooks, John Wheelock, Edwin Arlington Robinson, and Arthur Schlesinger. One name in particular, Twayne assumed, would sell more copies than the rest of the names put together. If we did not have permission to include Eliot's poems, we could pack it in; there would be no book, there would be no contract, without Eliot's poems.

I had reached this point—in talking with Twayne—when Eliot's letter to the *Advocate* arrived. So I had to write him a letter in two parts. Part one would apologize for piracy and dismemberment of his poems. Part two would ask permission to reprint the same poems in the *Harvard Advocate Anthology*, and help to support the magazine which had just stolen and disfigured them. Part one, written with some disingenuousness, expressed sorrow over the activities of earlier editors. In part two, I put it to him. As the new Pegasus, I had been invited to edit . . . et cetera. In order for the anthology to succeed, we needed . . . et cetera. The magazine was in financial distress . . . et cetera. I wrote in a style as supple as President Harding's. I probably signed myself with a middle initial. Also, I did not date the letter.

His answer was gentle, with only a touch of asperity. I cannot find this letter, but I believe I remember what he said: he gave me permission to reprint his poems; he retreated from his earlier rage, and justifiable anger, supposing that an undergraduate magazine existed as a place where young editors learn by making mistakes. In giving permission to reprint his poems, he made a shrewd reservation. I was to print any of his undergraduate poems that I wished—except that I was to omit one of them; not one poem in particular, any one poem. Then at some future time Eliot could himself reprint his undergraduate poems, claiming correctly that these poems were collected together in accurate and authorized versions for the first time. *Poems Written in Early Youth* (1967) refers to an earlier pamphlet issued "without permission, and with many misprints. . . ."

In months to come, Eliot and I corresponded a little. I sent him proofs, that he might assure himself of accuracy. The book was published in December, 1950, just after I met Eliot for the first time. I took him to an *Advocate* party that fall, on one of his visits to Cambridge. I borrowed a car to pick him up, though our building was no more than five hundred yards from the guest house where he stayed. I remember little of that party, but I remember picking him up. Two young women sat inconspicuous in the back seat of the convertible—one of them my date, the other a literary person from Bennington engaged to the roommate from whom I borrowed the car. As Mr. Eliot bent to enter the seat beside the driver, I realized that he had not observed the occupants of the back seat. I hastened toward protocol, waving urgently in the direction of the back seat and shouting, "Mr. Eliot, I'd like you to meet . . ." He twisted and jumped, seeing them, reaching for his hat, and rising all at the same moment, so that with an abrupt jerk upward he hit his head on the doorframe of the car and knocked his hat off.

We settled down and traveled to the *Advocate,* where a hundred undergraduates and teachers crashed to observe the lion, and the martini drinkers staggered shoulder to shoulder. When I had delivered Eliot I retired to a corner. From time to time I staggered forth, to bar or bathroom, and on one of these occasions I bumped into Mr. Eliot, sober and preparing to leave. He looked at me with a pleasant smile, and said that he understood that I would be attending Oxford next year. Actually, it was only a hope; I had not yet won the fellowship I looked for. I told him that I *might* be attending Oxford next year. Ignoring the conditional, he asked me to look him up when I got to London; perhaps I would drop in on him at Faber and Faber, and perhaps at that time I would let him see some of my poems.

In London in September I found a cheap hotel, an awkward little place off Upper Shaftesbury Avenue, not far from the British Museum. It was only a few blocks from Russell Square, which was the address of Faber and Faber, and Mr. Eliot's business address. I had found the hotel on a tip from friends, and its proximity was fortuitous. As soon as I had taken the suitcase to my room, my first day at the hotel, I walked out to find Russell Square and Number 24.

All summer I had carried suitcase and typewriter through Italy and France and Scotland, working from time to time at improving my old poems, and on occasion beginning a new one. But I didn't do much work; I felt a little separate from my poems, and typing up a manuscript for Eliot began to bring me back to them. I left the manuscript, and a note reminding Mr. Eliot of my identity—dated, the return address highly legible—with a gentleman in uniform at 24 Russell Square. I waited less than a week until a small blue envelope turned up in the mail table in the lobby, with the Faber imprint I looked for. Eliot asked the pleasure of my company, at three in the afternoon, on a specified day in September of 1951.

Of course he had been inviting young poets to call on him for more than twenty years. The memoirs of English poets tell how each of them, at some point or other, received an invitation to meet Mr. Eliot. As a publisher, he kept his eyes open for young writers. As a critic and editor, he wanted to make the estimate of young poets that conversation adds to the printed page. As an older poet, he was generous and kind. When the English poets received their blue envelopes, they knew that Eliot had been reading their poems in the columns of the English weeklies. The letter was a sign of approval or at least interest. In my case, I had no such assurance. His invitation to me was sheerest generosity, perhaps coupled with old school feeling toward Harvard and the *Advocate.*

On the appointed day, I walked around Russell Square for an hour or so, rehearsing paragraphs of literary banter, until the hour of three, and precisely at three I presented myself to the uniform in the foyer of Faber and Faber. I was shown to a small waiting room, and almost immediately summoned to the elevator which would take me to Mr. Eliot's floor. I must have seemed nervous, because the uniformed man reassured me that Mr. Eliot was an extremely *pleasant* gentleman, and did I *know,* that he was actually an *American* gentleman?—but really he was just like *one of us.* In my terror I must have spoken no more than a monosyllable, or I would have revealed my nationality.

Reassured, I was led down a rickety corridor to a small office and to Mr. Eliot. He stood and smiled and shook my hand and welcomed me. The office was neat and compact, manuscript in tidy piles, books. I sat at a chair beside his wooden desk, no room for other chairs. On the wall in front of him, where he sat, hung several photographs; I recognized Virginia Woolf. But I looked little at his photographs of others. I looked at the greatest living poet.

Eliot was only sixty-three, in the autumn of 1951, but he looked at least seventy-five. I don't think I noticed this anomaly, in 1951, because I did not take seriously the difference between sixty-three and seventy-five. But the man who saw himself as an aged eagle when scarcely forty had endured subsequent aging accordingly. His face was pale as baker's bread. He stooped as he sat at his desk, and when he stood he slouched like the witch in the gingerbread house. His head shook forward slightly, from time to time, almost as if he nodded toward sleep. He smoked, and between inhalations he hacked a dry, deathly, smoker's hack. His speech—while precise, exact, perfect—was slow to move, as if he stood behind the boulder of each word, pushing it into view. Eliot was *cadaverous,* in 1951.

I wish I could say that when we spoke panic drained from my marrow bones, and that I relaxed and enjoyed conversation with the great poet. It's not true; I enjoyed my visit, as one might enjoy having climbed to the top of Marble Arch, or having walked a tightrope across the Crystal Palace, but afterwards I was exhausted and drained and triumphant, rather than enlightened and charmed—as I might have been, had I not insisted on regarding my companion as monument more than man. But it was I who *acted* like marble. I remember little from the meeting, but I know that I was solemn; I was so convinced of the monumentality of this moment—"I will be speaking of this, ages hence"—that I weighed every word as if my great-grandchildren were listening in, and I feared to let them down by speaking idiomatically, or by seeing the humor in anything.

Mr. Eliot went through my poems. He had written little notes in pencil in the margins and these notes cued him to small remarks: "Good line, there"; "I think you can trim this one down a bit." I don't think Eliot told me anything about my poems that I didn't know. They were, I think, not good enough for him to help me with them. By this time he had for many years been dealing with younger poets, but few of them had been as young and unsettled as I was.

We talked a good bit about American poetry, as of 1951, a subject about which we both knew something. I praised Theodore Roethke, of whom he said little. I praised the Robert Lowell of *Lord Weary's Castle;* Faber was printing him in England. I praised Richard Wilbur, whom Eliot also admired, and whom he expected Faber to publish (Faber brought him out six years later). Wilbur was someone, Eliot said, that they were keeping an eye on. There were others; they had been keeping an eye on Wallace Stevens, for instance, and now they were about to publish his selected poems. The suggestion was that Wallace Stevens was a young or otherwise "new" poet.

Now Stevens was nine years older than Eliot; *Harmonium,* Stevens's first book, appeared in 1923, the year after "The Waste Land." When I sat in Eliot's office that day in 1951, I thought he was being ignorant about Wallace Stevens—mistaking him for younger than he was. Now I know better. He was not being ignorant, he was being *grudging.* He had never been quite certain about Stevens, perhaps because Stevens's gorgeousness could seem self-indulgent to Eliot, and the aestheticism provincial or frivolous.

The ignorance that Eliot affected was a mild putdown in a classic English manner. When Churchill pronounced "Marseilles" as "mar-sales," we observed not mispronunciation but condescension. There was a *tone* to Eliot's "error" about Stevens which I failed to pick up because I had not learned English speech. And if I had picked it up, I might have recalled something Stevens had said about Eliot, a year or so before. Now the one remark recalls the other—two aged lions displaying claws for each other, each in characteristic manner. When I asked Stevens, on a Saturday, if he could stay over in Cambridge until Monday and attend the *Advocate* party for Eliot, he refused, saying that it would have been nice, really, because he had never met Eliot; but he had to get back to the office. Actually, he went on, he had never read Mr. Eliot very much; he was afraid it would influence his work.

My leg was pulled. I believed him. I never considered that there was war on Olympus, or even harsh words; instead, I allowed myself to consider that the great were *weird.*

There were reasons enough for breaches between Eliot and Stevens—breaches which Eliot, by planning a Faber edition, started in 1951 to close. There is always strain between the people who stay home and the people who go away. Our attention centered so much on American writers abroad, in the first third of our century—Henry James remaining in England and taking citizenship; Pound, Eliot, and for a time Robert Frost; Gertrude Stein in Paris, Pound in Paris for five years, Hemingway, MacLeish, Fitzgerald; Pound working out middle age in Italy's Rapallo—that we ignored the many writers who stayed home. Writers gathered in New Orleans and Chicago, on the West Coast, in Boston, and most copiously around New York. Some figures prominent in New York have become obscure—Mina Loy, Alfred Kreymborg, Waldo Frank, Gorham Munson, Matthew Josephson—but others remain in the pantheon, like Marianne Moore, William Carlos Williams, E. E. Cummings, Hart Crane, and Wallace Stevens. One of the persistent myths about Wallace Stevens, like the idea that Ezra Pound grew up in Idaho, is the notion that his poetry arose *in vacuo* from an insurance office and a Hartford suburb. To be sure, Stevens lived in Hartford during his later years and worked as vice-president at Hartford Accident and Indemnity. But he spent years crucial to his life as a poet in New York, from 1900 to 1916, among the poets of Greenwich Village and other company not associated with insurance. He was thirty-six when he moved to Hartford. In the years before the Great

War—climaxed by the Armory Show of 1913—there were picnics at Alfred Kreymborg's in the country with William Carlos Williams motoring over from Rutherford, and crowds descending from Greenwich Village including Marianne Moore with her bright red braided hair. There were parties, arguments, affiliations and disaffections. The friendship between William Carlos Williams and Wallace Stevens was central to American poetry—like so many friendships: Pound and Eliot; Eliot and Aiken; Pound and William Carlos Williams and H.D.; Ransom and Tate and Jarrell and Robert Lowell.

William Carlos Williams made his hatred of "The Waste Land" well known; it set his own work back, he said, by twenty years. Eliot never concealed his distaste for Williams. All the homebodies, I think, resented the exiles, and when the exiles returned—not only Malcolm Cowley but Archibald MacLeish and many others—they returned with guilt which turned into reproof toward the writers who remained abroad. The distaste for Henry James, displayed by Americanist critics in the thirties and forties, was evidence of the same battle.

But back to 24 Russell Square, in September of 1951.

We talked, as he put it, about "our literary generations." We talked a little about England, of which I knew nothing, and of Oxford and Cambridge. Then it was four o'clock, or nearly; it was time for Eliot to conclude our interview, and take tea with his colleagues. He stood up, slowly enough to give me time to stand upright before he did, granting me the face of knowing when to leave. When this tall, pale, dark-suited figure struggled successfully to its feet, and I had leapt to mine, we lingered a moment in the doorway, while I sputtered ponderous thanks, and he nodded smiling to acknowledge them. Then Eliot appeared to search for the right phrase with which to send me off. He looked me in the eyes, and set off into a slow, meandering sentence. "Let me see," said T. S. Eliot, "forty years ago I went from Harvard to Oxford. Now you are going from Harvard to Oxford. What advice can I give you?" He paused delicately, shrewdly, while I waited with greed for the words which I would repeat for the rest of my life, the advice from elder to younger, setting me on the road of emulation. When he had ticked off the comedian's exact milliseconds of pause, he said, "Have you any long underwear?"

I told him that I had not, and paused to buy some on my dazzled walk back to the hotel. I suppose it was six months before I woke up enough to laugh.

That year at Oxford I won the Newdigate, broadcast a poem on the BBC, sold poems to the *World Review,* and published two pamphlets with the Fantasy Press. When the *TLS* reviewed the pamphlets, with a generous condescension, Eliot wrote me a congratulatory note on prize and publication. He suggested that I drop by for another visit, on a future trip to London. Thus in the autumn of 1952, I called on him again at Faber and Faber, as I did several times in the future. Now the visits begin to blur into each other, my remembered notes less distinct. The second time I was perhaps not quite so overwhelmed, not quite so humorless. In the spring of 1953 I saw him again, at an evening devoted to Ezra Pound, held at the Institute of Contemporary Arts. Pound was still under guard, indicted for treason but judged mentally unfit for trial, at St. Elizabeth's in Washington. The ICA meeting—a rally supporting the notion that Pound should be set free—was chaired by Eliot, and included short talks by Herbert Read and J. Isaacs, and readings of Pound by Peter Russell and me. Peter Russell read Pound because he was a leading English Poundian; I read Pound because I was a poet with a certified American accent. R. P. Blackmur sat in the front row, and Eliot's friend John Hayward. The occasion was invigorating and without issue. Eliot was kindly and passionate, but said nothing exceptional. There was nothing exceptional about the meeting, barring one incident. In the course of his talk, J. Isaacs praised F. R. Leavis. *Mildly.* Whatever else you thought of Leavis, he said, you had to give him credit for his words on

"Mauberley." But this faint praise nearly caused a riot. On the platform we heard shouts of "Shame!" from the back of the hall, and then some scuffling and more shouts. Two people were ejected from the premises of the ICA on Dover Street in the West End. Later we discovered that they were John Davenport—Dylan Thomas's friend—and Graham Greene.

From 1954 to 1957, I was back at Harvard as a Junior Fellow in the Society of Fellows; Junior Fellows, who may come from any discipline, spend three years doing what they please. The society consists of ten Senior Fellows—professors largely, from various fields, whose duties are dinner and the election of new Junior Fellows—and about twenty-four Junior Fellows, of whom perhaps three-quarters are in residence at any time. The Junior Fellows are often impressive. At my first dinner I sat next to a young man and asked him what he did. "Mathematical linguistics," he said, to my bewilderment; I had met Noam Chomsky.

On Monday nights we all had dinner together. We started with sherry in the front room of our quarters in Eliot House, a tall brown paneled room with the stiffness of a common room. Then we repaired to the adjacent dining room, where we sat at a long table shaped like a flattened U, and ate good food. Guests were important. It was an unwritten rule that dinner guests be eminent. Edmund Wilson turned up about twice a year. I remember an evening spent talking with Vladimir Nabokov when *Lolita* was still unpublished in the United States, restricted to its two volume green paper Olympia Press edition. Mr. Eliot visited Cambridge about once a year, and while he was there he would take dinner with us. Once, someone asked Geoffrey Bush if he had sat next to Eliot at dinner, the night before.

"I couldn't," said Geoffrey. "John Hollander was sitting on both sides of him."

It was only coincidence that Geoffrey did not attribute the stunt to me. It must have been the year when I hardly spoke to Eliot, except for a greeting over sherry.

One Monday morning—when I knew Eliot was coming to dinner that night—I came to Harvard Square early, to spend a lazy day wandering among bookstores and drinking coffee. I was walking near the Harvard Book Store when I was greeted by the anthologist Oscar Williams, who was visiting Cambridge from New York. I knew him only slightly, and had found him friendly but insinuating. I knew it would be foolish to mention Eliot's presence in town. Someone had told me that Eliot despised Williams for his self-promotion; Eliot made a rule that none of his poems were to be reprinted in paperback anthologies, in order to avoid being printed by Williams. The anthologies were good ones, as anthologies go, somewhat disfigured by the editor's predilection to print quantities of his own poems. (Randall Jarrell once praised Williams's gall in a review, remarking that it really took something to think you were five times as good as Thomas Hardy.) His anthologies printed photographs of poets—I think the first to perform that dubious service—and one became familiar with cameo-fringes of photographs of great poets, perhaps showing in sequence Emily Dickinson, William Shakespeare, Oscar Williams, Walt Whitman, and Homer.

This morning Williams suggested coffee, so we sat together at a counter on Massachusetts Avenue and talked poetry a little, and he presented me with a signed copy of his latest paperback, and after half an hour we drifted apart. When I arrived at the Society of Fellows that night, the first person I saw drinking sherry was Oscar Williams. In a bookstore later in the day he had met a young astrophysicist, a Junior Fellow who, realizing that Williams was a poet and anthologist, felt that it was only polite to invite him to dinner with Eliot. The astrophysicist, however, had never met Eliot, and felt unconnected with poetry; by the time I arrived he was uncomfortable. He hurled Oscar Williams in my direction and fled.

Eliot was chatting with Arthur Darby Nock at the table which held the sherry. It became obvious that I must perform an introduction. Eliot turned slightly at my approach, recognized me, smiled pleasantly, and said something like, "Ah, yes. How pleasant to see you again."

I said, "Mr. Eliot I would like you to meet Oscar Williams"—a barefaced lie.

Eliot put out his hand, smiling, and did a double take. The smile withered, like a speeded-up film of a flower touched by frost. The hand withdrew a little, and then returned to be embraced and pumped by Oscar Williams's hand. The voice—more English, I thought, than I had ever heard it, with an "a" in the last syllable as broad as the Mississippi—laid out a sentence as if mounting a butterfly on a piece of velvet: "Ah, yes," said T. S. Eliot to Oscar Williams, "I recognize you from your photographs."

My stomach curled into itself; Eliot's sentence would, I thought, have extracted the backbones from an army of Gaul. But Williams was nothing daunted. With a friendly grin he acknowledged Mr. Eliot's equality. Egalitarian, he said, "Yes, I recognize you from yours, too."

The conversation had extended nearly as far as it could go. Eliot was prepared for one further move, before he returned to Professor Nock, who was standing at the periphery of this circle, benign and uncomprehending. "It is a distressing fact," said Eliot, "of growing older"—I had the momentary sense that he was searching for an end to his sentence, a conclusion that would give a spin to his heel, as he swiveled away from his new acquaintance—"that one comes to resemble one's photographs." As Williams rushed to agree, Eliot nodded lightly in my direction and turned back to Professor Nock, who resumed a conversation interrupted midsentence.

The third year of my fellowship Eliot missed his annual visit; he got married instead.

When I left Cambridge to teach at the University of Michigan, I quickly found occasion to write him. The Department of English wanted Eliot to read his poems at Michigan, and I knew that he liked to pay for his annual American visit by doing a poetry reading or two. I wrote him and asked if he would come to Ann Arbor for a reading. In the course of the letter, I said that I regretted not seeing him the year before. When his refusal arrived, Eliot made characteristic humor out of his inability to make his usual transatlantic trip the year before. An alteration of his domestic arrangements, he told me, necessitated a relocation of his residence—or words to a similar Latinate music.

A year later we met in New York, and I interviewed him for the *Paris Review*. For some time that magazine had been interviewing novelists, beginning with the first issue's interview with E. M. Forster. The *Paris Review* invented the contemporary literary interview, printed in dialogue form, which twenty-five years later has become a cliché of literary quarterlies. Running low on major novelists, the magazine in 1959 was ready for poets, and asked me (I was poetry editor) to begin the series by interviewing Eliot. In the spring of 1959, Eliot visited the United States with his bride, and we arranged to conduct the interview at Mrs. Louis Henry Cohn's apartment. Mrs. Cohn and her late husband, dealers in rare books and manuscripts, had been friends of Eliot for some years, and the Eliots stayed with her when they visited New York.

I came to New York a day early, staying with Robert and Carol Bly; the night before the interview, Louis and Dorothy Simpson came to dinner. Neither Simpson nor Bly had met Eliot; both admired him; both wanted to meet him. Thus I arrived at Mrs. Cohn's apartment, the next morning, equipped not only with a deck of questions on three-by-five cards, not only with a cumbersome tape recorder, but with two "tape technicians." As introductions were made and the interview started, Bly and Simpson affected working-class invisibility, and checked such technical details as electric plugs with great professionalism. As the morning wore on they dropped their guards. When Mrs. Cohn brought out the Scotch—and Eliot lectured us all, briefly, never to destroy Scotch whiskey by adding ice cubes—they sat on the sofa and drank their drinks and laughed and joined in the conviviality.

I went to my card file, which served me well. When Eliot's answers provoked further questions, I followed the lead of his talk. Then when his answers slowed down—or when we refreshed our drinks—I flipped ahead in my cards, weeding out the questions already answered or bypassed, and organizing the ones that remained. Eliot answered my questions, as one might have predicted, in *paragraphs*—as if he had known the questions, as if he had prepared his answers. Nowadays writers are used to questions, from audiences after poetry readings as well as from journalists with tape recorders, but Eliot belonged to an earlier, possibly more responsible, era: if you had something to say about poetry you wrote an essay. So his fluency in speech, responding to my interrogation, came neither from the lecture platform nor from the experience of being interviewed; it came instead from years of good conversation. Of the several interviews I have conducted, the one with Eliot required the least revision.

I saved until last the question I wanted most to ask, but feared to. I shouldn't have hesitated.

I was twenty-nine that year, about to publish my second book of poetry, beginning perhaps to grow up. When I was adolescent I conceived of growing up as climbing a mountainside, but implicit in the idea of a mountain was the idea of a plateau. One would reach this plateau at some point in one's twenties—one would be "a poet," one would marry and settle down—and then one would walk over this plateau until one died. I suspect most adolescents hold onto some such notion, which derives from the values placed on age by our elders. "You'll understand when you grow up." It also derives from the wish to relax, to stop struggling, to give up the struggle. When I was twenty, I thought that when I published poems in a good magazine, I would know that I was good; when I was twenty-five, and my things had appeared in the *Hudson Review* and *The New Yorker,* I still didn't know. When I had a book, I hoped, *then* I would know that I was good. From the age of fourteen I had been trying to be a good poet. When did you get to find out whether you were any good or not? Finally now, approaching the margin of thirty, I thought I knew the answer. Reading Eliot's essays had helped. Here is the last exchange in the interview:

> INTERVIEWER: One last thing. Seventeen years ago you said, "No honest poet can ever feel quite sure of the permanent value of what he has written. He may have wasted his time and messed up his life for nothing." Do you feel the same way now, at seventy?
>
> ELIOT: There may be honest poets who do feel sure. I don't.

In editing the interview for publication, I omitted a couple of phrases. When I first asked him if he now felt sure of his work, he answered quickly, "Heavens, no! Do *you?*" I hastened to assure him that I didn't.

When we arrived at the apartment that day, and I laid eyes on the Eliot for the first time in two years, I was shocked. I described his appearance a decade earlier; at the age of sixty-two or -three, he had been pale, stooped, and cadaverous, with a hacking cough; now, at the age of seventy—but with a new young wife—he looked like George Sanders. Now he looked debonair, sophisticated, lean, and handsome, with a fine tan just acquired in the Caribbean. All during the interview he threw his head back to laugh a hearty, vigorous laugh. Gone was the cough, gone the appearance of extreme old age.

Instead, he was a fond husband. Mrs. Eliot wasn't with us when we started the interview, but joined us in progress—an almost matronly young woman, fleshy and warm. As soon as she arrived, Eliot became more animated. When his answers were especially well phrased, he glanced in her direction as if he wanted to catch her response to his wit. When we interrupted the questioning for a drink, Eliot moved to the sofa to sit beside his wife. They held hands, and continued to hold hands for the rest of the morning. A close friend of theirs later told me that he had seen Eliot at a dinner party eating his soup left-handed, with some difficulty, because he was seated on his wife's left, and his right hand was engaged with her left hand under the table.

In writing about Eliot, I want mostly to tell what he was *like,* as I knew him; to provide notes on a man I encountered. But now I will suggest a biographical or psychological notion about which I have no real knowledge.

Eliot's first marriage was painful for husband and wife. It nearly ruined Eliot's life, and whether the marriage did it or not, Vivien Eliot's life was a ruin. This bad marriage was crucial to Eliot's poetry. In 1915, Eliot was not a poet. He had written some poetry, including "Prufrock"; he was considered a poet of the first order by Ezra Pound and by his old friend Conrad Aiken—but Eliot himself was uncommitted to the art. He was a Ph.D. candidate in philosophy at Harvard, and it was obvious to the people he met—in 1915 in England—that his interests were academic and philosophical, that he would take his degree, and that he would become an eminent professor of philosophy in an American university. Like many talented young people, he had seemed to grow away from poetry as he grew older. Then he met Vivien Haigh, married her abruptly and almost surreptitiously in a registry office, decided to remain in England, abandoned his doctorate and with it his American academic career. Instead, he took what work he could find to support himself, and wrote poems. This combination of events *identifies* Vivien, England, and the life of poetry.

Vivien Eliot was blessing and curse, Muse and death's head. She gave and she took away. She was insightful, clever, witty, vivacious, depressed, nervous, and mad. Eliot was—as they say in popular songs—crazy about her. Why so? It is dangerous to write poetry, as most poets believe. We may well be punished, as Prometheus was punished for his impious gift. Adrienne

Rich published a book at twenty, and was immediately stricken with arthritis which has harassed her the rest of her life. I have written about Dylan Thomas. Some people court their own punishment by falling in love with it or by marrying it. Typical of the marriages of writers of genius (and other artists) is the intensely creative woman artist who loves the neurotic, possibly psychotic man; she cannot live without him, he is her secret Muse, bringing her poetry—and at the same time tearing her life apart. The roles reverse when the artist is male; and the same murderous relationship may occur when the artist is homosexual.

Why did Eliot, in particular, need to marry a death-muse? Eliot's mother was a poet. Because of the sounds of poetry, and its infantile associations, poetry is often the Mother. To marry the Mother is at the same time wholly forbidden and wholly desirable. It is clear from Eliot's poems that impotence, or at any rate a sense of sexual incompetence and coldness, obsessed him during his marriage to Vivien. Recently some writers have suggested an earlier homosexual episode in Eliot's life, to which his marriage was a reaction. Possibly. Of course the sexual debility was there before Vivien arrived, only waiting for her to activate it. Eliot married Vivien in order to be impotent, to suffer, and to write poems. When he separated from her, he chose a monastic grief. However, she was not through with him, but waited for him outside Faber and Faber; and once walked through London with a book jacket of Eliot's stitched to her hat; and once attended one of his lectures carrying a placard: "I am the wife he abandoned." Fifteen years after the separation, she died, in 1947, in a mental hospital in London. It was ten years before Eliot could rise from the grave to marry again.

The marriage, the conversion, the separation, dour years of devotion and self-denial, and the remarriage all parallel events in Eliot's poems and plays. I do not suggest that the life explains the poems; I suggest that Eliot's doctrine of impersonality was the purest camouflage, whether he was aware of subterfuge or not. His poems before Vivien are young, literary, clever, without psychic depth or intellectual profundity. "The Love Song of J. Alfred Prufrock" is the best of these; and combines a young man's self-mockery with his reading of French symbolists and Henry James. Prufrock's fear of the body points toward the Fisher King—but only a little. Mostly it is Prufrock's style that matters in this poem, from his opening gesture toward realism—"Like a patient etherized on a table"—to his final Tennysonian mellifluousness, which one can take straight as "beautiful poetry" or (better) crooked as self-judgment by pastiche. With the poems written after marriage, Eliot approaches emotions *outside* literature. Although the exo-skeleton of "The Waste Land" is anthropological, and some of the materials derive from reading, the poem is as personal as confessional poetry—and perhaps more so, because this confession is not a literary device. "The Waste Land" is the twentieth century's monument to the nervous breakdown:

> On Margate sands,
> I can connect
> nothing with nothing.

Although we have known for decades that Eliot went to Margate to recover from "nerves," we have mostly refused to read the poem he wrote. The monument to breakdown is by no means generalized; it is the breakdown of a man who has read widely, certain lines sticking in his brain and accruing personal and nonhistorical significance. It is a breakdown associated with forbidden sexuality. For one man the Oedipal conflict may result in satyriasis and promiscuity; for another in homosexuality; for another in impotence. The barrenness of "The Waste Land," and the Fisher King's dilemma, suggest the inability to conceive offspring if nothing else. And the fantasies—when the poem anticipates not so much confessional poetry as surrealism—make a nightmare of babies and of female death-kissing sexuality:

A woman drew her long black hair out tight
And fiddled whisper music on those strings
And bats with baby faces in the violet light
Whistled, and beat their wings
And crawled head downward down a blackened wall. . . .

An earlier version of this scene is the typist's weary sexual encounter with the clerk; which is how—with sordidity and squalor, without pleasure—we imagine the adult sexuality of our parents.

What is that sound high in the air
Murmur of maternal lamentation. . . .

As Eliot's religious conversion takes place in the poetry—before the separation from Vivien; the conversion makes the separation morally possible—we see Eliot in all genuineness give up hope for any kind of regeneration, be it sexual or spiritual. The track of this abnegation is called "Ash Wednesday." It is a superb poem, as great as "The Waste Land," though not so engrossing. In a later poem like "Journey of the Magi," he could give us in objective story a personal, retrospective account of the difficulties of conversion—but it was "Ash Wednesday" 's loss of hope, which allowed hope to be born, that dramatically displayed the motion of the soul and created the great locus of the conversion. And after conversion, the "Four Quartets," which explore the spiritualized emotions of a Christian, contain further autobiography, but relate to the earlier poems like the more rarified "Paradiso" to the painful "Inferno."

Domesticity precedes ideology, for all men and women. The feelings between parents and children, siblings, men and women as lovers or as spouses—these relationships penetrate the life of genius as much as they penetrate the lives of the rest of humanity. To insist on the primacy of the family affair is neither to denigrate nor to reduce the poem or the idea: that Marx entertained notions about his father, which informed the structure of Marx's thought, says nothing of the validity of Marxism. But who writes about Marx, and ignores the family affair, ignores the man. Of course Eliot wanted us to "ignore the man"—and from his wish arises the New Critics' dogma indexing the biographical heresy. But Eliot's own doctrines of impersonality, heaven knows, should alert us to suspect that his own poems are personal and biographical. I do not say that when we read his poems we should derive his life from them; I do say that when we read his poems, we must be conscious that they are "personal," as well as historical or doctrinal, or we do not read them.

Working over the interview with Eliot was easy. On April 6, I sent him a typescript of the interview, with new questions suggested by the text, and with eighteen queries. When I changed my question to fit his answer, I asked his indulgence; when I found a word awkward or ambiguous, I suggested another word or asked him to fix it; when I didn't understand a reference, I asked for explanation. His reply of four pages, dated 16 April, accompanied the text of the interview on which he had made corrections. Because he spoke a decent prose, he needed to make only small revisions. Speaking of Conrad Aiken to the tape recorder, he had called him "a kind creature," and when the phrase turned up in type it looked condescending; it had not sounded so in speech, and Eliot revised "creature" into "friend" for print. When at the end of the interview he told me that he was still unsure of the value of his work, he went on to say that "no intelligent writer knows if he is any good." When he looked at it typed up, it sounded dogmatic; he cut it out. He answered my eighteen queries mostly by revising the text. He corrected my spelling of Omar Khayyám. He changed prepositions, removed a passage which he claimed no longer to understand, made substitutions for single words. One paragraph—about formal verse as counter-revolution—he wholly recast. He answered my six new questions so that five of them entered the text—two questions about his old theories of poetic drama, another about revising other people's poems, another about the poet and nuclear annihilation, and another about meeting Yeats. The sixth exchange I decided not to add to the interview; I had asked him, on the insistence of a *Paris Review* editor, if he had ever given thought to writing fiction; his answer: "Never."

The interview appeared in our twenty-first issue, later the same year, together with poems by Ted Hughes, Geoffrey Hill, and by both of my tape technicians.

During the interview I had asked Eliot whatever happened to the manuscript of "The Waste Land," and he told me the familiar story of how it had disappeared after John Quinn's death. (In 1968, Eliot dead three years, the manuscript turned up—and now has appeared in book form, elegantly edited by Mrs. Eliot, complete with Pound's cuts and comments—discovered after all in John Quinn's papers, which had been deposited at the New York Public Library and never thoroughly investigated.) In 1959 we assumed that Quinn's papers had been searched, and that the manuscript was irretrievably lost.

Shortly after doing the interview, I heard a rumor. The manuscript had been found! Someone was offering it to the Morgan Library for $200,000. Thinking that I needed to footnote the text, I wrote Eliot to ask if it was true. It was the first he had heard of it; and it did not please him. He asked me to investigate. There followed a comic series of letters. The Morgan Library denied that it had been offered the text; instead, they had heard that Yale was dickering for it. When I wrote Yale, Yale denied all knowledge, but had in fact recently heard that the Morgan was negotiating for it; perhaps if I wrote them again. . . ? Then another letter arrived from Yale, and the information was startling. The manuscript had been found, and it was being offered to a large university in the West. I kept Eliot apprised. It depressed him. When the price in the rumor dropped to $100,000, he professed to have lost interest, the sum was so small.

When the rumors petered out, he decided again that the manuscript was lost forever, and died, I suspect, satisfied that his drafts would never turn up.

In the autumn of 1959 I went to England with my family, and lived in the village of Thaxted until the summer of 1960. Eliot wrote in October, pleased with the interview, which had just appeared; he asked me to visit him in the spring; just now, the Eliots were off to the United States. But when spring came we went to Italy, where I interviewed Ezra Pound, and I did not talk with Eliot that year. Back in Ann Arbor, I had occasion to invite him again to read his poems at Michigan. But now we wrote about another subject too. First, I had a letter from Charles Monteith, Eliot's colleague at Faber and Faber, asking me to revise Michael Roberts's *Faber Book of Modern Verse,* and add some new poets to it. Michael Roberts brought modern poetry to England with his Faber collection in 1936. I had met dozens of poetical Englishmen who had discovered poetry through Roberts's anthology. After the war, as new poets emerged and published, the collection fell out of date. Roberts died in 1948, and left behind some notes toward a new edition, which Ann Ridler used in making a second edition (without American poets) in 1951. By 1963 Faber wanted a third edition, American poets included. Faber asked me to do the edition for a flat fee, which is contrary to writerly economics, and the fee was minuscule: one hundred pounds. When I wrote back to accept the task, I asked for more money. I did not get it. I suppose that I would have done it for nothing, if Eliot had asked me to do it; I suppose Faber knew that.

But I bring up the subject not just to say the obvious—my edition appeared in 1968—but to give another note on T. S. Eliot:

In a letter that began by telling me he could not come to Ann Arbor, Eliot continued by saying that he was pleased I would do the new edition of Roberts's work. Then he added that of course he and his colleagues wanted my own work to be represented in the anthology. Perhaps, however, it would be best for me not to make the final selection of my poems, but to leave space for them, and forward to Faber a larger selection of my poems appropriate for selection. Then Faber could choose among them, and print a note at the front of the anthology advising the reader that the editor's poems were included at the insistence of the publisher, and had in fact been selected by the publisher. This procedure, he suggested at the end of a paragraph, might allow me to avoid the criticism which had been directed at a certain contemporary anthologist.

I suppose that you do not become the leading literary figure of the English-speaking world without shrewdness. Possibly Eliot considered that I might choose horrid poems, even in the context of my own work, and wanted therefore to reserve judgment to himself. I doubt it. The subterfuge existed solely to allow the note to be printed at the front of the book.

I wrote Eliot immediately to say that, although I was grateful for the suggestion, I would not print my own poems in this edition of *The Faber Book of Modern Verse.* Eliot answered to say that he approved my decision. I doubt that he expected me to accept his scheme; I think he enjoyed the scheming.

In 1963 I returned to England for a year, and saw Eliot for the last time. When I arrived in Thaxted that summer Eliot wrote that he was "still a hobbling convalescent," but that he spent three afternoons a week at the office. He suggested that I come up to town and have a cup of tea with him. I saw him on August 28, 1963. He looked frail, sickly, and happy. He met me at the door of his office, smiling and making a pleasant noise—I suppose "chortle" is onomatopoeia for it. Old Possum had turned into Old Codger. His motions were deliberate, and his head shook a little; but this was not the "old man" of sixty-two, whom I had met in this same office twelve years before. This age was genuine, and not an image of self-denial. He was affectionate, calling me "Donald" as he had not done before (in his letter I had remained "Mr. Hall") and telling me that our *Paris Review* interview was the best one that had ever been done with him. Talk of his interview led us to talk of my interview with Pound, and then to Pound himself. Eliot spoke of his old friend with sadness, with evident affection, and with an objectivity which seemed almost medical. He said that of course Pound was a megalomaniac. The doctor at St. Elizabeth's had pronounced on Pound's megalomania, Eliot told me, and diagnosed him very well. Pound's new self-denigration was merely the other side of megalomania. Then Eliot slipped a little to the side of what he had been saying, remembering, I think, past annoyances over Pound's judgment; annoyed but not angry, affectionate still, as one remains affectionate toward a brother who always gets himself into trouble. Pound was always an extremely poor judge of people, he told me; extremely poor.

Then he rambled on about an English poet, flatterer of Pound's, whom I will call Peter Beckwith, because it does not resemble his name. (I will change another name and circumstance in a moment. That afternoon, Eliot expressed numerous suspicions of people and their motives.) He was afraid now, he told me, that Peter Beckwith was trying to exploit Pound, and he explained what he thought Beckwith was up to. Eliot's mind was full of worries about the exploitation of old poets and dead ones. He feared that Professor Buttermarch, at a prominent American university, was conspiring with a dead poet's surviving son-in-law to snatch manuscripts from the poet's widow. He said fierce things about Buttermarch, who was an opportunist—Eliot told me, his voice tense with anger—and a dangerous man, who made a career of duping widow executors of literary husbands. There was panic in his voice, as he looked into his own death and imagined the birds gathering around the corpse, and around his young widow.

We talked about his plans for this winter. He needed for his lungs' sake to leave wet London. They would go to Nassau. No, they would not visit Cambridge again, he said sadly, in answer to my question, because his sister had died the winter before. It was his brother's widow who had died, the last remaining close tie to Cambridge. No, they would go only to Nassau, and they didn't like it much, but they knew what to expect. They had tried Barbados once, two years before, but they had undergone an unpleasant experience. The manager at the hotel had become angry at them, and ruined their visit, because they refused to be exploited. The manager had wanted to have a huge party for them, and introduce them to everyone he knew, but the Eliots wanted to rest, not to meet a hundred strangers. Eliot told the manager that they would be perfectly happy to visit him and his wife at their house, but please not to have a large party, where they would have to meet all sorts of people. The manager, he told me again, had wanted to *exploit* them.

He brought up the subject of the illness which had almost killed him in London the winter before. One evening an ambulance had rushed him to the best hospital in London for bronchial troubles, he told me, where he had a private room without charge. The old Tory praised National Health. They treat one so marvelously there, he said. But it was Valerie who had saved his life. His eyes filled with an old man's sentimental tears as he told me that his wife had saved his life.

I noticed again the pictures on the office walls. Looking with me, he mentioned Marianne Moore with affection and levity, praising her as a performer: no one, he said, could drop papers on a platform with more skill than she could. There was the same photograph of Virginia Woolf I had noticed in 1951. There were drawings of Goethe and Blake, in which Eliot fancied a resemblance around the eyes. There was a new large photograph, signed with a flourish by Groucho Marx. Eliot told me that he and Groucho had never actually met, but they had exchanged photographs, and that they ought to be meeting soon, since Groucho said that he would be coming through London. He asked me if I would like to meet Groucho Marx. I regret to say that I won't be telling *that* story; I heard no more of it.

I asked Eliot if he could come out to Thaxted. Perhaps by spring he would be strong enough; certainly, he said, we must see a great deal of each other. I told Eliot that my wife was singing in the choir at Thaxted Church; my son was being enlisted to wear a white robe and walk in procession; and I was learning to ring bells. He laughed a slow laugh for a long time. I must beware, he said, of becoming a church warden, since once you became a church warden it was very hard to stop being one. "I was a church warden for twenty-five years before I could get out of it." Then he talked about ritual and doctrine again, about Tractarians and Dr. Pusey. But ritual without doctrine, he added, was nothing; I changed the subject.

I asked him if he was writing anything, and he said with some wistfulness that he was not. He had been too ill to write anything; he hoped he would be able to write something that winter. He would like to write another play, but first, he had to write an introduction to the paperback edition of *The Use of Poetry and the Use of Criticism,* the book made from his Charles Eliot Norton lectures at Harvard in 1932. He had read over the book just recently, and discovered with pleased surprise that it was a good book. I said that in the past he had deprecated it; he corrected me, saying he had been *modest.* He mentioned that he had hurried to finish writing *The Use of Poetry and the Use of Criticism,* because he had been about to give another series of lectures at Virginia. He did not mention the title of *After Strange Gods,* but shook his head and said that the Virginia lectures had turned into a bad book, a bad book, a bad book.

The hour of four o'clock approached, as it had done before. I rose, and Eliot remained sitting. Benign and fragile, he smiled and said goodbye, and said again that we would certainly see a great deal of each other that year, and I left. I can still see him sitting in his chair.

A year and a half later, in January of 1965, I read in the paper that he was dead. And I read in the paper, and heard from friends, about the service in Westminster Abbey, which Pound attended. Everything was as it should be. Eliot suffered in early and middle life, turned Christian, lived through a "hard coming" to Christianity, and through painful middle age; but in old age he found honor, joy in a second marriage, and he died full of years and glory. The price men and women pay for being artists, Eliot paid when he was middle-aged. He wrote great poems; then he set out, I think, to make a good death, and made one.

FRAGMENTS OF EZRA POUND

1. Rome: Sunday

In 1960, while I was spending a year in England, the *Paris Review* sent me to Italy to interview Ezra Pound for its series of interviews called *Writers at Work.* When I knocked on the door of the Roman apartment where Pound was staying with friends, I was apprehensive.

In awe of his poetry, aghast at his politics, I understood that he talked politics more than he talked poetry. A few years back the *Paris Review* had nearly scheduled an interview, while Pound was still in Washington. (He had spent 1945–1958 in the United States, mostly in the insane asylum at St. Elizabeth's Hospital in the District of Columbia, where he had been confined as mentally unfit to stand trial for treason; during the Second World War, he had remained in Italy and broadcast for Italian radio.) In 1956 he first agreed to be interviewed, then suddenly exploded and reneged, declaring that the magazine was part of the "pinko-usury fringe." Usury was the Devil in Pound's theology; the race of the Devil was mostly semitic. In 1956 the *Paris Review*'s masthead included two Jewish names. In St. Elizabeth's, friends of mine had told me, Pound had railed about "the most dangerous man in the world," whose name appeared to be "Weinstein Kirchberger," which took me a while to translate.

When I knocked on the door, I feared what would answer my knock: madness, rebuff, cruelty, arrogance.

Pound answered my knock. There was no mistaking him. His face was large and jagged, constructed in sharp triangular sections, like modular architecture. This was the face that his friend Gaudier-Brzeska carved in marble in 1914, and that Wyndham Lewis painted in 1938 as if it were metallic. Both sculpture and painting appeared to be influenced by cubism; now I saw that Pound's face looked as if *it* were influenced, as if it had learned its shape by emulating Cézanne's geometry. The beard, which was gray and came to a sharp point, continued the angles of the face, and long hair flared to his shoulders and rose thickly on his head: a magnificent head.

But his eyes, which looked into me as we stood at the door, were watery, red, weak. "Mr. Hall," he said to me in the doorway, "you—find me—in fragments." As he spoke he separated the words into little bunches, like bursts of typing from an inexperienced typist: "You have driven—all the way—from England—to find a man—who is only fragments."

He beckoned me down a long corridor into a pleasant corner room, full of sunlight and books, where we sat opposite each other. Looking in his eyes, I saw the fatigue. Later I watched his eyes and mouth gather from time to time a tense strength, when he concentrated his attention on a matter gravely important. Fragments assembled themselves in half a second, turned strong, sharp, and insistent; then dissipated quickly, sank into flaccidity, depression, and silence. In 1960—though I could not know it then—Pound was verging on the brink of silence, that personal inferno where he lived out the last decade of his life.

In his sunny room, heavy with tables, two sofas, and big comfortable chairs, suitcases lay under a desk in a corner. Three books spread themselves out on a lamp table next to an easy chair: a Confucius in Chinese, a copy of Pound's own *Women of Trachis,* and Robinson's edition of Chaucer. (Robert Frost kept Robinson's Chaucer in his Vermont cabin.) Pound sat on a sofa and told me about his friend Ugo Dadone, owner of this flat on the Via Angelo Poliziano, formerly a general in an African campaign, injured and left for dead in the desert—Dadone nearly as fragmented as Pound. Over one of the sofas I notice a signed photograph of Gabriele D'Annunzio, in his flying costume.

As Pound rambled, I listened to the voice more than to the words. Theatrical, flashy, he rolled his *rrr*'s grandly, and at the end of each sentence kept the pitch high until the final word, which he dropped in pitch while he retained volume. This melody lent a coda to every sentence, a coda I remembered from the sixteen r.p.m. records at Harvard's Poetry Room. As an undergraduate I had spent hours listening to that voice, wrapt inside great earphones in a blue chair at the Lamont Library. Pound made the recordings on a brief visit to the United States in 1939, undertaken in his megalomania with the hope and expectation that by talking to the right people he could prevent the Second World War.

When Pound visited the United States in 1939 I was ten, and perfectly ignorant of him. When we declared war on Italy in 1941, I was thirteen, and determined to be a writer. By the time American and Italian soldiers were shooting at each other, I wanted to be a poet for the rest of my life, I loved Ezra Pound's poetry, and I reviled him as a traitor and a Fascist sympathizer.

The Second World War—which began in Europe when I was almost eleven, and ended in Japan when I was almost seventeen—was the bread of my adolescence, the milk of my growing up. When I hayed in New Hampshire in the summer months, I cocked the point of my scythe toward the hairy ditches, where I imagined escaped Nazi prisoners of war hid by day. When I read the newspaper, I could not conceive that a peacetime paper would have enough news to fill its pages. Every night on the farm we listened to a radio shaped like a cathedral as Gabriel Heatter told us that the skies were black over Europe with young Americans bombing German cities in just vengeance. Every movie was a war movie, every radio show was performed before servicemen, every Book-of-the-Month Club Selection was dedicated to the war effort. At high school the heat went off at noon, even in the dead of winter. In gym the boys all learned to box, toughening themselves for war, and the finals of the heavyweight division were held in the auditorium in front of the whole school. A large blond senior named George Taubel knocked out an awkward, strong young man, a good athlete, named Bill Herbert, knocked him cold on the auditorium stage, and a year later—less than a year—Bill Herbert was dead in a wave of Marines invading a Pacific island.

Although I tested the possibilities of pacifism, and although when I was fourteen or fifteen I began to shock my friends by calling myself a socialist, I *knew* that the United States was right and that Germany, Japan, and Italy were wrong. Like almost everyone of my generation—and like no one fifteen years younger—I never doubted my country's general virtue. Perhaps the Great War had been a trade war—like Troy, like the Russo-Japanese—but *this* was a war for justice. Evil was Hitler, and Hitler was Evil. I feel embarrassed to write it—after Lebanon and Guatemala and Chile; after Korea; after Vietnam—but the evil we apprehended was entirely *out there;* none of it was *in here.* When in Boston one day I watched a parade—I think it was Memorial Day, perhaps 1944—and watched march past the wiry, lean, intense squad of men who were the only survivors of the first wave that waded onto the beaches of Iwo Jima, I wept and could not stop weeping, aware perhaps of Bill Herbert and the other dead whom I had known, aware also of my own fears. For I was sure that I would myself go into the army, and fight in the same war, which I assumed would go on forever.

And when I bought T. S. Eliot's *Collected Poems,* at fourteen, for two dollars, I drew a circle around Ezra Pound's name in the dedication to "The Waste Land"—"For Ezra Pound *il mig-*

lior fabbro"—and in the white space of the page wrote the word which signified my critical judgment: "Nerts!"

I bring my politics into this story because I suppose they are part of the story, and not because my politics were sensitive or unusual. Like most people's, my politics are conventional, naïve, uninformed, and fickle. And although my view of the morality of nations has suffered some sophistication, unavoidable in the last thirty years, I have not rid myself of prejudices acquired in youth. I find it difficult to meet Germans; I avoid setting foot in that country. Although I do not retain intellectual conviction of moral superiority, I retain hard feelings; I want to *growl* at Germans, and the hair stands up on my back, like a cat seeing a dog.

If my politics were conventional and primitive, my poetics were not. Shortly after I wrote "Nerts!" in Eliot's *Collected Poems,* I began to read Pound. I read him in anthologies like Louis Untermeyer's, who wrote angry introductions to Ezra Pound but printed him nonetheless. I read him in textbooks. I read his own collections published by *New Directions.* When the war was ending I met someone who had known Pound a little, and who supported my growing admiration. At the same time, his anecdotes encouraged me to dismiss the politics as madness. This man had visited Rapallo in the mid-thirties on his honeymoon. After a vigorous game of tennis, Pound confided to him that the hills above the tennis courts were inhabited by spies with binoculars, sent from Wall Street to keep an eye on E. P., whose economic ideas would ruin the Wall Street bankers' conspiratorial hold on the world's wealth.

For me, poetry is first of all sounds. I discovered early that Pound, who could do other things as well, had the greatest ear among modern poets. For the sheer pleasure of sound—the taste of it in one's mouth—no one comes near him. Early in life I discovered Pound's "The Return," a perfect symbolist poem; what I loved was the noise it made, rubbing its syllables together as a grasshopper rubs its legs.

See, they return; ah, see the tentative
    Movements, and the slow feet,
    The trouble in the pace and the uncertain
    Wavering!

See, they return, one, and by one,
With fear, as half-awakened;
As if the snow should hesitate
And murmur in the wind,
        and half turn back;
These were the 'Wing'd-with-Awe',
        Inviolable.

Gods of the wingèd shoe!
With them the silver hounds,
        sniffing the trace of air!

Haie! Haie!
    These were the swift to harry;
These the keen-scented;
These were the souls of blood.

Slow on the leash,
        pallid the leash-men!

I suppose one says something about symbolism in "The Return" if one mentions a defeated Pantheon, but a symbolist poem is not an allegorical poem—the symbol, it has been noted, is a *new word*—and I would as lief think of tired hunters, or Greece replaced by Rome, or Rome defeated by Goths, or Pennsylvania overwhelmed in the fourth quarter by Cornell. I print this poem here not in order to paraphrase it but—I will embarrass my readers, who have put away childish things—to chew and suck upon it. How the diphthongs and long vowels move together, a slow march down the page, dip and pause and glide. I can read it again and again, each time with vast refreshment of senses and world-love—as I can look again and again at Matisse's "The Red Studio."

Early on, I found and enjoyed Pound's vigorous ballad about Christ, "Ballad of the Goodly Fere," and his Provençal and Renaissance monologues, like the violent "Sestina: Altaforte"—"Damn it all! all this our South stinks peace." Later I discovered the energetic translation of the "Seafarer," then the quietness of the Chinese poems and imitations, and realized that Pound's ear had found yet another music: he had discovered the lyric potential of *flatness.* Later, I studied the quatrains of "Hugh Selwyn Mauberley," academically the most accepted of Pound's poems, with its eloquent stanzas on the Great War. Later still, I discovered that I preferred the looser lines of "Homage to Sextus Propertius," where he became a sort of sarcastic Whitman.

I will not try to quote, I will just assert the extent of his invention and adaptation. If he found a lyrical flatness in his translations from the Chinese, in Japanese poetry he found the tiny lyric as quick as a fly, like "In a Station of the Metro." He invented the free verse epigram, writing about "Les Millwins," or about sexual satisfaction as a bathtub draining. And he invented, in the *Cantos,* a device for containing the modern world in the borders of a single poem.

Or that is what, in his grand ambition, he tried to do. Perhaps he did not accomplish this ambition, but if he did not, he wrote in the *Cantos* thousands of lines of magnificent poetry—"ear, ear for the sea surge / murmur of old men's voices"—by which he gathered together and juxtaposed the elements of a universal culture. Chinese history and Confucian ideology found parallels and divergences with American Adamses and Renaissance Medicis, with Elizabethan jurists and twentieth-century anthropologists, with his own economic doctrines of Social Credit, with Mussolini's Fascism—and with the poet himself caged outdoors at the end of a war in Pisa, reasonably convinced that he awaited execution.

Then, too, I began to learn another side of Ezra Pound's character.

The history of literature chronicles considerable generosity. Although poets are frequently as vain as actors and although rarely one encounters a poet genuinely vicious to his fellows, most poets help each other out. Thus poets often come in groups, and especially when they are young they work tirelessly to rewrite each other's poems. They try to live in each other's vicinity, and when they must live apart, they revise each other's work through the mails. The collected poems of our best poets contain lines written by their friends. Vernon Watkins and Dylan Thomas could recall lines each had written for the other, which critics had singled out as typical of the man who had not written them.

Pound was a catalyst to other poets. His presence made poets out of people who might otherwise never have survived into poetry. Greatly as I admire the poetry of William Carlos Williams, I am not sure that he would have been a poet without Ezra Pound. Pound's energy and conviction, at any rate, pulled H.D. and William Carlos Williams further into poetic commitment, when the three students knew each other at the University of Pennsylvania. Later, when Pound met older writers already committed to the art, he bullied editors into publishing them, he reviewed them, he invented public relations devices like "Imagism" in order to attract attention to them, he raised money for them, and got them out of jail—and on one occasion sent one of them a pair of old brown shoes.

Pound discovered Eliot, through the agency of Conrad Aiken, when Eliot had written Prufrock but little else, and seemed destined to become an American professor of philosophy. He argued Harriet Monroe into publishing Prufrock in *Poetry;* he encouraged and cajoled Eliot into further poems; when Eliot's work at the bank seemed to burden him, he set out to support Eliot by subscription (which embarrassed Eliot, who put a stop to it); when Eliot fumbled toward "The Waste Land," Pound's solid and magnanimous critical intelligence cut that poem into its shape.

I could tell story after story illustrating the accuracy of Pound's taste, and the generous energy with which he promoted the writers he admired. Nor was his taste limited, when it included D. H. Lawrence and James Joyce, as well as Eliot and the Imagists; Ford Madox Ford and Yeats among the elders; Ernest Hemingway, Louis Zukofsky, Basil Bunting among the youngers; most astonishing of all, it included Robert Frost, whose literary predilections might have made him The Enemy. (If Pound's first task, as he says in a *Canto,* was to "break the pentameter," Frost wasn't helping.) But Pound knew quality even when it turned up in a sonnet, and he leapt to promote Robert Frost—who disliked him and avoided him—without worrying about the politics of literary styles.

In the history of literature, no writer equals Pound in accuracy of taste, or in energetic magnanimity.

When the *Pisan Cantos* appeared in 1947, most readers considered them the best *Cantos* since the first thirty. I found them moving in the extreme, with their moral uncertainty, their mingling of defiance and despair. Whatever the politics of the man who wrote the poems, the *Pisan Cantos* included great poetry. The *Pisan Cantos* also included paranoiac anti-Semitism. When Pound was awarded the Bollingen Prize for the *Pisan Cantos,* there was a noisy scandal. Haters of modern poetry suddenly discovered how much they detested Fascism. All the old arguments about art and morality marched forth, generally in their stupidest uniforms.

I have never found it difficult to split poem from poet. Perhaps it is *nasty,* that it is not difficult; but it is not difficult. Instead, I find it often essential. If a poet is great, the poem is the poet at his or her greatest, and the man or woman in person will never equal the poem created. Poets know that their poems are more important than they are—when they are writing the poem. The great poets may tell lies all day and all night—to sexual objects if seduction is the necessity; to audiences, if they demand public love; to admirers, if they require to be surrounded by toadies—but when they write their poems they do not lie. I have heard poets on platforms speak the most outrageous hypocrisy about their work—Robert Frost was worst—and then I have gone home and read true poems.

Conversely, I have known a hundred poets who were decent and apparently honest people in daily life—playing poker, serving on committees, raising children, defending beleaguered friends, even judging other poets—who when they took up their Bics stole the voices of dead poets and the ideas of live friends. And I have known sophisticated, intelligent poets who wrote lying, bumpkin poems, pretending to be *sincerely* inarticulate.

When Pound wrote the *Pisan Cantos,* it did not astonish me that the poem rarely resembled the harangues recorded from Rome radio. Neither the *Pisan Cantos* nor "The Return" nor "Homage to Sextus Propertius" appeared to be works of someone who found Wall Street representatives in the hills above his house, or believed in the Protocols of the Elders of Zion, or thought that he could prevent the Second World War by holding select audiences with Senators.

One mistake constant to the political mind is to underestimate the diversity and discontinuity of the psyche.

One mistake common to the nonpolitical mind—or to the politically naïve or lazy or apathetic—is the converse error: to consider that we may disregard a man's or woman's politics, relegate politics to some shabby subdivision of the mind, or cancel it out by compensating for it: as if the beauty of Pound's greatest poetry "made up for" the nastiness of his social and racial ideas. It was verifiably an American named Ezra Pound who said on Roman radio, May 5, 1942:

> The kike, and the unmitigated evil that has been centered in London since the British government got on the Red Indians to murder the American frontier settlers, has herded the Slavs, the Mongols, the Tartars openly against Germany and Poland and Finland. And secretly against all that is decent in America, against the total American heritage.

The same Ezra Pound wrote, years earlier in *Canto IV:*

> Beneath it, beneath it
> Not a ray, not a sliver, not a spare disc of sunlight

Flaking the black, soft water;
Bathing the body of nymphs, of nymphs, and Diana . . .

The same Ezra Pound wrote, years later, in a fragment from *Canto CXV:*

A blown husk that is finished
        but the light sings eternal
a pale flare over marshes
        where the salt hay whispers to tide's change . . .

And how do I fit these pieces together? I do not fit these pieces together; they *are* together, in the mystery of a man's character and life. All I will do, for now, is recite that life, in stick-figure fashion:

a young man grows up vowing to be a poet, emigrates, publishes great poems, sets himself up wholly as an aesthete;

when his friends, and millions of others, die in the Great War, he detaches himself from aestheticism, looking for causes of war and outrage;

for a while his poems gain in resonant seriousness; then a new tone begins, a tone of paranoia and irascibility;

he finds causes in economics, devils in bankers and later in Jewish bankers, and a cure in his own economics;

his interest in poetry declines; he considers himself evolved into statesman and economist; his friends withdraw, finding him mad;

having discovered a hero in Benito Mussolini, he broadcasts from Italy, to his old country at war with Italy, speeches often murderous with hatred;

imprisoned, in fear of death, abject, the poetry returns, the old voice ringing out the noble line;

but that is not the end of the story, as it should be;

the madness or the obsessions remain, in his long imprisonment; and the poetry remains, intermittent, sometimes trying to fly on one wing, sometimes flying on two;

and with release from prison nothing resolves itself, politics and poetry confused and unremedied;

until finally, convinced of failure and error, the old man sinks into silence, ten years of speechless despair, interrupted rarely by his own voice, like a voice that speaks from a tomb;

or like the tiny voice of the Sybil, quoted by Eliot at the start of "The Waste Land," who, centuries old, shriveled as a raisin, enduring, is asked by boys what might she desire; who answers, *I want to die.*

When I wrote my first letter to Ezra Pound that winter—writing from England, proposing that I visit him and interview him for the *Paris Review*—I addressed him at his daughter's place, the Schloss Brunnenburg, a castle in Merano of the Italian Tirol, formerly Meran of the Austrian Tirol. He had lived in this castle—with his daughter Mary, his wife Dorothy, and Mary's husband, the Egyptologist Boris de Rachewiltz—much of the time since his return to Italy. Mary was Olga Rudge's daughter, not Dorothy Pound's. In the thirties in Rapallo, Pound had spent five nights a week with his wife, and two with Olga Rudge.

Merano's climate and isolation—the literal climate, not the metaphorical one—did not appeal to Pound. ("It's fine—" he told me once, "if you can live—on mountain scenery.") At some point, he and Dorothy rented a flat in Rapallo, striving to return to the place where they had lived so many years before the war. It didn't work out; they rented the flat on a Sunday, and on Monday discovered that the ground floor was deafeningly occupied by a boiler factory. On another occasion, a young woman in her twenties moved in with Dorothy and Ezra; this experiment worked no better than the boiler factory.

A few days after I posted my letter to him, I received a postcard dated "2 Dec 59," which read:

Shd/one distinguish between magazines that wish to print one, and those that only want one to be interviewed?

Yrs
E Pound

The asperity was what I feared and expected; it did not surprise me; but the message surprised me. Did Ezra Pound really want to publish in the *Paris Review?* Apparently he no longer considered the magazine an operation of the "pinko-usury fringe"—but why did he want his work to appear there? My assumption was that Ezra Pound could print poems anywhere.

But he couldn't, of course. American magazines that pay noticeable sums for poems—*The New Yorker, The Atlantic, Harper's, Ladies' Home Journal*—would not have welcomed a poem by Ezra Pound in 1959. *The New Yorker,* for instance, was still disinclined to print a poem which Mr. Ross would not have understood. Pound published his poems in the *Hudson Review,* or in *Poetry,* and received for a *Canto,* I suppose, something like a hundred or two hundred dollars.

He required little money to live on; all his life he lived, as he put it, "on low overhead." But he could not make a living, selling *Cantos* at fifty cents a line. And I doubt that his royalties amounted to more than a few thousand dollars a year, in 1959. Teachers did not assign his books in American university classes; his work was too hard for the professors, because the notes had not yet been published. He received some income from anthology rights—but, again, I doubt that the annual accumulation was more than three thousand dollars. His politics kept him out of some anthologies, and diminished the extent of his representation in others. Political disrepute and a reputation for obscurity combined to limit his income from poems.

He was worried in 1959 that he would not have enough money to support himself and his family. I suspect that this worry was unreasonable—Pound had generous and affluent friends; also, he had accumulated savings while incarcerated—but it was real enough to him, as he faced old age.

In 1959 the *Paris Review* was trying to represent a generation. As poetry editor, I had returned poems by prominent older poets, in order to hold the *Paris Review* to its discovered shape. We published Robert Bly before anyone else did; we published James Wright, Louis Simpson, and James Dickey early in their careers. Because I lived in England early in the fifties, we published Geoffrey Hill and Thom Gunn.

It made no sense to publish Pound, as his postcard seemed to request. On the other hand, the *Paris Review* sold copies not by printing Robert Bly or Geoffrey Hill, but by exploiting its elders: each issue carried an interview with a celebrated older writer. Maybe it made sense, in the issue which contained the Pound interview, to print new work discussed in the interview. I wrote Pound asking what he had to offer; I wrote George Plimpton asking if we could pay Ezra Pound for some unpublished work. Pound's answer came first, typed on both sides of a postcard, dated "i Dec." He had been going through boxes of manuscript which had survived the war in Rapallo. He wrote about some things he had found:

> Guy in Ind. wanting to print letters and forgotten translations of Heine, (probably for free,) but would serve as chronicle of past times and no reason for me to keep up american universities that never pay me anything
>
> I am, frankly, looking for people who will feed the producer, whereas they mainly want me to help them . . . time and again by the dozen.
>
> No doubt the supported think such an attitude very crass.

(Pound knew nothing of me or my circumstances. I was free-lancing that year. Maybe he assumed that I was supported for my year in England by a Guggenheim or a Fulbright; most of the American poets or academics he met in Italy were supported by grants.)

> Shd/a man of my age be able to USE even the little he gets? (news to you probably that such conditions exist).

In the letter I found what I later witnessed in his conversation; he appeared to try out a nasty or domineering tone; then he qualified himself and apologized:

Worry IS bad for the temper.
cordially yours   and pas de bile
E Pound

On the front of the postcard, at right angles to the address, he typed a postscript that wandered into obscurity, and announced his new diffidence:

this communication NOT very communicative, and not fit to post, but am being rushed to a train, and if I dont send it, you wd/have to wait God knows how long for even partial answer, and probably incomprehensible enquiry into matters unlikely to have been broached in yr/presence.

He was already thinking of me—as he thought of everyone—as a student to be coached in the ways of the world; and he mocked himself for his habit.

Through December and January I prepared myself for the interview. My Pound books remained in Ann Arbor; Charles Monteith at Faber and Faber sent me everything they had in print, and I read Pound all over again. Meantime George Plimpton turned up some money in New York, and I was able to tell Pound we could pay for a Poundian portfolio. (We could not pay for the interview itself; we had paid no one else to be interviewed.) I was delighted that we might help him with his finances. By now, Pound had become anxious over what we could print:

Heaven knows where I will be, and if anything more than fragments will be available.

This was Pound's first use of the word "fragments."

The mess made of proofs for *Thrones,*

—the latest collection of *Cantos,* about to be published—

Due to my incapacity to attend to 'em,

—the incapacity unexplained, as it always would be—

is no harBINGer for new composition, but we can hope. (*)

The asterisk led to the bottom of the page:

I mean there are fragments of new Cantos. but . . . whether fit to release???

These fragments were substantially the poetry later collected as *Drafts and Fragments of Cantos CX-CXVII*.

I lived in the landscape of Ezra Pound, week after week. I read and reread most of what had been written about him, criticism which was largely unsatisfactory; some of it was marred by pedantry, often pedantry curiously lacking in documentation and certainty; and much of it was marred by passions: Pound inspired loathing or he inspired discipleship. Early in February the BBC Third Programme rebroadcast three interviews with Ezra Pound done a year earlier by D. G. Bridson, who had visited Merano with his tape recorder and a television crew. Bridson was a knowledgeable and intelligent interviewer, and the radio programs were excellent. The television program used film of Pound walking, Pound with his grandchildren, Pound with his bust by Gaudier; the sound for the television program was Pound's detached voice, abstracted from the radio interviews; I was able to see the television tape at the BBC television studios, and take a look at the castle where I expected to see him.

I listened to the radio program several times, and it was encouraging. Pound made sense, and spoke with vigor, only a year past. My anxieties lessened a little.

Late in January, Pound rode south from Brunnenburg to Rome, where he put up at Ugo Dadone's apartment in the Via Angelo Poliziano. He expected his visit to be brief. He didn't want to leave Rome, but thought he had to, and expected to see me in Brunnenburg. On February 8 he wrote a postcard: "Aiming to get to Brunnenburg by 25th—what is latest date you need certitude?" In a February 14 letter, he said he had "committed the folly of reserving the sleeping car for Thursday." He expected to arrive at Brunnenburg by February 19, "and shall await you there." Then on February 17 came a cable: "Come to Rome Merano icebound Pound."

We sat in the sunny room and talked. I had not brought my tape recorder with me, that afternoon. I feared that he might object to the recorder; poets were always blaming technology for something or other, and this man was not only a poet but a paranoid. I wanted to avoid offending him, whom I expected to be ready to take offense.

We talked for an hour, and I saw no paranoia, no gibbering, no brutality, no readiness to take offense. I saw fatigue, or rather I saw energy and fatigue in constant war, in which fatigue continually overpowered energy, only to have energy revive itself by a fragile and courageous effort of will, and fly its quick flag, later to fall back again under the dour attack of tiredness. The alternatives were precipitous and the fatigue seemed more than physical; it seemed abject despair, accidie, meaninglessness, abulia, waste. He would walk up and down the small, bright room, sit in a chair and read to me from manuscript, alternating pairs of spectacles as if he were juggling in a circus; then suddenly his face would sag, his eyes turn glassy like a fish's, and he would collapse onto a sofa and into silence; then he would jump up in five minutes and begin the cycle again, his speech newly vigorous and exact.

We talked for an hour and a half, that Sunday afternoon. I had expected to see him only for a few minutes, to make an appointment to interview him the next day. I had expected him to be busy and arrogant, perhaps to set aside two hours for me tomorrow, like a dictator posing for his bust. I had expected him to lay down the rules by which we would play the game. Instead, I found him *worried* about the interview, the way I used to worry about final examinations. He worried about the questions I would ask, afraid I would ask hard ones, afraid he could not answer them thoroughly, with wit, with full recollection.

I was surprised at the seriousness with which he took the interview. Most writers take interviews lightly, as gossipy interludes between bouts of composition and revelry. When a writer is interviewed, he or she has answered two-thirds of the questions before, and much of the time can play a prerecorded tape for answer, while the busy mind composes a shopping list. But Pound undertook the interview with anxiety, for two reasons that I became aware of: in the past, even the recent past, interviews had caused him trouble, when he was misquoted or selectively quoted or when he had been tactless. On his release from St. Elizabeth's two years before, reporters had asked him what he thought of Robert Frost's part in the negotiations, and Pound reportedly answered that, well, it had taken Frost long enough. I suppose he made a flippant, mock-arrogant answer to a provocative question—he was in fact grateful to Frost—but the newspapermen reported that he had exposed his nastiness again.

The other reason for Pound's anxiety was harsher: he was not sure that what he said made sense.

And he was still obsessed about what the *Paris Review* could find to print. He told me again that the *Cantos* newer than *Thrones* were unfinished and therefore unprintable. He had not written a line since July. He had been in no shape to write, since last July. He spoke about blood pressure, and about pills that kept him alive; I formed the idea that he had suffered a stroke, though neither of us mentioned the word. Perhaps he suffered only from symptoms of high blood pressure.

Lacking new *Cantos* for the *Paris Review*—as he thought—he had assembled for my reading a miscellany of uncollected writing: letters to Louis Untermeyer, especially "An Autobiographical Outline," which he wrote in Rapallo in 1932, apparently addressed to Untermeyer as author of biographical notes, "in order to put the facts straight"; some old translations from Latin: Horace, Rutilius; translations from Heine; and his recent *Versi Prosaici,* which collected gists and piths from the *Cantos,* attempting to boil down Pound's most central references into dense, elliptical prose.

Then there was another packet, he told me, perhaps unsuitable for publication in the *Paris Review,* but vital for me to read. His eye seized on me, peering, interrogating, almost pleading. He pleaded that I listen, read, pay attention, and take seriously what he had to tell me. After a lifetime of influencing, sometimes bullying, first in literary causes and then in economic and political ones, he continued to look for disciples or converts. But in Rome in 1960, he was not trying to convince me of the efficacy of Social Credit, or of the intelligence of Benito Mussolini. Quite the reverse.

He had been waiting for me all day. At some hour before I arrived, he had taken a walk, and had left me a note in case I showed up while he was gone. Now he handed me the note:

I will be back by 4.30 or sooner—you can go up and glance at Versi Prosaici (unpublished)

Bunting letters

Letters to Untermeyer

incredibly stupid of me not to have sent you phone number.

Can you if at your convenience wait at Dadone's if anywhere near 4.30 at any rate leave yr. phone number

of course we shd. talk before I turn you loose on the disordered fragments

but the chairs are comfortable

only extracts possible for use and abusive expressions shd. be cancelled—I made peace with G.K.C. for example

at any rate the Bunting is worth reading i.e. for D. H.

yrs E. P.

use of violent language DEPLORABLE but I got something done. by or in spite of it. Bunt's scribbles have educational value for D. H. however rash it may be to turn you loose on 'em in absentia.

When I left him to return to the hotel for the night, I carried the note with me, together with the bundle of manuscript, and found the insults for G. K. Chesterton embedded in the Untermeyer letter. In the Bunting letters I found the education Pound intended for me—and it was an education I was not prepared for: Bunting writing Pound in the thirties had told him that Mussolini was no good, that Pound's thinking was cockeyed.

Pound had begun to educate me in the errors of Ezra Pound.

As he handed me the bundle to take back to the hotel, he said cryptically that Bunting knew a bit more in the thirties than E. P. did; only when I read the letters did I understand. In his self-accusation his tone was jaunty as he tried out the notion that a man could admit his errors and even survive them. But he could not sustain the jauntiness; nothing sustained itself. Fatigue came over him like a sudden shower, and he lay back in his big chair with his eyes closed, his leonine head leaning back, in the position he held for the Wyndham Lewis portrait of 1938, with the sculptural lines turning his face to stone.

His fatigue reminded me of my resolve not to waste his time, or to outstay my welcome. I stood up and said I had to go. He opened his old eyes, which bored straight into me with sudden energy, and he said very quickly, "*Must* you go?" The voice amazed me, the tone of it. He seemed disappointed, even sorrowful.

I rejected this interpretation. I told him I had to get back to my family; I would not tell him that I was leaving because he seemed exhausted. So he walked me to the elevator, and we agreed that I would arrive the next morning at nine o'clock with my tape recorder. I felt his anxiety build again. When the elevator arrived he held the door open for a moment. "You needn't think you're taking any of my time, you know," he said. "I'm at your service. I'm here to be interviewed."

Walking back to the hotel, I let the realities of the hour crash against my preconceptions. I told my wife, "I think he's *lonely.*" She had known of my fears, of my expectation of arrogance or even dismissal. I told her what I had seen and felt. We agreed that, if I still sensed his loneliness the next day, I would ask him to dinner with us.

2. Rome: Monday

The next morning I woke early, my family still asleep, and consulted the stack of three-by-fives I had collected for the interview. Next to them was my copy of the Faber edition of *Thrones,* which I was to review for the *New Statesman,* and which I was reading for a second time, taking notes in the margin. I found *Thrones,* like most of the *Cantos,* hard to read, obscure—not in thought or metaphor, not in its English diction, but obscure in reference, full of names I did not know, or recognized vaguely as familiar from earlier *Cantos;* and obscure as usual in its Chinese, Greek, Latin:

> OU THELEI EAEAN EIS KOSMOU
>   they want to burst out of the universe
> amnis herbidas ripas
>   Antoninus;
>   Julian
>   would not be worshipped
> "So thick the dead could not fall"
>   Marcellinus
> "dead chap ahead of me with his head split
>   could not fall."
>   XXIII, 6, and there also
> Assyrios fines ingressus, . . .

Without reference books, forgetting languages I had studied, I fluttered like a butterfly from flower to flower of comprehension. When I found a passage I could follow straight through, I marked it for possible quoting.

At eight o'clock I put down my copy of *Thrones,* and departed the hotel room carrying my tape recorder and my stack of three-by-fives. I walked quickly to the Via Angelo Poliziano, and had coffee and rolls in a café across from Ugo Dadone's flat, running through my questions again, looking at my watch every five minutes.

Pound answered the door dressed in pajamas, an old bathrobe tied loosely around them. His voice was quicker this morning, his gestures nervous and excited. He glanced at the tape recorder and groaned. It was a small battery-operated machine, primitive and inefficient, that I had rented in London. To Pound it was an instrument for torture; it put him on the block of his own, exact words.

As I set it up and tested it, in thc sunny room, he paced nervously up and down. He made sure again that I would print *nothing* without showing it to him first—something I had promised in my first letter. "What are you going to ask me?" he kept saying, as I fussed ineptly with the small machine. For him, the interview was a contest at which he would succeed or fail. I don't think he was competing with anyone else. He had read my interview with Eliot, and approved of it, but I never felt that he was competing with Eliot. He competed with a notion of himself; he put demands on himself that he feared he might not live up to. He feared not being witty enough, not being sharp and thorough and epigrammatic and right; he feared not making sense.

He lay down on the sofa when I started to ask questions.

Before I talk further about Monday, let me say a few things about the interview. Or let me say that there were two interviews. One occupied three days in a sunny room in Rome, early in March, 1960, an interview of roller-coaster alternations for Ezra Pound, triumph and despair, an interview which was incomplete sentences, gaps, great leaps over chasms, great Icarian plunges from sun to ocean. I will talk about that interview in these pages.

The other interview can be found elsewhere—the printed dialogue which appeared in the *Paris Review* two years later, neat and witty and energetic, with complete sentences and coherent paragraphs.

Any interview which looks coherent in print has found much of its coherence in editing. On an hour's tape, a single topic will surface three times at widely different places; with scissors and paste, the interviewer usually assembles one topic into one sequence. Interviewing Eliot or Pound or Marianne Moore or Archibald MacLeish, I would bring my stack of three-by-fives, and I would have my cards arranged in reasonable order. But when the interview began, the cards would reveal themselves as comfort blankets for the interviewer. I might ask only one or two questions from the cards, in a two-hour session; one question would start Pound or Moore or Eliot or MacLeish off, and he or she would begin to answer half a dozen other questions typed on other cards. Then the answer would give rise to another, related question, in the natural way of conversation. Eventually all my questions were answered, most without being asked.

In any interview, "the natural way of conversation" leads to doubling and redoubling of steps, and requires editing, joining like to like, eliminating repetition, and solving apparent contradiction. Pound knew all this, and as the interview continued he came to rely on the editing he knew I would do, the hours of scissors and paste which any interview requires—Eliot's not so much, and Pound's most of all. In all the three days, Pound seldom finished a thought; frequently, he did not finish a sentence. He would begin a long sentence, pause, stumble—and become aware of the rasp of the tape recorder. "No, no, no, no," he would say, and "Turn that damned thing off." (The quality of the tape was poor, but I managed to pull the words from it; when I made a copy, the quality diminished, and now all you can hear is, "Turn that damned thing off.") When I turned it off and took notes instead, the change didn't seem to help. Sometimes instead of answering my questions he talked about his difficulties in answering them. He was beset, he said, by the Jamesian parenthesis. He decided that the Jamesian parenthesis was a quality (or defect) of the American mind. Trying to answer my question he would go back to supply information required as a preliminary, then decide that he needed a qualification or a preliminary to his preliminary, then qualify the qualification—and no longer remember where he had started or where he was going.

Sometimes an hour later he would return to an old, failed answer, and pick up where he had left off. A few questions from Monday he finished on Wednesday. Each morning when I returned to him, he had made notes to complete paragraphs abandoned the day before; he worked on the interview all night, between fits of sleep. He worked on the interview after I had returned to England, and finished some of his best paragraphs or sentences in letters mailed from Italy to Thaxted.

Failure was torture for him, but he never suggested that we stop, that we cancel the interview "due to ill health" or whatever. He was determined to succeed, even when he seemed hopeless. He was determined to succeed for his own sake, surely, but also for reasons that I can only call generous. "I have brought you—all the way from England," he said in a despairing moment, "and I cannot—give you an interview."

But it was the old man's pride that seized me by the throat. It must have been on Tuesday or Wednesday that he spoke to me, out of one of his longer silences, when it had become apparent to both of us that he would never recover a steady eloquence, that the fragmentation was irreversible; he looked deeply into me for a moment, and said, "Don't—let me sound—so tired."

So I didn't. The interview contains no words that Pound did

not speak (or write) and no ideas or implications that he did not, I'm sure, intend; neither does it correctly represent, for any stretch longer than two inches of text, the dialogue that took place on the Via Angelo Poliziano.

Not all his pauses were failure and forgetting. Sometimes he paused for the right word and it came to him. When he assembled a sharp or clever phrase, he smiled and chuckled and looked at me for approval or confirmation. Sometimes a question raised in him recollection of scene or anecdote, and provided him opportunity to mimic, and these were his happiest moments. He loved to mimic, and like many poets he was good at it. He performed Eliot and Hemingway with special finesse and gusto.

Often he raised objections to my questions, because they dwelt on the past. He accused me of assuming that he had lived his life in order to talk about it. He had not spent his years, he told me, analyzing his own reactions to things. He objected to my questions, but without rancor. He objected to them when he found them difficult.

And I, on the other hand, floundered in the difficulty of his answers, even when occasional energy thrust him through complete answers. I would ask him a question, perhaps about coming to Italy in 1908, and his answer would begin with an anecdote about the first rotary snowplow, or about assayers in the Philadelphia mint. At first I thought he misunderstood my questions. Then when he persisted—when he was able to persist—from initial anecdote to finished answer, I would see the snowplow's or the mint's analogical relevance to Italy in 1908. Often he strung two or three anecdotes or pieces of information together—the ideogrammic method of the *Cantos,* by which differing items, juxtaposed, yield a generality nowhere stated. But often he could not persist or develop—he forgot, he lost himself—and I sat in silence across from him, with the fragment of an answer hanging in the air between us, like the landscape background of a painting, the foreground undone.

In excuse, when he failed, he sometimes blamed the years at St. Elizabeth's. If you get used to the company of nuts, he told me, you get out of the habit of making sense. Depression grew thicker in the room, until his accumulated complaints of failure bulked larger than the failures themselves. Gradually I realized that he was convinced of failure not only in the interview; I understood that he doubted the value of everything that he had done in his life.

Remember that this was 1960, that Pound had not yet told reporters that his work was nothing, that I who was interviewing him was thirty-one, and more innocent than I had right to be.

Pound was an old man, doubting the worth of what he had done. To my astonishment, he leapt to take scraps from my hand. I mentioned to him casually that Henry Moore as a young sculptor had taken comfort from Pound's book on Gaudier-Brzeska, with its insistence on the superiority of carving to modeling. He was moved almost to tears; it was something he had not known before. I didn't have the idea that he knew Moore's work—Pound's years of championing sculptors like Gaudier and Epstein, painters like Picabia, were well behind him—but he knew Moore's reputation, and he was touched by new evidence that he had done something worthwhile. He enjoyed the news for a while in silence. Then he spoke. "There is no doubt—that I have been some use—to some people."

One only says "there is no doubt" when one has felt doubt. So he doubted even his generosity, or his usefulness, to others—this man who had discovered or promoted or found publishers and patrons for the best writers of his time. In recent years, in anecdote or interviews, I had heard that Pound abused some of these old friends and protégés. There was, after all, the quoted remark about Frost. I was prepared for an elder who would denounce his peers and his protégés. But I heard no disparagements from Pound. When I brought up his reported remark about Frost, the recollection depressed him. He spoke of Frost with affection and gratitude, and of the wisecrack with regret and denial; stumblingly, he said he had been misquoted.

When he talked about Eliot, it was with relish and laughter, usually to recall some piece of wit that passed between them. His words about Eliot carried a quality that I recognized as the affection an older man feels for a younger. I did not recognize the quality at first, because from my position they were equally Olympian; what is an age difference on Olympus?

When he showed anger in our conversations, it was over institutional betrayals. He was especially angry at Harvard. He felt that the Harvard University Press had betrayed him. He had wanted to publish his translations of Confucius's Classic Anthology of Chinese odes with the Chinese *en face,* an expensive project. *New Directions,* his usual and long-faithful publisher, had deferred to HUP. Harvard published the book in English only, promising as Pound understood it to print an *en face* edition later. Pound lacked the suspicion, or the acumen, to demand a contract which specified how *much* later. The *en face* edition had not appeared by 1960; nor has it since.

He became angry with Harvard again because of something I told him. As I mentioned, he had recorded poems for the Poetry Room on his 1939 visit to the United States. On the label of a huge 16 r.p.m. disc, a note insisted, "Do Not Play Band Six." Naturally enough, when I first played these records as an undergraduate I immediately played Band Six. It was a marvelous reading of "Sestina: Altaforte," also known as the Bloody Sestina, where Pound in the mask of Bertrans de Born praises war. The reading began with the shouted line—I jumped in my blue chair, and my eardrum ached—"Damn it all! All this our South stinks peace." (Typical of Pound's contradictions, the poem was composed in the breathless quiet of the British Museum Reading Room.) In the 1939 recording, Pound banged a drum as he spoke the poem; because of 1939 low-fidelity, it sounded as if he were kicking a filing cabinet.

Innocently that morning, forgetting that I had defied a

handwritten prohibition, I filled a pause by praising his reading of the poem. Pound interrupted his silence with a black look. "So they're letting them listen, are they?"

I remembered my lawlessness then, and confessed it. He muttered again about Harvard's promises. I asked him the obvious question: why had he demanded that the poem be proscribed?

He paused a while, I suppose, to find the phrase.

"War," he said, "—is no longer—amusing."

We had agreed to work the morning only, and begin again the next day. As we talked I became convinced of what I had suspected—that he was lonely and eager for company. At some point halfway through the fragmented interviewing, I broke another silence to ask if he would have dinner with us that night. He waited to answer, collecting or recollecting. The *next* night, he told me, he was invited to the Chilian embassy. *Tuesday* night. Tonight, *Monday* night, Dadone was expecting him for dinner; but maybe . . . He asked me to wait a moment, and left the room to consult his host. When he returned he immediately began to complete a sentence, to answer an old question that he had abandoned earlier, leaving my invitation unanswered. When he paused again, exhausted with effort, prone on the sofa with closed eyes, I asked him if he would have dinner with us tonight.

"Oh, yes," he said, opening his eyes. "It's all arranged. Yes. Yes."

When I left him at noon I walked back to the hotel discouraged, with tapes and notes which added up to little. I felt compassion for the old man, but apprehension about our evening. I did not know what to expect of Pound, freed from the menace of interview, loosed on the town.

After lunch and a nap—the interview exhausted me too—I began my book review of *Thrones.* I found myself praising it whether I understood it or not, holding it up for praise.

We picked him up at Dadone's at seven o'clock, driving the

Morris Minor through Roman traffic, sedate at this evening hour. We asked him to choose the restaurant. He said in a humorous manner that, well, Crispi's ought to do—as if we should know that Crispi's would do more than *do;* as if he were referring to the Tour d'Argent in Paris, or to Lutèce in New York. He had attended on Crispi's before the war, he told us; just the other night he had returned for the first time, and it wasn't half bad. He implied that everything else, in Italian life, had declined precipitously.

He worried that he would direct us incorrectly, but he led us through Rome without hesitation or error, which cheered him up. As we strolled toward the restaurant door, I looked him over. This was a new Ezra Pound, shirt open at the neck, with a light coat and a great yellow scarf, carrying a stout stick. His large black hat sat back on his head, revealing his abundant gray hair, and he walked with his head thrown back, his beard strutting forth at a jaunty angle.

He chatted with the headwaiter in Italian, holding himself upright like a general, and requested a particular table by pointing at it with his stick. When he had consulted the menu he chose *osso bucco* for himself, and recommended it to the rest of us. Upon consultation we ordered a carafe of the house red wine. Pound drank little.

We conversed, the three of us, with Pound paying special and even flirtatious attention to Kirby, his eyes glinting as he looked at her, especially if he made her laugh. There were pauses and moments of awkwardness also, when he would stop in midsentence forgetting his way, but these lapses were less frequent in Crispi's than in Ugo Dadone's corner room. Once or twice he made confident references in anecdote to an obscure Parisian friend, or to a Washington caller—and when he saw that we did not understand he lapsed into momentary depression, guilty again of mental error. Then he would recover himself with another story.

Mostly, it was grandfather's night out, and he was happy and funny, and if he didn't want to talk about the past in the morning, by evening he loved to reminisce. He told more Eliot stories, mimicing Eliot with avuncular, mocking, affectionate accuracy. He remembered a song that he and Eliot made up back in the years just after the Great War. He sang stanzas of "The Yiddisher Charleston Band," in a vaudevillian Jewish accent, and seemed without fear that we would find him anti-Semitic. (The song was perhaps no more anti-Semitic than MacNamara's Band was anti-Irish; but I cringed when I heard the name of it; Pound's subsequent actions lent it a retrospective nastiness.) When the Yiddisher Charleston Band was playing—this was the song's burden—*everybody* danced. It was young Pound and younger Eliot doing music hall. King Bolo made his appearance in one verse, the protagonist of a rumored series of pornographic verses by the young Eliot—these verses have never turned up, to my knowledge; various references occur in memorabilia; when I asked Pound about them, he hinted there might be a copy in the Pound archives—and King Bolo was dancing the Charleston too. The only couplet I remember went:

> Mistah Cool-idge, de Pres-i-dent,
> He couldn't come but de fam-il-y vent.

In another stanza, Mary Magdalene put in an appearance, as singer or dancer. She was the only Biblical figure, as Pound sang it that night.*

When Pound sang this stanza, he dropped his voice, perhaps out of deference to the religious convictions of diners nearby. I found it hard to hear the words, and Kirby couldn't hear them at all. Pound was looking at her—singing to amuse her—and saw her visage assume an expression he misinterpreted. Her face pretended to hear and to enjoy, but it was

*John Peck informed me that this song was printed by Louis Zukofsky in *An Objectivists' Anthology* in 1932, attributed solely to Pound. The printed version largely coincides with my recollection of Pound's performance. In Zukofsky's anthology, however, it is "Calvin," not "Mistah"; and "Jheezus" and Mary each make an earlier appearance. I leave my version as it was; I will not allow a text to corrupt a recollection.

too honest to sustain the lie, and so she appeared pained or disapproving.

This verse concluded his song, or Pound chose to conclude it there. With a foxy, roguish expression on his face, he leaned toward Kirby, wagging his finger, and said, "Baptist?"

Ezra Pound considered that a postwar American woman, raised in Princeton, graduate of Radcliffe, would be shocked by the presence of a Biblical personage in a comic song. Suddenly, looking through his eyes at her, I understood the distorting glasses of his vision. He was looking through 1908 eyes: at the church picnic the young ladies wear straw hats over their white collars; they huddle together and giggle; now young Ezra Pound approaches, and with a fine sardonic air speaks with a daring levity—about the literalness of the Bible perhaps; or about the sanctity of the 4th of July—*"Oh!* Mr. *Pound!* The things you say."

He spoke of the United States, that night at Crispi's, with nostalgia and affection—but he did not speak of a United States I knew at first hand. He spoke of my grandparents' America. Leaving the country in 1908, he had returned briefly in 1910 and in 1939. His only lengthy visit had occurred within walls, and most of his St. Elizabeth's callers were neo-Fascist toadies. "The trouble with seeing nobody but visitors"—he said apropos his St. Elizabeth's socializing—"is that you never talk to the opposition." His visitors told him what they thought he wanted to hear, and his notion of contemporary American life was naïve. You could hear 1908 in his voice, in that eclectic accent which was Pound's version of the village eccentric. You could hear it in his canny guess, "Baptist?"

Pound was a dinosaur, strangely preserved into a later millennium, stretching his long bones out of dinosaur valley into the chrome city—and not noticing that things had altered.

He *missed* the United States. He wanted to return, to see the country outside asylum walls. His wife had been miserable there, he told us, and she did not want to return—but perhaps he could fly over for visits? Did we think someone would pay his way over, perhaps to visit a university?

I leapt to assure him: any number of colleges and universities would pay great sums to hear him read his poems.

He asked: could we help him? He did not know what to do, his friends did not seem to want him to return, and he did not know how to go about it.

Of course we would help him!

I had no doubts—right then and there—but that Pound could handle himself on a reading tour. There would be no pauses in a reading, when he had the text in front of him. And despite pauses in our interview, it was clear from our experience tonight that the old man was in decent shape. He could tell good stories, and I had heard nothing of Weinstein Kirchberger or Franklin Delano Rosenfeld.

And *this* was the man who had poured the foundations of modern poetry in English. In America little poets and big ones traveled from campus to campus all year, earning their livelihood reading their poems; why shouldn't the father of us all receive a thousand invitations from a thousand universities? I told him there would be no problem; I told him he could pick and choose among invitations. He was encouraged, but I could see that he remained skeptical. I told him that as soon as we returned to England, I would write letters and begin his career as rider of the poetry circuit.

Dinner done, we fought over the check for a moment. I won. We walked outside into the mild spring night. As we headed for the car, Pound made it obvious that he wanted the evening to continue, that he did not want to return to Dadone's right away. Did we want to walk?—but come to think of it, he no longer knew the area. Perhaps we would like to drive around Rome by moonlight? Had we done any sightseeing? No? Well, then, he would show us around, from the car, and when we had time we could return for a closer look by daylight.

We drove in directions and over avenues that I cannot remember. We drove past the Forum and the Colosseum, and through a square where "Muss" made speeches to the Roman crowds, past walls where the Duce had erected maps of the ancient Roman Empire and his new Italian one. Pound identified public buildings as we cruised by them, in the night largely free of traffic. "There's the synagogue," he said at one point; he never named a Methodist Chapel for us; he *did* point out St. Peter's.

Finally we drove by the new railway station and our hotel, into the Via Angelo Poliziano. Halfway down the street, an ice cream shop showed bright lights amid the darkness of the other, closed shops. *"Here,"* said Pound, long before we arrived at Number 80. "Stop *here.* I'll buy you an ice cream."

We three stood on the sidewalk together, dipping wooden spoons into cups of exquisite *gelati.* American music issued from the ice cream parlor's jukebox. Pound stood in the yellow light, his coat flung across his shoulders like a cape, his hat angled back on his head, his great stick under his arm, his scarf draped with flair around his neck. He stalked up and down a few feet, smiling as his wooden spoon delivered its mouthfuls, veering back and forth on his toes, stalking with youthful gait again for a moment.

3. Rome: Tuesday

When Kirby and I were alone Monday night, we talked over our evening. I had seen a happier man, but she was unconvinced. Pound had been silent and glum when he had not been entertaining us with stories, and she was afraid that he had been bored. Listening, I became half convinced, my old preconceptions returning.

I woke early again and finished a longhand draft of my review. I was seeing Pound at ten this morning and would stay with him until one, when he would take an afternoon nap to prepare himself for the Chilean reception tonight. In the afternoon, I thought, I could type another draft of my review, and maybe finish it tonight. Then the phone rang. It was an American novelist, whom I knew through the *Paris Review*. He had heard that we were in town, and invited us to a party that night.

Well, I decided, at any rate I can type up another draft this afternoon.

When Pound answered the door at ten o'clock, he was strutting with pride and energy. Leading the way back to his room, he bounced on the tops of his toes. He handed me sheets of paper on which he had written sentences to fit into yesterday's answers. He had been up for two hours, and he felt *much better* than he had felt the day before. I watched his energy and his buoyancy with delight, but also with reserve: I had seen ups and downs before.

He let me know the source of his elation. For Pound, our evening out had been a social triumph, proof that he was sane and normal, proof that he could function like anybody else. He kept returning to the subject of Kirby; he was charmed with her not only because he found her attractive, but because she was neither poet nor Fascist; she was, in Pound's eyes, a *normal American,* a phrase which he used two or three times in commendation. Five or six times during the morning he returned to the subject of the night before, not in conventional thanks but as illustration of his energy or competence. When he asked again about poetry readings, I said—not to discourage him but to help him prepare and be wary—that of course they would be tiring, and that he must protect himself from fatigue. "Well," he said with a twang of pride, "you saw me last night! . . ."

For him, our night's diversion had been a carnival discovered in the square of a Calvinist town. It was gaiety, it was health. He spoke of it again when he ruminated about returning to America for two months every winter; *that* was what he needed, more nights like last night. "I haven't had a relaxed evening like that since I left America," he said. "I want to be able to talk to bright, normal people. Europeans don't understand anything." Eating at Crispi's, buying the ice cream on the way home, he had behaved like bright, normal people, not like the lunatic they said he was; he ended a lively evening like anyone in America, with ice cream and a wooden spoon.

His elation spilled over into the notion of the coming evening. He was pleased to be invited to the Chilean embassy. Then I asked him if he could go out with us again the following night, Wednesday—our last night in Rome. He accepted at once.

I switched on the tape and began to ask him questions about politics. The day before I had asked him only about literature and literary associations. Some of his answers had moved toward politics, involving themselves in monetary policy. But I had not spoken of Mussolini and the broadcasts, treason or anti-Semitism. Now I entered the nightmare places, wasted country of blackshirts and jackboots, blitzkrieg and genocide.

Pound in 1960 was explaining himself, excusing himself. He pleaded in his defense his long friendship with Louis Zukofsky. Later when Pound disparaged his anti-Semitism as "suburban," I remembered how he had told me that some of his best friends were Jews.

He told how the St. Elizabeth's psychiatrists informed him about death camps, about which I doubt that he had known anything. He said that they tried to make him guilty. Hearing him excuse himself, I knew that they had succeeded. He let me know, gradually and reluctantly, that he doubted what he had done. Bunting knew more than Ezra Pound, he had told me. Now he said, "I guess I was off base all along." Now he was no longer defending his actions in themselves; he was defending the *sincerity* of his actions. He told me about trying to leave Italy and return to the United States, after the war started, a return blocked by American authorities. He told me he had not committed treason—his familiar defense—because there can be no treason without treasonous *intent.* And his intent—he insisted—was to defend the Constitution against President Roosevelt, the usurper. (If Mussolini had gone down in his estimation, there was no funicula which elevated Roosevelt.) In his patriotic defense of the Constitution, I heard again the accents of 1908. He reminded me of my Connecticut grandfather, conservative Republican brought up on 4th of July oratory.

All this time I said nothing. I could not agree when I didn't agree. The phrasing of the treason law—about giving aid and comfort to the enemy—seemed fairly straightforward. I could not agree that his friendship for Louis Zukofsky made null and void a hundred attacks on Yidds and kikes. So I said nothing, only listened and occasionally asked a question, and my silence drove Pound frantic. He demanded exoneration, forgiveness. I was drawn to the old man—but I could not tell him what he wanted to hear. Finally, after an hour of his excuses and my silence, he gathered himself to make the outrageous plea: "Do *you* think they should have shot me?"

He had me there. No, I did not think they should have shot him—and I told him so. He laughed a long time, his face flushing. When he stopped laughing he suggested we take a walk.

Pound wanted to buy a pad and notepaper. When a writer buys paper, it's an optimistic sign. The energy he gathered from his evening out was still upon him. Wearing his yellow scarf, carrying his stick, he led me four or five blocks to a stationery store. Pound extolled the Bic pen to me, widespread in Europe but not yet arrived in Ann Arbor. Then on the walk back to the apartment, the energy began to drain from him again. I think that the tension of talking politics had sustained him; now that we talked of other things the fatigue rolled over him again like a tide. As we waited for the elevator in the hallway his eyes closed, and I worried that he lacked the strength to walk to his room. Then he lay on his sofa bed and closed his eyes. It was eleven-thirty. I suggested that I leave him now and let him rest, but he told me that I had promised to stay until lunchtime. After lunch—he said slowly, as if he were speaking from sleep—he would take a long nap, to be ready for the Chilean party tonight. Now, he said, I should ask him more questions; we must continue our interview.

We did. I returned to some topics of the day before, and completed more answers. I asked a few new ones. Pound remained prone, his eyes closed, and there were long pauses again. I turned off the recorder two or three times. Once I thought he had fallen asleep. Then his eyes opened and caught me studying the face I thought asleep, and his eyes bored into me and would not let me go. "The question is"—the voice said, after a long silence—"whether I give up now—or have another twenty years to write in."

We continued to gaze at each other. After another long pause, he said, "All the time—I feel the hands of the clock—moving."

Then he swung his legs over the side of his bed and sat up, still looking hard at me, his face now level with mine. "From what—you see of me," he asked, "—do you think—I will be able to go on writing? Do you think—there is enough of me here—to work?"

I who had expected arrogance and contempt was asked to judge Ezra Pound's mental abilities.

From the time I was a small boy, I had loved the company of old people. From my ninth birthday, I had been aware of the hands of the clock, for myself but also and perhaps originally for the old people I loved, grandmothers and grandfathers and great-uncles and great-aunts in Connecticut and in New Hampshire. When I was a child, I felt closer to octogenarians than to children my own age. Now I felt close to Ezra Pound in his predicament. He stood where we would all stand, if we lived long enough, at the long and agonizing moment of power's loss, but not complete loss, when energy and understanding flash forth only to be overcome again, when hope and hopelessness reasonably alternate.

I would not lie to him, but said to Pound what he already knew: maybe he *was* too tired—I permitted myself the euphemism that Pound used—to work on *Cantos;* I did not know. For a long time he continued to stare, with an intensity that was almost devouring. Then he sighed, his body loosened its tension, and he remarked that really, all he needed was two months of relaxation like last night; that would fix him up.

Back at the hotel I worked over my review of *Thrones.* If I could not reassure the old man that he would write more *Cantos,* I would praise to the skies what he had already written. I wouldn't lie to him, but I might lie to others about him. I was feeling something like devotion. Some people in their old age demand or plead for a filial relationship to the young. I felt this plea in Pound, and I responded. By late afternoon, my typescript of the review was chicken-scratched with revisions. Soon the babysitter would arrive, and we would leave for the party. I had to get the review in the mail tomorrow. I wondered where I could find someone in Rome who could type up an English book review. At the desk, two young clerks told me there was no problem at all: they would type it. If it was a matter of the great poet Ezra Pound, the American who preferred to live in Italy, why should they not work late and without sleeping . . . ?

When we left to go to the party, one clerk was reading my English aloud to the other, who was hunting and pecking at a typewriter. When we returned at one in the morning a neat typescript of my review, with only a few exotic errors, was rolled in our mailbox.

At the party were all the literary Americans in Rome. I talked a good while with the host, and with Moreland and Saskia Hopkinson. It was relaxing to be away from Pound and among Americans my own age. I didn't need to listen so hard—and I did not have to keep on *feeling* all the time. It was the emotion—I realized—that drained me when I was with Pound.

Moreland had told the American literary colony about the interview. No one at the party had ever met Pound, and many were curious. I was called upon to testify to his mental condition, and to talk about his politics. I found myself exaggerating on the side of his health, normality, and coherence. Then I found myself in a brief, sharp argument. One tall and aristocratic figure, whom I knew to be an American translator from the Italian, resident in Rome, hung at the edge of several conversations without taking part. I noticed a lip that curled with increasing annoyance. Aware as I thought of the reason—and possibly a little drunk—I escalated my praise of Pound and Pound's poetry, until finally the translator could resist no longer. He leapt into the conversation, denouncing Pound and denouncing me for praising him, even for talking with him. Pound was a Fascist, an anti-Semite, a lunatic, a bully, and a bad poet.

I had provoked the fight I wanted, and quickly asserted the contraries. The people we stood among tried smiling, as if the argument were in good fun; it wasn't. I was angry, and realized that I had been spoiling for a fight with someone who denigrated Pound. Finally, when it seemed as if somebody might hit somebody else, the translator summed up my moral character in a word or two and walked out of the party.

It was time to go home. Driving home with Moreland and Saskia, I felt triumphant, as if I had defended my old father against attack. As my heart slowed down its pounding, I was aware that Saskia was proposing another social engagement. She suggested that, since the interview was going so well—I had exaggerated—perhaps tomorrow I would bring Pound to lunch at their home?

I doubted in reality I could; Pound would be tired after the Chilean party; whatever energy remained should go to the interview. Answering, I said that I would extend the invitation to Pound, and telephone them about it, but that I didn't think it would work out. I said that Pound had mentioned some errands he had to do; I lied, protecting Pound in his fatigue, trying to protect myself, I suppose, from sharing him with anyone else.

4. Rome: Wednesday

In the morning the desk clerk weighed my *New Statesman* envelope, I bought the stamps, and my review of *Thrones* took off by morning post. Then as we ate breakfast in our room, the telephone rang. It was Pound calling, at nine o'clock, an hour before I was scheduled to see him. His voice was vigorous, he sounded happy and strong. He asked if I would bring the car this morning; we could drive to the Circus Maximus and take a walk together; I should bring the tape recorder, and we could continue the interview on foot.

I wondered where he would lie down, when the fatigue took him over; but I enjoyed the new confidence of his proposal, and his hostly generosity—he wanted to show me Rome—and I said I would bring the car.

Then he asked if I had plans for the rest of the day.

I was confused. I said we still planned to have dinner with him.

He knew that—he said quickly—but he wondered about the *rest* of the day. We would be leaving Rome tomorrow, he said, and he wanted to see as much of us today as he could.

I told him we felt the same way.

I thought of Saskia's invitation to lunch, but I didn't mention it on the phone. I hung up and hurried through breakfast. Kirby agreed that I should tell him about our invitation, and sound him out. If he liked the idea, I would bring Pound to our hotel about noon, and pick my family up.

Now I finished breakfast and drove the car to Dadone's apartment. It was a deep spring day, bright sun, light air with a little breeze—the perfect weather of a Roman spring. Maybe Pound took vigor from the weather. The fragile elevator creaked upward, and when the door slid open I found myself facing Pound, who was waiting in the hallway outside the apartment. He was pacing, rubbing his hands together, smiling, and looked twenty years younger than he looked when I first saw him.

He took my arm and led me back to his sunny room, saying that he had something to show me. Scarf, hat, and stick lay together on a chair near the door, ready for our expedition. He shuffled through a clutch of papers—some of them notes toward answers to old questions, which he gave me later in the morning—to find what he wanted, and handed me two sheets of graph paper, scrawled over with a blue Bic. "This might help a bit," he said, "in case I konk out." I remembered that while we walked to the stationer's the day before, he complained that someone had sold him a pad of graph paper, when he had wanted plain. Now the graph paper looked purposeful, as the big hand spaced out notes toward the conclusion of the *Cantos,* curved over tight squares in the poet's calligraphy of space:

Provisional ending
          re nature of sovereignty
(if I konk out.)

nostos.
periplum.

vs. paradiso, difficult
        to find inhabitants
                for.

to clarify obscurities.
(vers. prosaici
as note.)

get clearer
definite ideas or dissociations already
expressed.

verbal formula to control
rise of brutality.

principle of order
vs. split atom

Early this morning—I found out later—he had read over his new *Cantos* and fragments. He was vigorous now, and happy with plans for work, as he had not been "since last July." His "Provisional ending . . . (if I konk out)" was a vital sign, not a morbid one: he was able to *conceive* that he could finish the *Cantos*. The conception carried with it doubts about what he had done—"clarify obscurities"—but it was humorous, when it acknowledged the difficulty in finding inhabitants worthy of Paradise; and the note touched again on the old verities of his life and work: "nostos" is home, and "periplum" is the voyage around the world, like Odysseus's around the Mediterranean, that the traveler must endure before returning home; and his provisions looked toward the accomplishment of a goal: "verbal formula to control rise of brutality"—the brutality or brutishness that Ortega ascribed to the vertical invasion of the barbarians. Brutality was loss of control for Yeats also, when the clawed falcon no longer hears the commands of its master; "principle of order vs. split atom" put the controlling mind on the one side, the violent atom with its destructive power on the other; and the atom was split "in fragments" and therefore not under control.

He named his enemy, making general or metaphysical what was also private or personal. The problem of finding or maintaining order in the universe is identical to the problem of finding or maintaining order in the self. In Canto XIII, from the first collection of *Cantos,* he quoted Confucius:

> If a man have not order within him
> He can not spread order about him;
> And if a man have not order within him
> His family will not act with due order;
> And if the prince have not order within him
> He can not put order in his dominions.

When I arrived—"Mr. Hall, you—find me—in fragments"—the atom had split, and all the King's horses and all the King's men couldn't put Ezra Pound together again. Now he dared to hope that he had the energy to reassemble both himself and the atom.

He spoke with a vigor that made anything seem possible. He settled his hat back on his head, flung his scarf around his neck, and took up his stick. Then he realized, with a short laugh, that he didn't know how to direct me to the Circus Maximus. He sat at the edge of his sofa bed, hat and scarf still on, and studied a map. Then suddenly it happened, horribly in front of my eyes: again I saw vigor and energy drain out of him, like air from a pricked balloon. The strong body visibly sagged into old age; he disintegrated in front of me, smashed into a thousand unconnected and disorderly pieces. He took off his hat slowly and let it drop, his scarf slid to the floor; his stick, which had rested in his lap, thudded to the carpet. His long body slid boneless down, until he lay prone, eyes closed, as if all the lights in a tall building went out in a few seconds, and the building itself disassembled, returning to the stone and water and sand from which it had come.

For a few minutes he said nothing, only breathing and sighing. If I had not seen similar catastrophes before, I would have thought he had suffered a stroke or a heart attack. After two or three minutes he opened his eyes and looked at me. I said nothing but looked back into the eyes that watched me.

After another two or three minutes, he mumbled, "I can't

do anything right." After another pause he added: "I get you to go the trouble—of bringing a car over here—and then I crump out on you."

It was no trouble of course and I said so. But now Pound was as depressed as he had been elevated. He had brought me "all the way down to Rome for nothing." I told him I had the material for the interview. He said, well, he didn't feel like going out now, so maybe I should ask him some more things. I did, and filled in some gaps, but Pound's depression was heavy. When a question reminded him of the *Cantos,* he doubted that he would live to complete them. He spoke again of the difficulty of finding inhabitants for a Paradiso, and now he was complaining of his incompetence. Maybe he was mistaken all along, he mumbled, to put Confucius at the top; maybe it should have been Agassiz. He looked at me as if I could decide for him.

Gradually, as we talked and I recorded his answers, he recovered a little. He swung his legs over the side of the bed and sat up. He had been invited to visit Chile, he told me with pleasure. He didn't expect he would go there, but he was glad to be asked; now if someone would ask him to the United States . . .

He was gathering strength again, to assault the Circus Maximus. He thought he would feel like it in another ten minutes, he told me. I asked if he could sign some books, in the meantime. I had brought them from England in the car, not with the idea that Pound would sign them—who would ask a favor from the ogre I had invented?—but in case I needed to consult them for the interview. Now I wanted his signature on them for the sake of myself and my grandchildren, and I knew that he would be pleased to do it. He wrote apologies in all the books, along with his signature. In the *Selected Poems* he wrote "Roman holiday," by which he meant to imply that there was nothing for me in Rome but a holiday. In his *Classic Anthology* he wrote, "This at least contains horse sense." In the collection of his letters he wrote, "to Hall having mercy," in

Rock Drill "to Hall persisting," and in *Thrones* "to D. H. attempting consolation." At the back of *Thrones* I later found another note in his hand, repeating his earlier shame about the errors in his text: "as to minor errata gawd help us."

When he finished signing—handing me each book with a smile, looking at me as I read the new line—he stood and put on his hat and picked up his scarf. Then he changed his mind, put them down on the bed, visibly deciding to do something else. He strode rapidly across the room, and pulled two suitcases from beneath a desk. He opened one and rummaged through it and closed it and opened the other. From the second suitcase he lifted a loose pile of papers and carried it to me where I sat on the sofa across from his bed. He sat down beside me and set the papers between us. The top page began with a roman numeral; I was looking at the drafts of new cantos.

Go ahead, he told me, read them.

These were the *Cantos* that he had worked over "until last July," and which he had read again this morning. These were essentially the lines collected in 1968 as *Drafts and Fragments.* I say "essentially" because he worked on them again in 1960, from March through June, and when I had returned to England mailed me further versions; and he did some further work until 1962; I cannot distinguish, in my memory, the versions I read that morning from the versions I read later. The differences, I believe, were not great.

There was also a sheet of paper that I remember whenever I think about form in the *Cantos:* it was a list of quotes and lines from earlier *Cantos;* it was headed "Things to be Stuck in."

I sat reading, rapt. Pound walked up and down, glancing at me, then lay down and closed his eyes. This time he seemed not to collapse but deliberately to rest himself. I read for half an hour, with enthusiasm becoming elation. In my review of *Thrones* I had praised him not so much for *Thrones* as for his whole career. Now I loved *new poems*—sounds, images, passages from the typescript in front of me. I interrupted my reading to tell him so—he made it obvious that he wanted to hear my opinion—and he sighed deeply and smiled.

I don't remember just what I said to him. But I have a note which I made later that day, which must represent how I felt. These were the best *Cantos* since the Pisan, I said; they returned to lyricism, and to personal vulnerability, his own life and his own concerns surfacing through the details of history. I was moved by the poetry of old age, by the acknowledgement of error or failure shining through a language that gave the lie to failure. I quote from the final versions:

> Can you enter the great acorn of light?
>   But the beauty is not the madness
> Tho' my errors and wrecks lie about me.
> And I am not a demigod,
> I cannot make it cohere.
> If love be not in the house there is nothing.
> . . .
> i.e. it coheres all right
>   even if my notes do not cohere.
> Many errors,
>   a little rightness,
> to excuse his hell
>   and my paradiso.
> . . .
> To confess wrong without losing rightness:
> Charity I have had sometimes,
>   I cannot make it flow thru.
> A little light, like a rushlight
>   to lead back to splendour.

There was also—and I remember reading it that morning, I remember the dazzle of it—the fragment of Canto 115 that begins:

> The scientists are in terror
>   and the European mind stops
> Wyndham Lewis chose blindness
>   rather than have his mind stop.

The operation that might have saved Lewis's sight might have impaired his intelligence. You must accept the punishment of persistent dark, if you are to see inwardly and to speak what you see. Canto 115 also contains lines I quoted earlier:

> A blown husk that is finished
>   but the light sings eternal
> a pale flare over marshes
>   where the salt hay whispers to tide's change

These poems were paradisal, elevated, and ultimately removed from the scene of personal failure, because there is something that persists and survives individual wreckage: "i.e. it coheres all right," and "the light sings eternal." In the note I wrote that afternoon, I said that I felt that the *Cantos* were almost finished, not finished by resolving all issues raised, but finished in their ascent; so I must have told him that these fragments were paradisal.

I sat on the sofa reading and rereading them, and I exclaimed over and over again, and pointed out lines that were especially beautiful. Pound asked me three or four times if I *really* liked them. I don't think he doubted me; he was positively leering with pleasure, but like most of us he could not hear enough praise.

After a few moments he tired again. I did not expect it this time. Horribly his body sagged again. He crossed the room to his sofa bed and sat down with his head in his hands. When fatigue took him over, it drowned his hopes; and the higher his hopes had been, the more profound his despair. I heard his old voice moving out from the darkness under his hands, like a voice from a cave. "The question is," he said—and paused a long time—"whether to live or die." I had no comment to make. I looked into his eyes. My heart broke for him, as he sat possessed again by the conviction of impotence, inability to *finish,* impotence intensified by the conviction that he had made huge mistakes, mistakes too gross to rectify, mistakes of life and of art. He looked across the room at another poet (for better or worse; he knew nothing of my work) with forty more years to make things cohere. After a long time he said, "There can be such—communication—in silence."

The sentiment was not original. I suspect, however, that little of his past life had been spent in silent communication; and most of the rest of his life he remained mute.

Then Pound's irony, that device which protects us when we become vulnerable, rose up and said, "Well, maybe nothing—is being communicated—to you," and the fatigue passed again, and he put on his hat and scarf. "Let's be going," he said.

We never made it to the Circus Maximus. He tried to direct me, using his map, but we circled helplessly in the Roman traffic, and the roads we wanted were never where we wanted them to be. After fifteen or twenty minutes of frustration, we found a place that looked ancient enough, and parked. (When we drove out again we discovered a sign, and learned that we had visited the Baths of Caracalla.) We walked for half an hour. I asked a few interviewer's questions, lifting the recorder so that it hovered between us at speech-level, and he answered me. But he did not want to talk about himself. He was conscious of having exposed himself, conscious of what he had shown. Walking around the ancient stones, he fabricated an interest in my "work"; how was it going these days?

I say "fabricated," I trust, without indignation. He was kind enough to wish to appear interested, but he didn't know my work, and I don't believe he retained much interest in the poems of anyone younger than himself. He would read his old friends and contemporaries—Eliot, Williams, Cummings, Marianne Moore—but I think he had to strain to be interested in Robert Lowell. Perhaps it pained him to lose touch—this was the man who had discovered excellence among the young before anyone else did—but it shouldn't have. As an artist grows older, he loses the ability to discriminate among the young. It is inevitable. He grows away, he grows apart—and eventually the faces and the poems blur together, and begin to look alike. I have known people to lose their ability to read younger poets while they were still in their thirties; most lose it around fifty; Eliot held onto it until his sixties, perhaps because as an editor discrimination was his profession. Pound lost interest, and then judgment, in the late thirties, when he was about fifty years old.

Still, I was touched that he asked the question, and I answered by speaking briefly of my endeavors in poetry at the moment, while he nodded to indicate his understanding.

It was eleven or eleven-thirty now. Pound's energy held up—and by now I realized that it would rise and fall whatever happened—so I asked him if he would like to eat lunch at the Hopkinsons' place, telling him briefly about Moreland: that he was associated with the *Paris Review,* that he was a novelist, that I had known him at Harvard, that he was rich and his wife beautiful. Pound said yes, let's do it; he was going to stick as close to us as possible all day; after lunch he would take a nap, he said, and then if he was up to it we would go back to Crispi's that night.

We drove back to my hotel, parked, and Pound waited in a café across the street while I went upstairs. My wife was beginning to feed the baby, and the process would take forty-five minutes or so. I telephoned the Hopkinsons, and told Saskia that we would arrive for lunch in an hour—a baby, a five-year-old boy, two parents, and an aged poet—if the invitation was still in order. It was.

I entered the café and found Pound drinking a cup of coffee. When I sat down, a waiter walked up to us, to take my order, and wagged his finger back and forth between us, saying a sentence in Italian, addressed to Pound, which ended with the word "figlio." Thinking he recognized a resemblance, the waiter asked Pound to confirm that I was his son. Pound looked at me and laughed lightly and said, "*Sì. Sì.*" When the waiter left to get my beer, Pound laughed again, and said, "Well, now that you're a member of the family . . ."

A moment later, the fatigue washed over him again. With no place to lie down, he propped his head on his fist, elbow on table, and leaned against the wall. His eyes closed occasionally, but he did not sleep. "Keep on talking," he said, and I did. Again I searched my mind for anecdotes that would please him. I asked him if he had heard about the Ezra Pound night at the Institute of Contemporary Arts, London 1953.

If he had heard, he did not remember. So I told him the story I have already recounted in "Notes on T. S. Eliot." Pound was amused to hear of the ruckus Graham Greene and John Davenport raised. ("Their asperities diverted me in my green time.") He was pleased to hear of the occasion itself, and of the cable Peter Russell and I addressed to him at St. Elizabeth's, which he did not remember receiving: "Ezra is a-comin in. Lhude sing Possum." (It was Pound who gave Eliot the nickname of Old Possum. Pound in his youth wrote a satirical poem about the London winter, parody of an old song, which began "Winter is icummen in, Lhude sing Goddamn. . . .")

I also told him my favorite of all knock-knock jokes. (First I had to explain the *genre.*) "Knock-knock." "Who's there?" "Ezra Pound." "Ezra Pound who?" *A capella, con molto brio*—"Ezra Pound to get you in a taxi, honey. I'll be there about a quarter of eight." I think he enjoyed the pun; I know he enjoyed the evidence the joke afforded him that his name was au courant. Yeats took pleasure, in his old age, to hear Dublin urchins singing a poem he wrote when he was young; Pound in exile delighted in the monument of a knock-knock joke. Then he told me a story which pleased him. When the jurist Roscoe Pound, no relation, was introduced to a collegiate audience as Ezra Pound, the audience cheered. Clearly Pound understood that they were cheering Ezra. I knew that the applause was ironic, and even based on the anomaly that a law professor was confused with a preconceived traitor. I did not disabuse him.

Instead—filling up the time, supplying what he needed—I

dredged up another story. In 1956, the year after I published my first book of poems, I was invited to an insane meeting of writers. President Eisenhower had instituted the People-to-People program, in which groups of American professionals—manufacturers, architects, farmers—gathered to recommend courses of action to the executive branch, actions to promote contact and understanding with people of foreign countries, especially countries of eastern Europe. William Faulkner was chairman of the writers' group and picked most of the prominent names in American letters. In addition, he named one young fiction writer (Harold Brodkey, it was) and one young poet. We met in Harvey Breit's apartment in New York. I call the meeting insane because of the group's diversity—Saul Bellow and Edna Ferber; Pound's old friend William Carlos Williams, and Pound's most hysterical detractor Robert Hillyer. This mixture, I suppose, was intended to be "a representative cross-section."

The gathering was drunken, argumentative, and inconclusive. Some of the proposals angered Saul Bellow and he walked out. Steinbeck brought a Hungarian novelist with him, and much of the discussion derived from the recent rebellion in Hungary. William Carlos Williams—loyal to Pound, though he found Pound's politics anathema—proposed that we recommend releasing Pound from St. Elizabeth's, which occasioned some antipathy. The evening ended, amid the debris of a thousand opinions, with Harvey Breit's parliamentary shrewdness. He suggested that a small subcommittee meet the next day to boil down all these valuable suggestions. He suggested that the subcommittee consist of William Faulkner, John Steinbeck, and Donald Hall. No one could object to Faulkner and Steinbeck because they were Faulkner and Steinbeck. Nobody could object to me because I was nobody.

Writers staggered out into the streets groping for taxis. I remember standing on a curb with William Carlos Williams—

who appeared sober—and telling him with sudden fluency how much I admired his work. Because I was known at the time as an iambic reactionary—though I did indeed love his poems—he may not have returned the admiration; he grunted.

We met the next morning in Saxe Commins' office, Faulkner's editor at Random House. We decided to limit ourselves to a few, simply worded recommendations to our President, possibly doubting his intellectual capacity. We agreed quickly to three proposals which had achieved befuddled consensus the night before. Then I proposed that we add a fourth: "Free Ezra Pound from St. Elizabeth's hospital." Steinbeck was quickly negative. I don't think that he cherished antipathy for Pound. He was afraid that the proposition would offend too many people, Congressmen for instance, and that we endangered our other proposals by including this one. Saxe Commins was nodding his head, and I thought my proposal had lost, when Faulkner suddenly sided with me, and the fourth proposal passed two-to-one.

But it was Faulkner's sentiment, and phraseology, which delighted me, not simply his assent. After Steinbeck finished his objection, Faulkner addressed the secretary who was taking down our proposals. "Yes," he said. "Yes!" He had been laconic the night before and so far this morning; now he almost chattered. "Yes! Say it this way. Take it down this way, young lady. 'While the Government of Sweden confers its highest honor on the Chairman of this Committee, the United States keeps its best poet in jail.' "

Telling the story to Pound, I left out the antipathy at the evening meeting, and emphasized that Steinbeck's reluctance was strategic. When he heard Faulkner's sentence he smiled, but Faulkner's vanity was not the lesson he took from the story—nor the one I intended him to take. As with Henry Moore, he had found another celebrated artist to count on his side, and another piece of praise to warm himself with. After a moment or two he said with a moved gruffness, "Please thank Faulkner when you see him."

The baby sat in the back of the Morris Minor station wagon, in her pram-top. My wife and son sat in the back seat. Pound and I sat up front and got lost. It wasn't wholly our fault, because a street prominent in our directions was blocked off for repair. We drove in circles for half an hour, trying to climb an inevitable hill which we could see but lacked access to. We stopped pedestrians and Pound interrogated them without success. Everyone was polite, even warm and jolly, but without skill in directing us. Some of the people seemed to have trouble with Pound's Italian. I had understood that his Italian was once excellent; perhaps it had deteriorated in thirteen years at St. Elizabeth's? I reminded myself that I sometimes had trouble with his English.

We arrived late enough for politeness, not so late as rudeness, and ate a magnificent lunch on a terrace, in a large house on top of a Roman hill, under the mild Roman sun of spring. Pound loved the sun. Before lunch and between courses he sank back in his chair, his head thrown back on a pillow, to soak it in. Sometimes the brightness bothered his eyes, and he had difficulty adjusting his hat to shield his eyelids. We all fussed over him, and an amused calm voice emerged from the covered face: "Grandpa can get out of the sun if he wants to."

Cold cucumber soup. Vitello tonnato. Salad. A light white wine. Fruit and cheese. Coffee.

After lunch we talked with Saskia and Moreland, and Pound dozed or listened, apparently content or even pleased to lie at the periphery of a conversation among "normal Americans." Occasionally he entered the conversation with a mysterious line, especially startling to Moreland and Saskia, who had not experienced these obscurities earlier. Moreland was master of a polite sound, resembling a laugh of assent, that stood in for a response. On several occasions Pound drew himself together to perform an anecdote, complete with mimicry, which he knew would please his audience—some story of Yeats or Wyndham Lewis or Joyce or Eliot. One of his own anecdotes upset him. Someone mentioned I Tatti, Bernard Berenson's villa outside Florence. Immediately Pound perked up, reminded of a story. One day at dinner, he told us, Berenson's young grandson had asked a question out of the blue: "Grandfather, what is a Jew?" Pound mimicked Berenson in answer, drawing himself up in severe dignity, turning slowly upon an invisible grandson, enunciating slowly and carefully: *"I'm—one."*

Mimicry made the story funny. We laughed, along with Pound—and then I saw him crumple again. Now it was not fatigue. He passed his hand over his mouth and his eyes, his face abject: misery, shame, guilt. "Oh," he moaned. "How did we get on the subject of race?"

When he sang us "The Yiddisher Charleston Band," and when he pointed out a synagogue, he had brought up the "subject of race" with us before; and of course in the interview I had asked about it, and heard him boast of his friendship with Louis Zukofsky. Apparently he feared to disgrace himself in front of Moreland and Saskia.

When we had drunk our coffee Pound looked tired. The five of us loaded ourselves into the Morris, and set out for the Via Angelo Poliziano with new directions. At first Pound sat back with his eyes closed. Then he opened them and spoke, "I hope I didn't hurt you with Mr. Hopkinson." I said he hadn't, not knowing what he had in mind. I suppose he was thinking of the Berenson story, or perhaps of the cryptic remarks. After a moment I asked him what kind of hurt he meant. Hopkinson was a rich man, he told me; we had to be careful with rich men. He mentioned Moreland's "Harvard man manner." I told him that the remoteness of the rich had always put me off.

"Yes," said Pound. "I suppose they have to protect themselves. Particularly if he thinks I may look on the *Paris Review* as a source of some of my sustenance."

When we parked in front of Dadone's Pound turned in the front seat and shook hands with Kirby, continuing to clasp her hand after he had shaken it once or twice, and spoke as if he might be saying goodbye. He looked terribly tired.

"I might not see you again," I said suddenly. "I hadn't thought of that."

"Well, I had," he said, and got out of the car. I followed him into the building where he pushed the button for the elevator. It was four o'clock in the afternoon. I told him again that we wanted to see him tonight, to return to Crispi's with him. He nodded his head, too tired to speak. I said I would telephone at seven, to see if he was able. He nodded again, and clasped both my hands, but said nothing, and when the elevator came he entered it silently and ascended out of sight.

At seven his voice was strong. He had slept well, he was ready for Crispi's, how soon could we come?

That night his conversation was steadier, more consistent than it had been before. Perhaps because he knew us better, perhaps because of a series of social triumphs, perhaps because of his nap, he never sank into a long pause. Maybe he was not so gay, not so entertaining as he had been on occasions earlier—but maybe he did not feel the necessity to entertain us. He talked mostly about the United States, how much he missed it, how much he wanted to visit the country. I assured him vehemently that he could visit as much as he wanted, paid by universities to read his poems. Oh, he told me, he required annual refreshment, at that national source. I told him he would have *no trouble,* moving from campus to campus, as a great poet reading his poems. Like Eliot he could read poems to pay for his annual return. He could read each year at some university near us, so that he could stay with us for a week or so each year. And not only would he visit the

United States for his refreshment, I assured him, he would make enough money on a two-month tour to support his family for a year.

We ate well, and drank more wine than we had drunk two nights before. We were excited and planned for the future: he would be working on the new *Cantos,* and he would send them to me; perhaps the *Paris Review* might use some of them with the interview; they would be badly typed; could I retype them for him? Of course I could, and of course the *Paris Review* would want them. And as soon as I could put the interview together, and get it typed, I would mail it to him for correction.

Perhaps before I had finished putting it together, he told me, he would have a few emendations for it, "things to be stuck in." For that matter, he said, maybe we could work together in England; the BBC was talking about broadcasting his opera *Villon;* maybe he could talk them into paying his fare to London, and he would stay with us in Thaxted.

The Priory had ten rooms, we told him, and he could have *two* rooms of his own, and stay as long as he liked.

Mostly our happy plans were for America. Pound asked questions about living in America, things that bothered him and that he needed to ask about. He could not drive a car; was it impossible, as certain Europeans insisted, to live in America without a car? I swore that I knew three young, male, otherwise sane Americans, all of them poets, who could not drive, and who survived without persecution or loss of citizenship. Then in the same tone he asked a different sort of question. "Tell me," he said, "how do you feel the influence of the American Communist Party in your daily life?" For a second I thought he was joking. I knew the American Communist Party up close, or I had in the past, and I knew that it had no influence at all on my daily life, or anyone else's, unless one chose to grant it influence. But he was wholly serious. He had spent all those years in St. Elizabeth's, being visited by people like John Kasper.

"None," I told him. "None at all. No influence at all."

He looked at me curiously, then nodded. I think he decided to consider me naïve.

"Why do you ask?" I said. "What do you see?"

Oh, he said, little things. For instance, a higher court had just decided that the NAACP did not have to surrender its membership lists to the Attorney General of the State of Mississippi.

I chose not to set him right. I didn't want to quarrel, or to upset him. Nor did I let his convictions about American Communists and the NAACP stop me from assuring him about his visits to the United States. There are things you do not wish to understand.

After dinner, we could not eat another ice cream, but we prolonged our evening with another tour of Rome. Pound said again, perhaps a little half-heartedly, that he should show us around because, after all, he had brought us all the way from England for this so-called interview. I told him again that the interview would work, that he would be surprised at how much he had told me. As we drove slowly among darkened streets, he named squares and buildings for us. With a quick gesture he pointed to a huge stone building, and said, "There's the scene of the crime."

"Where you made the broadcasts?" I said.

He nodded. "Where I handed in the texts."

A few minutes later we parked in front of Dadone's. All three of us walked into the foyer by the elevator and embraced each other. There were tears in Pound's eyes. We swore we would see each other soon—first in London or Thaxted, then in Ann Arbor when Pound was making his reading tours. The elevator arrived, and Pound—his hat cocked defiantly, his scarf astride his shoulder, his stick poked ahead of him—marched into it and swiveled his lined, stone, triangular face toward us, and mouthed goodbye as the elevator disappeared upward, and I never saw him again.

5. Thaxted, Ann Arbor

In the bustle of leaving Rome—feeding everybody, packing, clearing out the room; farewells to desk clerks who typed book reviews; tips; consulting maps, wheeling with assumed bravado through Roman traffic—I never lost sight of Pound's lined face miming goodbye. As we drove north, bypassing famous cities astride the *autostrada,* and the children subsided into sleep, my mind went over the last four days detail by detail—not over Pound's words tape-recorded for the *Paris Review,* but over gestures and motions of body, the look of old eyes, *gli occhi onesti e tardi,* and words unspoken in so eloquent a tongue. For the next few days, my mind existed in a place like the landscape of certain dreams, where experience wheels and hovers over one territory and will not go elsewhere—as when you finally slide into sleep after twenty-four hours straight driving across the American plain; slide into sleep only to continue driving, past dream grain elevators and dream acres of soybeans; so, driving through the changing landscape of Europe, I watched Pound's face over and over again, heard him speak in his slow and hesitant voice.

With my family deposited again in Thaxted, I drove to London, turned in the Morris, and left the tapes with a firm called Tape Typing, which had done earlier transcriptions for me.

Then I returned home by train and bus, slept twelve hours, and began what I had promised to do: I wrote two dozen letters to the United States, beginning my campaign to provide Pound an annual reading tour of North America. I wrote Pound's publisher James Laughlin; I wrote the Poetry Center in New York; I wrote Pound's connection at Yale, Norman Holmes Pearson; I wrote Harry Meacham in Richmond, Virginia; I wrote universities from coast to coast that booked poets for readings.

One morning the *New Statesman* arrived at my door, delivered with the newspaper, and the lead review was my piece about *Thrones.* "Ezra Pound," it began, "is the poet who, a thousand times more than any other man, has made modern poetry possible in English." All right. Commonplace, but all right. Then I started praising *Thrones,* and my tone became shrill: "In a better world, literary men would queue all night to get their copies of *Thrones.*" As I read my review, that morning, I felt the slack sensation in my body which tells me that I have failed again: for whom did I write that sentence? for the readers of the *New Statesman?* No, I wrote that sentence to be read by Ezra Pound. Much of the review in fact did not even bother to praise *Thrones,* but attacked the critics I presupposed to dislike *Thrones.* By this means—I would discover ten years later, in the pastures of psychotherapy—I was able to transfer my own unacknowledged dislike for *Thrones* to other, imagined critics, and by attributing my dislike to hated Philistines, express my own alienated feelings.

"In America," I said, "where Pound has been petrified into an industry by the academics, the first reviews have been either condescending or ignorantly respectful. In England they will copy everything but the respect, for England revels in a massive provincialism which must reject all evidence of the European mind." My review was three columns long. At the bottom of the second column—after scolding the English for six paragraphs—I finally claimed that "*Thrones* is a very good book," and for a few sentences I discussed the subject matter

Pound had undertaken. But when I quoted a lyric passage, and said, "In all, Canto 106 is one of the finest achievements of the *Cantos* . . . ," the weary book reviewer's cliché gave me away: I did not mean what I claimed to mean.

When the *New Statesman* arrived the next week I found myself attacked. Philip Toynbee—son of Arnold; Sunday book reviewer and literary journalist—wrote an angry and eloquent letter:

> Sir—It is hard to imagine a more stupefyingly useless review than Mr. Donald Hall's peripheral comments on Ezra Pound's Cantos. My irritation is probably due to my agreeing with Mr. Hall's general position on modern literature, but intensely disliking the snootiness of his self-approbation and his inability to say anything in the least helpful.
>
> We knew about Pound's unique achievement in the past. The question is whether the Cantos—and in particular the later ones—are great poetry, something very close to megalomaniac rubbish, or something in between. Mr. Hall believes that they are great poetry; but I can find nowhere in his three columns any serious attempt to tell us why.
>
> May I ask Mr. Hall a few questions? . . . Can he understand Chinese; and, whether he can or not, does he believe that the understanding of an English poem should depend on the answer to this question? Is he interested in Chinese economics? Does he think it reasonable or insane to believe that the *fundamental* evil of modern western society is the taking of interest on loans?

I did not answer Toynbee's questions.

Meantime I worked each day on the interview. The transcript from Tape Typing provided limited help, nor was it Tape Typing's fault. My tape equipment was primitive, and I had been careless using it. Windows had been open on those warm Roman days; one tape was crowded with children's games from the street outside, another with the repeated cries of a woman seeking a taxi. These noises filled long Poundian silences, and obscured the rare word. There were many holes.

Still, the typescript included whole speeches by Pound, and fragments he welded together over the days, and my own responses, which sometimes repeated Pound's words and reminded me of what he had said. I sat for days with the transcript of the interview—with its many gaps for unintelligibility, it looked on the page like a Canto—listening over and over again to the original tapes, supplying here a missing word, there an inflection which provided a question mark; or I would hear the one word in a sentence which would be mnemonic to the rest, making sense out of what had sounded like gargling; or making corrections. When I finally established a text, I assembled the parts into intelligible order, attaching to the incomplete answer of one day the completed paragraph of the next.

All spring Pound wrote me at least once a week, enclosing revisions of new Cantos, or old letters or translations the *Paris Review* might want to print; but also he sent me afterthoughts for the interview. Some of the afterthoughts repeated, word for word, phrases I already had on tape; he only *feared* he had not said this favorite sentence. Others varied in phrasing, and allowed me to take my pick. Others were wholly new, and I built them into the interview—as he wanted me to—as if he had said them in Rome.

"Also for interview," he would write in his longhand, then continue: "There are epic subjects. The struggle for individual rights is an epic subject, consecutive from jury trial in Athens. Thru Anselm vs Wm. Rufus. To Coke and Adams." I had the sequence—a little different, a little more detailed—on my tape; and he repeated further versions of the same statement in two subsequent letters. "If I am being 'crucified for an idea,' " he wrote another time, "it is probably the idea that European culture ought to survive me: that the best qualities of it ought to survive along with whatever other cultures, in whatever universality." And a footnote—to his word "idea"—continued to protest his new diffidence: "i.e. the coherent idea round which my muddles accumulated." In the interview, I placed the footnote between dashes, after "idea."

Another page came labeled "add to interview as dialog," and read:

> O.K. I am stuck. Question am I dead as
> Messrs A.B.C. etc might wish?
>
> An epic is a poem containing history.
> Modern mind containing heteroclite elements.
>
> Past epos has succeeded when all or a
> gt. many answers were assumed.
>
> At least between author and audience,
> or a great mass of audience.
>
> Attempt in an experimental age IS ergo,
> rash.
>
> One's temper is bad when asked to give
> specific answers prematurely re the as yet
> unexplored.
>
> As to obscurity what about the great
> example which occasionally mentions 3 authors
> at once?
>
> [D.H. can go into that. sounds megalo
> for me to do so. And keep hammering.
>
> one wop calls the 2 boiler makers a
> moral shock. Or something of that sort.]
>
> Two dabs sent yester—
>
> Question. how much REST is one allowed?
> Has rigor mortis set in??

I did indeed "add to interview as dialog," or I added much of it, mixing these lines with lines gathered from the recorder and from other written sources, letters and notes. I added "the" to the beginning of sentences, where his epistolary style omitted what he would have used in speech. When I mailed him the interview, after all, he could change anything he wanted to.

A recurrent theme of these letters was the struggle to find material for the *Paris Review* to print. We talked about using *Versi Prosaici,* which was dense but fascinating, but he discovered that it had already been printed in an English magazine, which bewildered and dismayed him.

> I don't know where or when they got text.
> I have probly/lost the U.S. copyright anyhow=ugh.
> gawd hellup all pore sailors

He ended the letter, "wd the attempt to translate Horace fill the bill?" Then a day or so later, brooding, guilty, he wrote again. He *knew*—true or not—that losing *Versi Prosaici* was his own fault, and he struggled with the notion like a fly stuck in axle grease. Letter after letter chewed over further possibilities, suggesting that we might print *Versi Prosaici* anyway, because the English magazine did not circulate widely, "but yr ed wd probly not think so/". Or maybe the letter to Untermeyer? He had second thoughts about the Horace translations: "Trouble with the Horace is that it was done *not* as best language, but to illustrate DIFFERENCE in style = H. in relation to quality of Catul. or Propert . . ." Ending a chaotic letter—begun on a strange typewriter, continued with Bic—he protests, "NOT drunk—just physically too weak to move."

But he began gradually to think that new Cantos might do it, for the *Paris Review.* "Will also see if a bit of new Canto can be released/" he wrote in one letter; his hesitation became not diffident but painstaking; "damn nuisance that on every or almost every page of 110–117 there is something unready or some sign that needs verification//". He began in fact to show some confidence, and he wrote in reference to criticism of the Cantos: ". . . you have seen enough to refute Alvarez re. its being no Fugue (? no stretti?) no pulling together of themes. mere free association." The English bookreviewer A. Alvarez, writing in a Sunday paper, had called the Cantos a "scrapbook," and decided that the "so-called fugal structure . . . has turned into something no more fugal than free-association."

Pound sent me Cantos as he worked them over, his typescript corrected in his hand, for me to retype and return. His manuscript corrections removed typos and corrected errors; I was to change "God" into "Gold." His corrections changed the look of the poem on the page; he put a capital A and a capital B on one page, a circle around each, and in a marginal note gave me the direction: "—A is above—B", meaning that two dashes should be directly aligned in the typescript, although three lines and a space separated them; the dashes themselves had been added in ink, so that the visual and emphatic parallelism appeared to be an afterthought, revision by means of punctuation and typography.

The *Paris Review* ended by printing Canto 116, and the superb fragment of Canto 115. Also, we printed the letter to Untermeyer under the title "An Autobiographical Outline." Also, we included two facsimiles—the first page of the *Pisan Cantos,* and a letter written to the censor from the Detention Camp, in which Pound explained that the new Cantos put into the mail were not some sort of Fascist code.

My days in England, toward the end of my year there, remained full of Ezra Pound. When I was not typing Cantos I was working over the final touches on the interview, removing repetitions, cutting the interviewer's loquaciousness, simplifying structure.

Because I was freelancing in England, I traveled up to London once a week or so. Wages waited in the West End. Whenever I could manage, I came up to London on a Wednesday, which was the day John Wain entrained from Reading on *his* freelancing errands. Wednesday was Wains-day at the Salisbury, a magnificent gin palace on St. Martin's Lane in the theater district; from noon until closing time at three, the Salisbury was a floating, crowded, hectic literary salon, with half the poets of England waving pints in the smoky air. A. Alvarez usually came, sometimes Ted Hughes, frequently Michael Hamburger and Christopher Middleton. John Wain had known Pound in Washington. (Wain originally met Pound under trying circumstances—at least as Wain tells the story. In the heyday of existentialist jargon, early in the fifties, the London *Observer* flew Wain to the United States to ask famous people about their "commitment" to one thing or another. Unaware of the American use of the term, Wain approached Pound in St. Elizabeth's Hospital and asked him if he was committed.) Wain—and everyone else at the Salisbury—wanted news of Pound, and by quotation and mimicry I brought the news. Among other matters I told how Pound wanted to visit the United States to read his poems. Immediately Wain was skeptical—skeptical of the wisdom of Pound's notion, skeptical of the reception he would receive from American universities.

He was not alone.

When I came up on Wednesdays I often did some work at the BBC. One of my producers was D. G. Bridson, old friend of Pound's who had done the interviews I consulted before I went to Italy. When I told him that Pound wanted to read poems in the United States he shook his head. At the same time I was working with Stephen Spender on a collaborative project. He had known Pound for thirty years, and had visited him in St. Elizabeth's whenever he had come to America. Stephen also thought it was a bad idea for Pound to do American readings. "They would crush him," Stephen said.

The people in the United States began to answer my letters about Pound's reading tour. From the universities I received cautious or negative answers. At first I was astonished. American university English Departments refused to listen to Ezra Pound read his poems? Then I reminded myself that English Departments at American universities never *had* wanted to listen to Ezra Pound, or to read him for that matter. Most of the university regards modern poetry as a nuisance, and certainly living poets as nuisances. Then there was the matter of Pound's—shall I say—controversiality. Not long before 1960, Senator Joseph McCarthy had found America's campuses trembling and acquiescent. Courage is not epidemic on university campuses.

But other letters gave me pause, as Wain and Bridson and Spender had given me pause. One came from a man who was perhaps Pound's greatest patron in the United States—no coward, obviously a dear friend—who begged me not to promote a visit by Ezra. He mentioned vaguely "the stress" and "the pressures to which he would be exposed." Finally, a political friend of mine, a leftist admirer of Pound, took me to task: "If he comes over, they'll picket him. They'll boo him off the stage. *Don't do it!*"

My enthusiasm and confidence, expressed to Pound in Rome, had been naïve. I was slow to accept the results, perhaps because I didn't want to write Pound and tell him. Then I wrote him that it seemed hard "to get anything done by letter from here." I had also looked into the possibility that the BBC might bring him to London for *Villon,* and was told that the BBC "doesn't do things like that." I passed the message on. Now Pound's letters no longer mentioned visiting the United States, nor coming to England. We talked only about Cantos and the interview, as I assured him that the typescript of his interview was almost ready. Late in spring, I had a letter from him like all the others, and I answered it, typing up a portion of a Canto for him; but he never wrote me again. I finished work on the interview, and sent it to him on May 30, and wrote a letter to go with it, hoping that he would correct and return it soon. After a couple of weeks I wrote again. I wrote again, and again.

Just before leaving England, that August, I had a letter from the Poetry Center in New York. When I wrote them suggesting Pound, I was forgetting or ignoring that the Poetry Center had its quarters in the Young Men's Hebrew Association. Leonard Lyons had printed an item in the Lyons Den suggesting that the Poetry Center of the YMHA would invite a well-known Fascist anti-Semite to read his poems. The Center had denied the charges, and asked me to be sure I said nothing to contribute to the brouhaha.

I returned to the United States out of touch with Pound, unable to find him a reading, author of fatuous praise of *Thrones,* and probably contributor to another small Poundian scandal.

In my excitement over a year of writing—and in my reluctance to return to teaching—I neglected to get reservations on a Cunarder or a French Line boat. We did not fly because we had a ton of baggage. At the last minute we found a cabin on a German ship that took ten days from Southampton to New York. The crew was surly, the food starchy and ill-cooked, but we made fast friends among passengers, and danced all night, and enjoyed the small momentary universe of the transatlantic passage. And for me, the ten days' sail was a decompression chamber; by the time we filed down the gangplank in New York, I was resigned to teaching again.

I taught Pound's poems to undergraduates that fall, and I talked about him all the time, to friends and students and to audiences when I read my poems. At the same time, I became gradually convinced that there would never be an interview in the *Paris Review.* No word arrived from Pound. Of course I retained a carbon of the manuscript interview I had sent him—but I would not print it without his revisions. A kind of message came to me indirectly. James Laughlin wrote me saying that Pound had been having a bad time—"acute depression, irritability, etc."—and was in a nursing home. Then Laughlin told me something else:

> His last letter to me appeared to refer to your interview, but I can't really make much sense out of it. He says: "Considerable effort to ruin me. Hall particularly interesting after article on British spectator re brainwash. Interview in state of fatigue when one mutters first

thing that comes into head." Can you figure out what this means? I'm sure you wouldn't have written anything in your interview that would be likely to upset him, and I wonder who it is whom he thinks is "trying to ruin him."

Even paranoids—as Delmore Schwartz was wont to say—have enemies. Pound's remark that considerable effort was being made to ruin him was about as paranoid as Yossarian's notion in *Catch-22* that the Germans were trying to kill him. But did he now number me among his enemies? I don't know. When I read Laughlin's letter, I believed so. Juxtaposition made it sound as if the interview was part of the conspiracy, a devious attempt to discredit him. Later, when I read his manuscript revisions of the interview, it was obvious that he had not read most of the interview with any such notion. His letter was confused. Considering his enemies, perhaps he remembered what I had written in the *New Statesman* about hostility toward him; and I think he confused the *New Statesman* with *The Spectator;* so that he may have intended to write something like: "Article in British Statesman re brainwash" of the public about Ezra Pound. But then, I wonder: why would I be "interesting after" such an article? I don't know, unless—after initially reading and correcting the interview in a friendly spirit—he later decided (in his irritability, depression—and paranoia) that by showing him "tired" I revealed myself to be one of the brainwashers, disguised as a friend.

A year later, at the end of September 1961, Dorothy Pound wrote me that she had found the corrected interview while she had been cleaning drawers in her husband's writing table. She told me that he had made numerous changes, but that apparently he had been unable to concentrate on editing the last third of the typescript. She asked me to print a footnote to the interview saying that Pound had lacked strength to complete his corrections. She noted that she had found no new Cantos, in her desk-cleaning, and added that as a precaution she was showing the interview to a lawyer in Boston.

A week or so later the interview arrived, annotated in his own hand on every page. (The corrections were thinner toward the end.) The changes were mostly further attempts to clarify, to define, or to set ideas in order. I added them to the text, even though they didn't sound like speech, whenever I could understand their position and function. On the second page of the interview, I had quoted Pound saying that he had tried "to make the Cantos historic but not fiction." Between "historic" and "but," on the typescript of the interview, Pound inserted a parenthetical example: "(vid. G. Giovannini, re-relation history to tragedy. 2 articles 10 years apart in some philological periodical, not source material but relevant)." I changed "2" and "10" to "two" and "ten"; I added a comma. Perhaps I should not have added the parentheses at all; but he appeared to want me to, and Dorothy had asked me to make the corrections. James Laughlin helped me to understand Pound's hand, and his abbreviations, but I remember at least one clause which I could not follow, and for which I could not find a place.

Occasionally Pound altered the text to soften dogmatism. When in speech he had told me, "Real free verse is . . . ," in revision he made himself say, "I think the best free verse came from. . . ." There were moments of fatigue, in his corrections. Reading one perfectly clear statement he had made—about judging poets younger than himself—he could not understand what he was getting at. "I don't know what I said," he wrote in the margin. "You can leave this as something needing clarification, that I am too tired to make now." And he changed an adverb describing how Ford Madox Ford rolled on the floor—to criticize the young Pound's diction—from "indecently" to "indecorously." Where he had said, "You used to go poking around in the smelting room," of the Philadelphia mint, he substituted the more formal "You could then be taken around in the smelting room. . . ." And he corrected spelling. The X that crossed out an ill-spelled syllable could be large and irritable. (Other misspellings were changed by pencil in Dorothy's hand.) Beside a few statements he put large question marks, as if he doubted that he had made them. At other times he miscorrected. I had him saying "I grew up in Philadelphia," and then revising himself, as we all do in speech, "the suburbs of Philadelphia." In the first sentence, he had changed "in" to "near." This made the first sentence accurate, but left the following clause redundant.

One footnote made an essential change. He had spoken of the advantage of a university where people "control opinion" or "control data"; this verb sounded Fascist; in a note on the margin he wrote that he was using the French "contrôler," "to verify." At another political moment, he had told me, "I don't know whether I was doing any good or not, whether I was doing any harm. And I probably was." On the manuscript, Pound circled, "And I probably was," saying, "Is this on tape? I don't think I said it." It was not on tape. I remembered him saying it. But I cut it out, because the next sentence came as close as Pound wanted to come—at this time in his life—to retracting his politics: "Oh, I was probably offside."

Paris Review number twenty-eight, "the Pound issue," was dated "Summer-Fall 1962."

Pound rarely spoke during the ten years that remained to him. When he did speak—sometimes of the silence itself—he spoke eloquently: "I did not enter the silence," he told someone, "silence captured me."

He stopped writing. He spent hours alone in his study, but after the middle of 1962 he wrote nothing substantial, and the final *Drafts and Fragments of Cantos CX–CXVII,* virtually complete in 1960, was finished by 1962. Yet he did not want to publish work he considered "drafts and fragments"; he allowed these lines into print in 1968 only to correct the errors of a pirated edition.

I read everything written about him; I think I missed nothing. There were a few interviews, in the last ten years: especially one long, intense conversation with Grazia Livi, published in *Epoca.* This interview was garbled into a news story, which made it known around the world Pound had "recanted," taking back everything he ever said or stood for. It was not so. Pound was depressed when he gave the interview; he said, "a strange day came and I realized that I did not know anything, indeed, that I did not know anything at all. And so words have become empty of all meaning." The old man was beached like a whale. He had lost touch with his own convictions and abilities. But he did not "recant"; he was convinced only of personal failure. He held hope, if not for himself, then for others' minds and spirits engaged in the endeavors he had undertaken: ". . . there is something in human consciousness that will endure, despite everything," he said, "and that will be capable of withstanding the forces of unconsciousness."

His sense of failure ran deep. "I know nothing at all," he went on. Doubting his memory, he said, "I have even forgotten the name of that Greek philosopher who said that nothing exists, and even if it did exist it would be unknowable, and if it were knowable it would be incommunicable." This sentence does not reveal a victim of senile dementia. The interview continues, miserable and lucid:

Is it . . . a truth to which you have come by suffering?

It is something to which I have come by suffering. . . . Yes, by an experience of suffering.

. . . .

What is it, now, that holds you to life, from the time that you have acquired a total certainty of uncertainty?

Nothing holds me any longer to life. Simply, I am "immersed in it."

. . . .

And do you manage to work still? Or does the great sense of uncertainty possess you to the extent that all creative efforts seem useless?

> No, I do not work anymore. . . . I do nothing. I have become illiterate and uneducated. I simply fall into a lethargy, at the beginning of winter, and to my own disgrace I do nothing but cultivate my greediness and laziness. . . . Yes, I fall into a lethargy, and I contemplate. . . .

He speaks with the tragic energy of a defeated king, like Oedipus the victim of his own errors—fallen, lamenting his smallness in the center of a stage which he dominates. He reminds me of Yeats' final vision of man's life, spoken from the mountain in "Lapis Lazuli"; or of the last Freud, daily wracked by cancer of the jaw, writing *Civilization and Its Discontents.*

Later in his despair he came closer to "recanting." He told Daniel Cory that the Cantos were "a botch," because "I knew too little about so many things. . . . I picked out this and that thing that interested me, and then jumbled them into a bag." As late as 1967, Pound told Allen Ginsberg that "my poems don't make any sense." Ginsberg argued with him. Perhaps Pound wanted to be argued with, but he was adamant and witty in response: "At seventy," he argued back, "I realized that instead of being a lunatic, I was a moron."

It was at the end of this conversation that Pound came to the remarkable conclusion, frequently quoted: "But the worst mistake I made was that stupid, suburban prejudice of anti-Semitism."

Pound's domestic life had been irregular. I mentioned that in the thirties he had alternated between his wife Dorothy and his mistress Olga on a regular schedule. As late as 1959, he asked a handsome young woman to marry him, and traveled with her for a time. It didn't work out. Dorothy wasn't having any divorces. (Dorothy was not only the wife; she was the Committee for Ezra Pound. "Complications re/Committee," Pound wrote Hemingway during this interlude.) In 1962, Olga fetched Ezra from a private clinic near Merano, and for the rest of his life she took care of him. It was not—as I understand it—that Pound chose to run away from his wife and live with Olga. He was past that. Dorothy was too old to take care of him, and he needed care. Olga, Mary, and Dorothy could not get along—much less live in the same house together. Dorothy remained with Mary at the Castle. Only Olga—or a nursing home—could have taken care of the old man.

Summers Ezra and Olga spent at Sant'Ambrogio, where Olga kept a small house; she and Pound had lived there thirty years before. Dorothy spent summers nearby in Rapallo. September to June, Ezra and Olga lived in Venice, in a narrow house on a narrow street behind the Santa Maria della Salute. Pound's study was the top floor, the middle floor was their bedroom, and the ground floor was a small living room and kitchen. Olga Rudge had owned the house since 1928.

In magazines I read about their life together. Pound stayed in bed mornings until ten or eleven, and after a late breakfast walked along the Giudecca Canal. Sometimes he spent hours in his study, reading, sometimes recording poems—his own and other people's—into a Grundig tape recorder. In the study he kept the bust which Gaudier-Brzeska carved of him in 1914. Sometimes he and Olga ate lunch at Raffaelle's, sometimes at Pensione Cici. After lunch another walk, perhaps along the Grand Canal. He played long games of chess. Friends stopped by; Pound would not speak, but seemed pleased by the company. Sometimes with a literary visitor Olga filled the silence by playing a record of Pound speaking his own poems, the disembodied voice floating out over the disenvoiced body.

Unknown visitors came also—pilgrims and exploiters—including one who pitched a tent outside the house. (As Ralph Waldo Emerson grew older, he was beset by admirers visiting Concord. He complained of the thousand strangers seeking audience: "Whom God hath put asunder, why should man put together?") Many would-be visitors—Olga observed—worshipped Pound without having read his poetry; she told one such that she would procure a visit if he could recite *one* line of Ezra Pound's. He couldn't. Others wanted to read Pound their own poems and take his praise away with them. Others were academics looking for an imprimatur to their books on Pound. Others were promoters announcing that they had already booked a hall in London for a poetry reading; they flashed airline tickets. An acquaintance of mine, finding himself in Venice, sought out the house and knocked at the door. He expected to meet Olga Rudge and be turned away. To his astonishment, the door opened to reveal Ezra Pound in bathrobe and slippers. In his confusion, the young man burbled, "How are you, Mr. Pound?" Pound looked down at him for a moment, out of the *hauteur* of his silence, and then uttered a single word, in the melody which sometimes resembled W. C. Fields: "Senile," he said.

If the wit belied the word, Pound, like anyone in his eighties, was beset from time to time by the illnesses of aging. He had surgery for cataracts. He underwent treatment, and perhaps surgery, for his prostate. He visited the clinic of Doctor Paul Niehans in Switzerland, where sheep cells were injected into his bloodstream; he did not feel rejuvenated. Still, for a man of his age he did well. Part of the life with Olga was travel. She had the vigor, and Pound had the appetite. Both had a little money. Paradoxical checks arrived for Pound from American social security, and increasing royalties were forwarded by the faithful Committee for Ezra Pound in Merano to the menage in Venice.

Ezra and Olga went to Delphi; they visited James Joyce's grave in Zurich and near Trieste the castle where Rilke wrote the Duino Elegies; in Paris they took in the Salle Gaudier-Brzeska at the Musée de l'Art Moderne. In June of 1969, at the age of eighty-five, Pound flew with Olga to New York for a fortnight, surprising his old friends. This trip—six years after he and I had talked about an annual visit—was his only return to this country, from 1958 when he left St. Elizabeth's until he died in 1972.

He returned to Hamilton at graduation, and received an

ovation. At the New York Public Library he inspected the manuscript of Eliot's "Waste Land" with his own deletions, corrections, and comments. He saw Marianne Moore at the Library, and called on Mary Hemingway, widow of his old friend. He walked through Greenwich Village, and saw Patchin Place, where E. E. Cummings had lived. In Wyncote he visited the house where he had lived as a boy. He entertained the notion of a trip to Hailey in Idaho, to visit the place of his birth; but time and energy ran low; he returned to Venice.

In Italy he sometimes attended the Spoleto Festivals, reading Marianne Moore's poems one year, his own another. Politics spoiled the 1965 Festival for him, as Yevgeny Yevtushenko left the stage rather than share it with Pound. He avoided politics, except for occasional disavowals like his words to Allen Ginsberg about anti-Semitism. One of his last pieces of writing was a change of economic terminology:

> re USURY
>
> I was out of focus, taking a symptom for
> a cause.
>
> The cause is AVARICE.

The old moralist on his deathbed named as the enemy neither the banker nor the Jew but one of the Seven Deadly Sins. Readers of the Cantos—with their poetic denunciations of greed and profit, selfishness and exploitation—had long noticed that the author often sounded less right-wing than socialist, less Fascist than Old Testament prophet.

But his old politics informed his silent world in a thousand ways. Each year the Nobel was announced, and each year Ezra Pound was passed over. His friends received it—Eliot in 1948, Hemingway in 1954, Beckett in 1969—and Stalinist poets received it, but the former Fascist did not. Perhaps he would never have received it anyway; neither Tolstoy nor Joyce nor Conrad nor Lawrence nor Proust won a Nobel Prize. Certainly Pound thought about it. Back in 1935 in Rapallo, James

Laughlin remembers, he used to say that he would use his Nobel Prize money to become a chef.

Another prize eluded him, and the scandal afflicted his last months. The American Academy of Arts and Sciences yearly awards its Emerson-Thoreau Medal "for outstanding contributions to the broad field of literature over the recipient's entire lifetime." Robert Frost received the medal, and T. S. Eliot; Hannah Arendt, John Crowe Ransom, Katherine Anne Porter. In January of 1972, the Academy's nominating committee recommended that Pound receive the award; Leon Edel was chairman of the committee, which included John Cheever, Lillian Hellman, James Laughlin, Harry Levin, Louis Martz, and Lewis Mumford. (Lillian Hellman did not vote; Lewis Mumford opposed Pound's nomination, and suggested Henry Miller instead.) As soon as the nomination was revealed to the Academy at large, the opposition gathered strength. A Harvard sociologist named Daniel Bell led the way, saying, "We have to distinguish between those who explore hate and those who approve hate." Irving Howe (not an Academy member) concurred, declining to "close the books of twentieth-century history, certainly not as long as any of us remain alive who can remember the days of the mass murder"—thus perpetuating the notion which connects Pound with Hitler's extermination camps.

Meeting in April, the council of the American Academy rejected the nominating committee's advice. Five members of the Academy thereupon resigned—including Malcolm Cowley and Allen Tate. Katherine Anne Porter returned her medal to the Academy. Harry Levin, who had defended the nomination with energy and anger, wrote after the rejection:

> The majority of the council, in overriding the recommendation, has attempted to rationalize its decision by repeated assertions that art cannot be isolated from morality. This is misleading, if not disingenuous, in its implication that Pound and his proponents were irresponsible esthetes. There was never any disagreement over the principle involved. Members of the committee never questioned the

assumption that esthetics is grounded in ethics. Pound, like his master, Dante, is not only an artist but an impassioned moralist.

The Cantos have a moral vision behind them; but they are uneven and fragmentary as well as ambitious and brilliant; and they are marred by flaws both esthetic and ethical. To assess such work on balance is a delicate problem, which requires historical knowledge and critical experience. . . . What remains to be regretted is the lack of cultural perspective, the willingness of educated minds—twenty-three years after the controversy over the Bollingen Prize—to protract a mistaken personal episode at the expense of a creativity which will outlast the rebuff.

Pound's advocates were defeated by the old voices that had been largely silent since Pound's return to Italy, repressive and Philistine voices which had been loudest during the Bollingen controversy of 1948.

Then to Harry Levin came one last comment on the scandal. The summer after the vote had gone against him, Pound met friends of Levin's in Venice. Out of the years of silence, near death, he raised himself to utter a brief message for Levin:

"It matters."

The old poets had been dying for some time—men of 1914 and younger men and women. Wyndham Lewis died in 1957 while Pound was still at St. Elizabeth's. Hemingway killed himself in 1961. Cummings died in 1962. In 1963 Frost died, and Pound's oldest friend, Willlam Carlos Williams. In January 1965, T. S. Eliot died, and only Marianne Moore was left of Pound's generation. She died on February 5, 1972—nine months before Pound—and he read her poem "What Are Years?" in a memorial service at the Protestant church in Venice.

Eliot's death touched Pound the most. He and Olga flew to England for the memorial service at Westminster Abbey. Then he wrote his final words on his old friend:

His was the true Dantescan voice—not honored enough, and deserving more than I ever gave him. I had hoped to see him in Venice this year for the Dante commemoration at the Giorgio Cini Foundation—instead: Westminster Abbey. But, later, on his own hearth, a flame tended, a presence felt.

Recollections? let some thesis-writer have the satisfaction of "discovering" whether it was 1920 or '21 that I went from Excideuil to meet a rucksacked Eliot. Days of walking—conversation? literary? le papier Fayard was then the burning topic. Who is there now to share a joke with?

Am I to write "about" the poet Thomas Sterns Eliot? Or my friend "the Possum"? Let him rest in peace. I can only repeat, but with the urgency of 50 years ago: READ HIM.

After two days in London, Pound flew to Dublin and saw Yeats's widow Georgie, determined, it seemed, to visit all the islands once more.

He lived inside his silence as if silence were the Mediterranean, and he the shipwrecked Odysseus of silence.

Once a reporter asked him, "Where are you living now?"

He answered, "In hell."

"Which hell?" the reporter asked.

Pound pressed his hand over his heart. "Here," he said. "Here."

When Grazia Livi interviewed him in 1963, just after he went to live with Olga in Venice, Livi began by telling Pound that she had been afraid to meet him. I suppose Livi feared what I had feared—that Pound would be arrogant, Fascistic, intolerable—but Pound misunderstood the fear's cause; Pound said, yes, he understood that fear: "Everything that I touch, I spoil."

Because interviewers asked him about poems and politics—and because Pound in his depressed answers belittled his poems and his politics—people have assumed that Pound's silence derived from his notion that he had spoiled or botched his artistic and intellectual life. Doubtless he felt as much, but there were profounder abysses: he said it was by "touch" that he spoiled everything. "If love be not in the house," he wrote in Canto 116, "there is nothing."

In 1971 Mary published *Discretions,* a memoir of her father and mother, and of her own growing up. It is a brilliant book—the author devoted to her father, corrosively angry at her mother. The publication shattered Olga, and shattered Ezra as well because of his double devotion to Mary and Olga, assassin and victim. The women around Ezra Pound hated each other. Now Dorothy had quarreled with Mary, and no longer lived at Castle Brunnenburg, but summered in England near her son Omar. Winters she returned to Rapallo, but in the last four years of Pound's life, she saw her husband only four times: old gray ghosts of the married couple—Ezra and the Committee for Ezra—past passion and frail in their ninth decade, hardly speaking to each other, hardly able to speak.

One day Pound broke silence, saying to a friend, "I have never made a person happy in my life." Certainly he blamed himself—with an omnipotence like Robert Frost's, and like many people's—and he could reread his Confucius of Canto XIII with a particular misery:

> If a man have not order within him
> He can not spread order about him;
> And if a man have not order within him
> His family will not act with due order, . . .

The hell in Ezra Pound's chest had to do with Mary, with Dorothy, with Olga, and with others; and the hell within Robert Frost's chest, in the middle of triumph and honors denied Pound, had to do with Elinor, Elliott, Carroll, Irma, Marjorie, and Lesley. At the end of the lives of our great poets, the domestic life is a desert of anguish—perhaps on account of choices made for the sake of the self and its passion and its poetry, choices which in the retrospect of old age appear destructive and cruel. For some poets—possibly for all—life's hell is a wound self-inflicted, as punishment for defying the Platonic censor's prohibition of poetry.

As for Eliot? Eliot died without a hell in his chest. Eliot lived through his hell in middle life—tormented by an insane wife for whose insanity he took responsibility, tormented by her as by a Fury—and searched for rectitude, and found it, married again, and died happy.

Ezra Pound died in his sleep two days after his eighty-seventh birthday. That week, he had enjoyed his birthday party, drinking and eating with everyone, and he had attended a Noh play, and Peter Brook's production of *A Midsummer Night's Dream.* His funeral took place on San Gregorio, with Mary and Olga in attendance; Dorothy was too weak to make the journey from England. His coffin went by gondola to the island of the dead, San Michele, where he was buried near Diaghilev and Stravinsky. Island of the exiled dead.

When he died I rehearsed in memory my time with him in Rome, and my feelings about him and about his poetry. I went to an old drawer where I keep such things, and extracted my little collection—the interview with his corrections, his letters to me, carbons of the typing I had done for him, letters from other people about him. On the back of the interview I found lines written in Pound's handwriting which I had forgotten. Lying in his bed in some rest home, or in the Castle; facing without knowing it ten years of shoreless silence ahead of him, estrangement from wife, daughter's estrangement from mother, years of hopeless sailing around his world ("gawd hellup all pore sailors"), the old man—Odysseus without Ithaca, without Penelope, without Telemachus—had written lines of poetry extracted from the first Canto, written a half century past, and which spoke to me now, the word from the grave, the word at the bottom of all the other words:

Shall return
thru spiteful Neptune,
lose all companions

No man completes his life or his Cantos; we are all fragments. But some men sail the seas. He sailed, not to Paradise; he returned to his personal Inferno, a hell constructed by the arrogance and madness of his middle age. At the same time, the vessel of his sailing reached home port: not Dante's Paradise but Homer's Ithaca. By means of the great and noble language of poetry, Ezra Pound assembled the best of himself and of the cultures he loved and studied. We shall find him forever in this Ithaca.

Conclusion: Gladness and Madness

In the *Paris Review* interview, I reminded Eliot that he had written, seventeen years before, "No honest poet can ever feel quite sure of the permanent value of what he has written. He may have wasted his time and messed up his life for nothing." Eliot confirmed that he was still unsure. Of course all three old poets died unsure, and two of them feared not only that they had messed up their own lives but that they had messed up or destroyed the lives of others. The fourth poet, dead before forty, died convinced that he had not written as he might have written; convinced as well that he had made a mess of things.

Artists of vast ambition seldom die happy. They have given in to no other adversary, why should they give in to age and death? While they kept life and energy, the disparity between goal and achievement, depressing when dwelled upon, could be overcome by work or by plans for work. When death is imminent, or when old age drains ability and energy, depression becomes chronic. One remembers Leonardo's melancholy question, at the end of his life, "Tell me if anything ever was done."

Most people avoid this despair at the end of life by following simple maxims: don't be ambitious; take it easy; be a *good* father, mother, citizen, teacher, farmer, salesman, thief; settle for Thane of Cawdor. When I was an undergraduate, I had as a teacher a poet who had published several volumes, and when I was nineteen I looked up to him with awe. One night I was eating and drinking at his house, and I talked pompously about *greatness* in poetry, and I irritated him. Suddenly his sharp voice said, "Hall, why don't you stop trying to be *great,* and just be *good.*" I felt ashamed, I accepted his rebuke, and I heard his voice in my ear for a long time. Now I think that he was wrong.

You will never be any good as a poet, unless you arrange your life and your values in the hope of writing great poems—always knowing (and if you do not know it you are a fool) that you may well have "messed up your life for nothing." And you will probably feel that in pursuing your ambitions you have messed up the lives of others, or that you have encouraged their destruction for the selfish sake of your art. Some time ago Louis Simpson wrote a cautionary tale in "A Dream of Governors." When the Prince was young he killed a dragon and married the Princess. Now the King is old and fat, and the land he rules is peaceful. Bored, he visits the witch who lives over the dragon's grave, and begs her, "Bring evil on the land / That I may have a task." Whatever the reason, Wordsworth's couplet retains the truth of general observation: "We Poets in our youth begin in gladness; / But thereof come in the end despondency and madness."

For the ambition of poets is larger than the ambition to become King of Scotland. Poetry exists to extend human consciousness, to bring materials and insights from the unconscious dark into the light of language. ("Where id was, let there ego be.") In my words on Dylan Thomas, I described this movement as evolutionary. I will repeat, and expand:

We must add the thesis of pre-verbal, irrational thinking to the antithesis of secondary rationalism. We do not wish to abandon reason—it is a common mistake to think that poetry urges this abandonment, even among poets who accomplish their true task—for the darkness of the wood; we will not give up appendectomies, theology, tractors, and Montaigne; the rush backwards into darkness is madness, drugs, drunkenness, and suicide. Instead, we add thesis and antithesis to make synthesis, retaining reason but adding unreason to it, making a third thing; *homo poeticus.* Poets are psychic revolutionaries. Because they belong to the society they wish to overthrow, they often punish themselves. In their role as society's protectors, they torture and sometimes execute themselves as revolutionaries bent on overthrowing government. Plato expelled the poets from his Republic of reason. All poets have dictator Plato inside themselves, attempting repression of the internal Orpheus.

We have been told to lay aside childish things. Poetry is not a childish thing, not regressive to an earlier state; it is synthetic and therefore revolutionary. But it must frequent infantile sources—it must live among them on familiar terms—or it will have nothing to superadd to the conventional adult mind. Poetry in its nature requires one perpetual return to the infant's crib—in its *form.* By form I do not mean such things as sonnets and tragedies, but the million minute resolutions of vowel and metaphor, consonant and idea, by which a poem finds its requisite wholeness and resolution. In "The Relation of the Poet to Daydreaming," Freud shrugged form aside for a later day (which never came) but hinted that form relates to forepleasure. And forepleasure is the adult relic of infantile polymorphous perversity, that sexualization of the infant's whole body.

The formal resolutions of a poem begin in the crib, when the infant croons sweet noises, not trying to speak but taking pleasure in tongue and lips. Here begins the mouth-pleasure of poetry. At the same time the infant stretches and contracts limbs, arms and legs moving in still dance. Here begins the muscle-pleasure of poetry, rhythm and motion. Adults who make poems include many adult matters in their poems. They must. But if they do not touch down at the crib they do not write poems. Touching down at the crib—accomplished most often by sound—*validates* poetry, and acts like a catalyst to the adult mind of the reader, loosening the mind until it can receive the messages that come from the baby mind that inhabits all of us—the mind possibly of Australopithecus, possibly the mind of squirrel and fish.

For the poet this journey backward is wonderful and frightening. It breaks rules. It violates taboos. Because mouth-pleasure allies itself with desire to ingest the mother (and through her the rest of the world), lyric poetry is full of images of cannibalism (sometimes disguised as theophagy, sometimes as nuclear and nutritional pantheism; sometimes not so disguised; Eliot's poems are full of cannibalism, Pound and Thomas also; Frost not so much). Lyric poetry lives close to the mother, and to the conflict which emerges from that closeness. I think that poets' destructiveness—turned inward mostly, scattering itself outward also—derives from this taboo-breaking journey to recover the infant and add this mind to the adult's. Guilt over destruction derives originally from guilt over eating mothers up.

So the old age of artists may be troubled by opposite things: Wordsworth's "despondency and madness" may come from despair of future ambition, or from guilt over the results of past ambition. Nothing alleviates the guilt, except *possibly* new rectitude sought and followed from middle life.

Perhaps there are ways to evade the other thing, ambition's despair. If you are as lucky as Yeats, you can die writing your best work. In the last letter he wrote before he died, he said that he was resting after writing much verse; but shortly, "I will begin to write my most fundamental thoughts." Or there is the wisdom of a short story by Henry James called "The Middle Years." The novelist Dencombe is dying in his middle years, convinced that his work has failed, despairing that he lacks "the second chance" of a long life, in which to do the great work which he feels is "in him." Dying, he meets a doctor who loves his published work, treats him and comforts him, and argues with him and finally convinces him that having done what he has done is "the only thing." If you've doubted, Dr. Hugh tells him, "If you've despaired, you've always 'done' it."

At last, shortly before his death, Dencombe himself understands: "A second chance—that's the delusion. There never was to be but one. We work in the dark—we do what we can—we give what we have. Our doubt is our passion and our passion is our task. The rest is the madness of art."

APPENDIX
THE PARIS REVIEW *INTERVIEWS WITH T. S. ELIOT AND EZRA POUND*

T. S. Eliot

INTERVIEWER: Perhaps I can begin at the beginning. Do you remember the circumstances under which you began to write poetry in St. Louis when you were a boy?

ELIOT: I began I think about the age of fourteen, under the inspiration of Fitzgerald's *Omar Khayyam,* to write a number of very gloomy and atheistical and despairing quatrains in the same style, which fortunately I suppressed completely—so completely that they don't exist. I never showed them to anybody. The first poem that shows is one which appeared first in the *Smith Academy Record,* and later in *The Harvard Advocate,* which was written as an exercise for my English teacher and was an imitation of Ben Jonson. He thought it very good for a boy of fifteen or sixteen. Then I wrote a few at Harvard, just enough to qualify for election to an editorship on *The Harvard Advocate,* which I enjoyed. Then I had an outburst during my junior and senior years. I became much more prolific, under the influence first of Baudelaire and then of Jules Laforgue, whom I discovered I think in my junior year at Harvard.

INTERVIEWER: Did anyone in particular introduce you to the French poets? Not Irving Babbitt, I suppose.

ELIOT: No, Babbitt would be the last person! The one

poem that Babbitt always held up for admiration was Gray's *Elegy*. And that's a fine poem but I think this shows certain limitations on Babbitt's part, God bless him. I have advertised my source, I think; it's Arthur Symons's book on French poetry,* which I came across in the Harvard Union. In those days the Harvard Union was a meeting place for any undergraduate who chose to belong to it. They had a very nice little library, like the libraries in many Harvard houses now. I liked his quotations and I went to a foreign bookshop somewhere in Boston (I've forgotten the name and I don't know whether it still exists) which specialized in French and German and other foreign books and found Laforgue, and other poets. I can't imagine why that bookshop should have had a few poets like Laforgue in stock. Goodness knows how long they'd had them or whether there were any other demands for them.

INTERVIEWER: When you were an undergraduate, were you aware of the dominating presence of any older poets? Today the poet in his youth is writing in the age of Eliot and Pound and Stevens. Can you remember your own sense of the literary times? I wonder if your situation may not have been extremely different.

ELIOT: I think it was rather an advantage not having any living poets in England or America in whom one took any particular interest. I don't know what it would be like but I think it would be a rather troublesome distraction to have such a lot of dominating presences, as you call them, about. Fortunately we weren't bothered by each other.

INTERVIEWER: Were you aware of people like Hardy or Robinson at all?

ELIOT: I was slightly aware of Robinson because I read an article about him in *The Atlantic Monthly* which quoted some of his poems, and that wasn't my cup of tea at all. Hardy was hardly known to be a poet at that time. One read his novels, but his poetry only really became conspicuous to a later gener-

* *The Symbolist Movement in Literature.*

ation. Then there was Yeats, but it was the early Yeats. It was too much Celtic twilight for me. There was really nothing except the people of the 90s who had all died of drink or suicide or one thing or another.

INTERVIEWER: Did you and Conrad Aiken help each other with your poems, when you were co-editors on the *Advocate?*

ELIOT: We were friends but I don't think we influenced each other at all. When it came to foreign writers, he was more interested in Italian and Spanish, and I was all for the French.

INTERVIEWER: Were there any other friends who read your poems and helped you?

ELIOT: Well, yes. There was a man who was a friend of my brother's, a man named Thomas H. Thomas who lived in Cambridge and who saw some of my poems in *The Harvard Advocate.* He wrote me a most enthusiastic letter and cheered me up. And I wish I had his letters still. I was very grateful to him for giving me that encouragement.

INTERVIEWER: I understand that it was Conrad Aiken who introduced you and your work to Pound.

ELIOT: Yes it was. Aiken was a very generous friend. He tried to place some of my poems in London, one summer when he was over, with Harold Monro and others. Nobody would think of publishing them. He brought them back to me. Then in 1914, I think, we were both in London in the summer. He said, "You go to Pound. Show him your poems." He thought Pound might like them. Aiken liked them, though they were very different from his.

INTERVIEWER: Do you remember the circumstances of your first meeting with Pound?

ELIOT: I think I went to call on him first. I think I made a good impression, in his little triangular sitting room in Kensington. He said, "Send me your poems." And he wrote back, "This is as good as anything I've seen. Come around and have a talk about them." Then he pushed them on Harriet Monroe, which took a little time.

INTERVIEWER: In an article about your *Advocate* days, for the book in honor of your sixtieth birthday, Aiken quotes an early letter from England in which you refer to Pound's verse as "touchingly incompetent." I wonder when you changed your mind.

ELIOT: Hah! *That* was a bit brash, wasn't it? Pound's verse was first shown me by an editor of *The Harvard Advocate,* W. G. Tinckom-Fernandez, who was a crony of mine and Conrad Aiken's and the other Signet* poets of the period. He showed me those little things of Elkin Mathews, *Exultations* and *Personae.*† He said, "This is up your street; you ought to like this." Well, I didn't, really. It seemed to me rather fancy old-fashioned romantic stuff, cloak-and-dagger kind of stuff. I wasn't very much impressed by it. When I went to see Pound, I was not particularly an admirer of his work, and though I now regard the work I saw then as very accomplished, I am certain that in his later work is to be found the grand stuff.

INTERVIEWER: You have mentioned in print that Pound cut *The Waste Land* from a much larger poem into its present form. Were you benefited by his criticism of your poems in general? Did he cut other poems?

ELIOT: Yes. At that period, yes. He was a marvelous critic because he didn't try to turn you into an imitation of himself. He tried to see what you were trying to do.

INTERVIEWER: Have you helped to rewrite any of your friends' poems? Ezra Pound's, for instance?

ELIOT: I can't think of any instances. Of course I have made innumerable suggestions on manuscripts of young poets in the last twenty-five years or so.

INTERVIEWER: Does the manuscript of the original, uncut *Waste Land* exist?

ELIOT: Don't ask me. That's one of the things I don't know. It's an unsolved mystery. I sold it to John Quinn. I also gave him a notebook of unpublished poems, because he had

* Harvard's literary club.
† Early books of Pound, published by Elkin Mathews in 1909.

been kind to me in various affairs. That's the last I heard of them. Then he died and they didn't turn up at the sale.

INTERVIEWER: What sort of thing did Pound cut from *The Waste Land?* Did he cut whole sections?

ELIOT: Whole sections, yes. There was a long section about a shipwreck. I don't know what that had to do with anything else, but it was rather inspired by the Ulysses Canto in *The Inferno,* I think. Then there was another section which was an imitation *Rape of the Lock.* Pound said, "It's no use trying to do something that somebody else has done as well as it can be done. Do something different."

INTERVIEWER: Did the excisions change the intellectual structure of the poem?

ELIOT: No. I think it was just as structureless, only in a more futile way, in the longer version.

INTERVIEWER: I have a question about the poem which is related to its composition. In *Thoughts after Lambeth* you denied the allegation of critics who said that you expressed "the disillusionment of a generation" in *The Waste Land,* or you denied that it was your intention. Now F. R. Leavis, I believe, has said that the poem exhibits no progression; yet on the other hand, more recent critics, writing after your later poetry, found *The Waste Land* Christian. I wonder if this was part of your intention.

ELIOT: No, it wasn't part of my conscious intention. I think that in *Thoughts after Lambeth,* I was speaking of intentions more in a negative than in a positive sense, to say what was not my intention. I wonder what an "intention" means! One wants to get something off one's chest. One doesn't know quite what it is that one wants to get off the chest until one's got it off. But I couldn't apply the word "intention" positively to any of my poems. Or to any poem.

INTERVIEWER: I have another question about you and Pound and your earlier career. I have read somewhere that you and Pound decided to write quatrains, in the late teens, because *vers libre* had gone far enough.

Eliot: I think that's something Pound said. And the suggestion of writing quatrains was his. He put me onto *Emaux et Camées.**

Interviewer: I wonder about your ideas about the relation of form to subject. Would you then have chosen the form before you knew quite what you were going to write in it?

Eliot: Yes, in a way. One studied originals. We studied Gautier's poems and then we thought, "Have I anything to say in which this form will be useful?" And we experimented. The form gave the impetus to the content.

Interviewer: Why was *vers libre* the form you chose to use in your early poems?

Eliot: My early *vers libre,* of course, was started under the endeavor to practice the same form as Laforgue. This meant merely rhyming lines of irregular length, with the rhymes coming in irregular places. It wasn't quite so *libre* as much *vers,* especially the sort which Ezra called "Amygism."† Then, of course, there were things in the next phase which were freer, like "Rhapsody on a Windy Night." I don't know whether I had any sort of model or practice in mind when I did that. It just came that way.

Interviewer: Did you feel, possibly, that you were writing against something, more than from any model? Against the poet laureate perhaps?

Eliot: No, no, no. I don't think one was constantly trying to reject things, but just trying to find out what was right for oneself. One really ignored poet laureates as such, the Robert Bridges. I don't think good poetry can be produced in a kind of political attempt to overthrow some existing form. I think it just supersedes. People find a way in which they can say something. "I can't say it that way, what way can I find that will do?" One didn't really *bother* about the existing modes.

Interviewer: I think it was after "Prufrock" and before "Gerontion" that you wrote the poems in French which ap-

* Poems by Théophile Gautier.

† A reference to Amy Lowell, who captured and transformed imagism.

pear in your *Collected Poems.* I wonder how you happened to write them. Have you written any since?

ELIOT: No, and I never shall. That was a very curious thing which I can't altogether explain. At that period I thought I'd dried up completely. I hadn't written anything for some time and was rather desperate. I started writing a few things in French and found I *could,* at that period. I think it was that when I was writing in French I didn't take the poems so seriously, and that, not taking them seriously, I wasn't so worried about not being able to write. I did these things as a sort of *tour de force* to see what I could do. That went on for some months. The best of them have been printed. I must say that Ezra Pound went through them, and Edmond Dulac, a Frenchman we knew in London, helped with them a bit. We left out some, and I suppose they disappeared completely. Then I suddenly began writing in English again and lost all desire to go on with French. I think it was just something that helped me get started again.

INTERVIEWER: Did you think at all about becoming a French symbolist poet like the two Americans of the last century?

ELIOT: Stuart Merrill and Viélé-Griffin. I only did that during the romantic year I spent in Paris after Harvard. I had at that time the idea of giving up English and trying to settle down and scrape along in Paris and gradually write French. But it would have been a foolish idea even if I'd been much more bilingual than I ever was, because, for one thing, I don't think that one can be a bilingual poet. I don't know of any case in which a man wrote great or even fine poems equally well in two languages. I think one language must be the one you express yourself in in poetry, and you've got to give up the other for that purpose. And I think that the English language really has more resources in some respects than the French. I think, in other words, I've probably done better in English than I ever would have in French even if I'd become as proficient in French as the poets you mentioned.

INTERVIEWER: Can I ask you if you have any plans for poems now?

ELIOT: No, I haven't any plans for anything at the moment, except that I think I would like, having just got rid of *The Elder Statesman* (I only passed the final proofs just before we left London), to do a little prose writing of a critical sort. I never think more than one step ahead. Do I want to do another play or do I want to do more poems? I don't know until I find I want to do it.

INTERVIEWER: Do you have any unfinished poems that you look at occasionally?

ELIOT: I haven't much in that way, no. As a rule, with me an unfinished thing is a thing that might as well be rubbed out. It's better, if there's something good in it that I might make use of elsewhere, to leave it at the back of my mind than on paper in a drawer. If I leave it in a drawer it remains the same thing but if it's in the memory it becomes transformed into something else. As I have said before, *Burnt Norton* began with bits that had to be cut out of *Murder in the Cathedral.* I learned in *Murder in the Cathedral* that it's no use putting in nice lines that you think are good poetry if they don't get the action on at all. That was when Martin Browne was useful. He would say, "There are very nice lines here, but they've nothing to do with what's going on on stage."

INTERVIEWER: Are any of your minor poems actually sections cut out of longer works? There are two that sound like "The Hollow Men."

Eliot: Oh, those were the preliminary sketches. Those things were earlier. Others I published in periodicals but not in my collected poems. You don't want to say the same thing twice in one book.

INTERVIEWER: You seem often to have written poems in sections. Did they begin as separate poems? I am thinking of "Ash Wednesday," in particular.

ELIOT: Yes, like "The Hollow Men," it originated out of separate poems. As I recall, one or two early drafts of parts of

"Ash Wednesday" appeared in *Commerce* and elsewhere. Then gradually I came to see it as a sequence. That's one way in which my mind does seem to have worked throughout the years poetically—doing things separately and then seeing the possibility of fusing them together, altering them, and making a kind of whole of them.

INTERVIEWER: Do you write anything now in the vein of *Old Possum's Book of Practical Cats* or *King Bolo?*

ELIOT: Those things do come from time to time! I keep a few notes of such verse, and there are one or two incomplete cats that probably will never be written. There's one about a glamour cat. It turned out too sad. This would never do. I can't make my children weep over a cat who's gone wrong. She had a very questionable career, did this cat. It wouldn't do for the audience of my previous volume of cats. I've never done any dogs. Of course dogs don't seem to lend themselves to verse quite so well, collectively, as cats. I may eventually do an enlarged edition of my cats. That's more likely than another volume. I did add one poem, which was originally done as an advertisement for Faber and Faber. It seemed to be fairly successful. Oh, yes, one wants to keep one's hand in, you know, in every type of poem, serious and frivolous and proper and improper. One doesn't want to lose one's skill.

INTERVIEWER: There's a good deal of interest now in the process of writing. I wonder if you could talk more about your actual habits in writing verse. I've heard you composed on the typewriter.

ELIOT: Partly on the typewriter. A great deal of my new play, *The Elder Statesman,* was produced in pencil and paper, very roughly. Then I typed it myself first before my wife got to work on it. In typing myself I make alterations, very considerable ones. But whether I write or type, composition of any length, a play for example, means for me regular hours, say ten to one. I found that three hours a day is about all I can do of actual composing. I could do polishing perhaps later. I sometimes found at first that I wanted to go on longer, but when I looked at the stuff the next day, what I'd done after the three hours were up was never satisfactory. It's much better to stop and think about something else quite different.

INTERVIEWER: Did you ever write any of your nondramatic poems on schedule? Perhaps the *Four Quartets?*

ELIOT: Only "occasional" verse. The *Quartets* were not on schedule. Of course the first one was written in '35, but the three which were written during the war were more in fits and starts. In 1939 if there hadn't been a war I would probably have tried to write another play. And I think it's a very good thing I didn't have the opportunity. From my personal point of view, the one good thing the war did was to prevent me from writing another play too soon. I saw some of the things that were wrong with *Family Reunion,* but I think it was much better that any possible play was blocked for five years or so to get up a head of steam. The form of the *Quartets* fitted in very nicely to the conditions under which I was writing, or could write at all. I could write them in sections and I didn't have to have quite the same continuity: it didn't matter if a day or two elapsed when I did not write, as they frequently did, while I did war jobs.

INTERVIEWER: We have been mentioning your plays without talking about them. In *Poetry and Drama* you talked about your first plays. I wonder if you could tell us something about your intentions in *The Elder Statesman.*

ELIOT: I said something, I think, in *Poetry and Drama* about my ideal aims, which I never expect fully to realize. I started, really, from *The Family Reunion,* because *Murder in the Cathedral* is a period piece and something out of the ordinary. It is written in rather a special language, as you do when you're dealing with another period. It didn't solve any of the problems I was interested in. Later I thought that in *The Family Reunion* I was giving so much attention to the versification that I neglected the structure of the play. I think *The Family Reunion* is still the best of my plays in the way of poetry, although it's not very well constructed.

In *The Cocktail Party* and again in *The Confidential Clerk,* I went further in the way of structure. *The Cocktail Party* wasn't altogether satisfactory in that respect. It sometimes happens, disconcertingly, at any rate with a practitioner like myself, that it isn't always the things constructed most according to plan that are the most successful. People criticized the third act of *The Cocktail Party* as being rather an epilogue, so in *The Confidential Clerk* I wanted things to turn up in the third act which were fresh events. Of course, *The Confidential Clerk* was so well constructed in some ways that people thought it was just meant to be farce.

I wanted to get to learn the technique of the theater so well that I could then forget about it. I always feel it's not wise to violate rules until you know how to observe them.

I hope that *The Elder Statesman* goes further in getting more poetry in, at any rate, than *The Confidential Clerk* did. I don't feel that I've got to the point I aim at and I don't think I ever will, but I would like to feel I was getting a little nearer to it each time.

INTERVIEWER: Do you have a Greek model behind *The Elder Statesman?*

ELIOT: The play in the background is the *Oedipus at Colonus.* But I wouldn't like to refer to my Greek originals as models. I have always regarded them more as points of departure. That was one of the weaknesses of *The Family Reunion;* it was rather too close to the *Eumenides.* I tried to follow my original too literally and in that way led to confusion by mixing pre-Christian and post-Christian attitudes about matters of conscience and sin and guilt.

So in the subsequent three I have tried to take the Greek myth as a sort of springboard, you see. After all, what one gets essential and permanent, I think, in the old plays, is a situation. You can take the situation, rethink it in modern terms, develop your own characters from it, and let another plot develop out of that. Actually you get further and further away from the original. *The Cocktail Party* had to do with Alcestis simply because the question arose in my mind, what would the life of Admetus and Alcestis be, after she'd come back from the dead; I mean if there'd been a break like that, it couldn't go on just as before. Those two people were the center of the thing when I started and the other characters only developed out of it. The character of Celia, who came to be really the most important character in the play, was originally an appendage to a domestic situation.

INTERVIEWER: Do you still hold to the theory of levels in poetic drama (plot, character, diction, rhythm, meaning) which you put forward in 1932?

ELIOT: I am no longer very much interested in my own theories about poetic drama, especially those put forward before 1934. I have thought less about theories since I have given more time to writing for the theater.

INTERVIEWER: How does the writing of a play differ from the writing of poems?

ELIOT: I feel that they take quite different approaches. There is all the difference in the world between writing a play for an audience and writing a poem, in which you're writing primarily for yourself—although obviously you wouldn't be satisfied if the poem didn't mean something to other people afterward. With a poem you can say, "I got my feeling into words for myself. I now have the equivalent in words for that much of what I have felt." Also in a poem you're writing for your own voice, which is very important. You're thinking in terms of your own voice, whereas in a play from the beginning you have to realize that you're preparing something which is going into the hands of other people, unknown at the time you're writing it. Of course I won't say there aren't moments in a play when the two approaches may not converge, when I think ideally they *should.* Very often in Shakespeare they do, when he is writing a poem and thinking in terms of the theater and the actors and the audience all at once. And the two things are one. That's wonderful when you can get that. With me it only happens at odd moments.

INTERVIEWER: Have you tried at all to control the speaking of your verse by the actors? To make it seem more like verse?

ELIOT: I leave that primarily to the producer. The important thing is to have a producer who has the feeling of verse and who can guide them in just how emphatic to make the verse, just how far to depart from prose or how far to approach it. I only guide the actors if they ask me questions directly. Otherwise I think that they should get their advice through the producer. The important thing is to arrive at an agreement with him first, and then leave it to him.

INTERVIEWER: Do you feel that there's been a general tendency in your work, even in your poems, to move from a narrower to a larger audience?

ELIOT: I think that there are two elements in this. One is that I think that writing plays (that is *Murder in the Cathedral* and *The Family Reunion*) made a difference to the writing of the *Four Quartets.* I think that it led to a greater simplification of language and to speaking in a way which is more like conversing with your reader. I see the later *Quartets* as being much simpler and easier to understand than *The Waste Land* and "Ash Wednesday." Sometimes the thing I'm trying to say, the subject matter, may be difficult, but it seems to me that I'm saying it in a simpler way.

The other element that enters into it, I think, is just experience and maturity. I think that in the early poems it was a question of not being able to—of having more to say than one knew how to say, and having something one wanted to put into words and rhythm which one didn't have the command of words and rhythm to put in a way immediately apprehensible.

That type of obscurity comes when the poet is still at the stage of learning how to use language. You have to say the thing the difficult way. The only alternative is not saying it at all, at that stage. By the time of the *Four Quartets,* I couldn't have written in the style of *The Waste Land.* In *The Waste Land,*

I wasn't even bothering whether I understood what I was saying. These things, however, become easier to people with time. You get used to having *The Waste Land,* or *Ulysses,* about.

INTERVIEWER: Do you feel that the *Four Quartets* are your best work?

ELIOT: Yes, and I'd like to feel that they get better as they go on. The second is better than the first, the third is better than the second, and the fourth is the best of all. At any rate, that's the way I flatter myself.

INTERVIEWER: This is a very general question, but I wonder if you could give advice to a young poet about what disciplines or attitudes he might cultivate to improve his art.

ELIOT: I think it's awfully dangerous to give general advice. I think the best one can do for a young poet is to criticize in detail a particular poem of his. Argue it with him if necessary; give him your opinion, and if there are any generalizations to be made, let him do them himself. I've found that different people have different ways of working and things come to them in different ways. You're never sure when you're uttering a statement that's generally valid for all poets or when it's something that only applies to yourself. I think nothing is worse than to try to form people in your own image.

INTERVIEWER: Do you think there's any possible generalization to be made about the fact that all the better poets now, younger than you, seem to be teachers?

ELIOT: I don't know. I think the only generalization that can be made of any value will be one which will be made a generation later. All you can say at this point is that at different times there are different possibilities of making a living, or different limitations on making a living. Obviously a poet has got to find a way of making a living apart from his poetry. After all, artists do a great deal of teaching, and musicians too.

INTERVIEWER: Do you think that the optimal career for a poet would involve no work at all but writing and reading?

ELIOT: No, I think that would be—but there again one

can only talk about oneself. It is very dangerous to give an optimal career for everybody, but I feel quite sure that if I'd started by having independent means, if I hadn't had to bother about earning a living and could have given all my time to poetry, it would have had a deadening influence on me.

INTERVIEWER: Why?

ELIOT: I think that for me it's been very useful to exercise other activities, such as working in a bank, or publishing even. And I think also that the difficulty of not having as much time as I would like has given me a greater pressure of concentration. I mean it has prevented me from writing too much. The danger, as a rule, of having nothing else to do is that one might write too much rather than concentrating and perfecting smaller amounts. That would be *my* danger.

INTERVIEWER: Do you consciously attempt, now, to keep up with the poetry that is being written by young men in England and America?

ELIOT: I don't now, not with any conscientiousness. I did at one time when I was reading little reviews and looking out for new talent as a publisher. But as one gets older, one is not quite confident in one's own ability to distinguish new genius among younger men. You're always afraid that you are going as you have seen your elders go. At Faber and Faber now I have a younger colleague who reads poetry manuscripts. But even before that, when I came across new stuff that I thought had real merit, I would show it to younger friends whose critical judgment I trusted and get their opinion. But of course there is always the danger that there is merit when you don't see it. So I'd rather have younger people to look at things first. If they like it, they will show it to me, and see whether I like it too. When you get something that knocks over younger people of taste and judgment and older people as well, then that's likely to be something important. Sometimes there's a lot of resistance. I shouldn't like to feel that I was resisting, as my work was resisted when it was new, by people who thought that it was imposture of some kind or other.

INTERVIEWER: Do you feel that younger poets in general have repudiated the experimentalism of the early poetry of this century? Few poets now seem to be resisted the way you were resisted, but some older critics like Herbert Read believe that poetry after you has been a regression to out-dated modes. When you talked about Milton the second time, you spoke of the function of poetry as a retarder of change, as well as a maker of change, in language.

ELIOT: Yes, I don't think you want a revolution every ten years.

INTERVIEWER: But is it possible to think that there has been a counterrevolution rather than an exploration of new possibilities?

ELIOT: No, I don't see anything that looks to me like a counterrevolution. After a period of getting away from the traditional forms, comes a period of curiosity in making new experiments with traditional forms. This can produce very good work if what has happened in between has made a difference: when it's not merely going back, but taking up an old form, which has been out of use for a time, and making something new with it. That is not counterrevolution. Nor does mere regression deserve the name. There is a tendency in some quarters to revert to Georgian scenery and sentiments: and among the public there are always people who prefer mediocrity, and when they get it, say, "What a relief! Here's some real poetry again." And there are also people who like poetry to be modern but for whom the really creative stuff is too strong—they need something diluted.

What seems to me the best of what I've seen in young poets is not reaction at all. I'm not going to mention any names, for I don't like to make public judgments about younger poets. The best stuff is a further development of a less revolutionary character than what appeared in earlier years of the century.

INTERVIEWER: I have some unrelated questions that I'd

like to end with. In 1945 you wrote, "A poet must take as his material his own language as it is actually spoken around him." And later you wrote, "The music of poetry, then, will be a music latent in the common speech of his time." After the second remark, you disparaged "standardized BBC English." Now isn't one of the changes of the last fifty years, and perhaps even more of the last five years, the growing dominance of commercial speech through the means of communication? What you referred to as "BBC English" has become immensely more powerful through the ITA and BBC television, not to speak of CBS, NBS, and ABC. Does this development make the problem of the poet and his relationship to common speech more difficult?

ELIOT: You've raised a very good point there. I think you're right, it does make it more difficult.

INTERVIEWER: I wanted *you* to make the point.

ELIOT: Yes, but you wanted the point to be *made.* So I'll take the responsibility of making it: I do think that where you have these modern means of communication and means of imposing the speech and idioms of a small number on the mass of people at large, it does complicate the problem very much. I don't know to what extent that goes for film speech, but obviously radio speech has done much more.

INTERVIEWER: I wonder if there's a possibility that what you mean by common speech will disappear.

ELIOT: That is a very gloomy prospect. But very likely indeed.

INTERVIEWER: Are there other problems for a writer in our time which are unique? Does the prospect of human annihilation have any particular effect on the poet?

ELIOT: I don't see why the prospect of human annihilation should affect the poet differently from men of other vocations. It will affect him as a human being, no doubt in proportion to his sensitiveness.

INTERVIEWER: Another unrelated question: I can see why

a man's criticism is better for his being a practicing poet, better although subject to his own prejudices. But do you feel that writing criticism has helped you as a poet?

Eliot: In an indirect way it has helped me somehow as a poet—to put down in writing my critical valuation of the poets who have influenced me and whom I admire. It is merely making an influence more conscious and more articulate. It's been a rather natural impulse. I think probably my best critical essays are essays on the poets who had influenced me, so to speak, long before I thought of writing essays about them. They're of more value, probably, than any of my more generalized remarks.

Interviewer: G. S. Fraser wonders, in an essay about the two of you, whether you ever met Yeats. From remarks in your talk about him, it would seem that you did. Could you tell us the circumstances?

Eliot: Of course I had met Yeats many times. Yeats was always very gracious when one met him and had the art of treating younger writers as if they were his equals and contemporaries. I can't remember any one particular occasion.

Interviewer: I have heard that you consider that your poetry belongs in the tradition of American literature. Could you tell us why?

Eliot: I'd say that my poetry has obviously more in common with my distinguished contemporaries in America than with anything written in my generation in England. That I'm sure of.

Interviewer: Do you think there's a connection with the American past?

Eliot: Yes, but I couldn't put it any more definitely than that, you see. It wouldn't be what it is, and I imagine it wouldn't be so good; putting it as modestly as I can, it wouldn't be what it is if I'd been born in England, and it wouldn't be what it is if I'd stayed in America. It's a combination of things. But in its sources, in its emotional springs, it comes from America.

INTERVIEWER: One last thing. Seventeen years ago you said, "No honest poet can ever feel quite sure of the permanent value of what he has written. He may have wasted his time and messed up his life for nothing." Do you feel the same now, at seventy?

ELIOT: There may be honest poets who do feel sure. I don't.

Ezra Pound

INTERVIEWER: You are nearly through the *Cantos* now, and this sets me to wondering about their beginning. In 1916 you wrote a letter in which you talked about trying to write a version of Andreas Divus in Seafarer rhythms. This sounds like a reference to *Canto 1.* Did you begin the *Cantos* in 1916?

POUND: I began the *Cantos* about 1904, I suppose. I had various schemes, starting in 1904 or 1905. The problem was to get a form—something elastic enough to take the necessary material. It had to be a form that wouldn't exclude something merely because it didn't fit. In the first sketches, a draft of the present first *Canto* was the third.

Obviously you haven't got a nice little road map such as the middle ages possessed of Heaven. Only a musical form would take the material, and the Confucian universe as I see it is a universe of interacting strains and tensions.

INTERVIEWER: Had your interest in Confucius begun in 1904?

POUND: No, the first thing was this: you had six centuries that hadn't been packaged. It was a question of dealing with material that wasn't in the *Divina Commedia.* Hugo did a *Légende des Siècles* that wasn't an evaluative affair but just bits of history strung together. The problem was to build up a circle of reference—taking the modern mind to be the mediaeval mind with wash after wash of classical culture poured over it since the Renaissance. That was the psyche, if you like. One had to deal with one's own subject.

INTERVIEWER: It must be thirty or thirty-five years since you have written any poetry outside the *Cantos,* except for the Alfred Venison poems. Why is this?

POUND: I got to the point where, apart from an occasional lighter impulse, what I had to say fitted the general scheme. There has been a good deal of work thrown away because one is attracted to an historic character and then finds that he doesn't function within my form, doesn't embody a value needed. I have tried to make the *Cantos* historic (Vid. G. Giovannini, *re* relation history to tragedy. Two articles ten years apart in some philological periodical, not source material but relevant) but not fiction. The material one wants to fit in doesn't always work. If the stone isn't hard enough to maintain the form, it has to go out.

INTERVIEWER: When you write a *Canto* now, how do you plan it? Do you follow a special course of reading for each one?

POUND: One isn't necessarily reading. One is working on the life vouchsafed, I should think. I don't know about method. The *what* is so much more important than how.

INTERVIEWER: Yet when you were a young man, your interest in poetry concentrated on form. Your professionalism, and your devotion to technique, became proverbial. In the last thirty years, you have traded your interest in form for an interest in content. Was the change on principle?

POUND: I think I've covered that. Technique is the test of sincerity. If a thing isn't worth getting the technique to say, it is of inferior value. All that must be regarded as exercise. Richter in his *Treatise on Harmony,* you see, says, "These are the principles of harmony and counterpoint; they have nothing whatever to do with composition, which is quite a separate activity." The statement, which somebody made, that you couldn't write Provençal canzoni forms in English, is false. The question of whether it was advisable or not was another matter. When there wasn't the criterion of natural language without inversion, those forms were natural, and they realized them with music. In English the music is of a limited nature. You've got Chaucer's French perfection, you've got Shakespeare's Italian perfection, you've got Campion and Lawes. I don't think I got around to this kind of form until I got to the choruses in the *Trachiniae.* I don't know that I got to anything at all, really, but I thought it was an extension of the gamut. It may be a delusion. One was always interested in the implication of change of pitch in the union of *motz et son,* of the word and melody.

INTERVIEWER: Does writing the *Cantos,* now, exhaust all of your technical interest, or does the writing of translations, like the *Trachiniae* you just mentioned, satisfy you by giving you more fingerwork?

POUND: One sees a job to be done and goes at it. The *Trachiniae* came from reading the Fenollosa Noh plays for the new edition, and from wanting to see what would happen to a Greek play, given that same medium and the hope of its being performed by the Minorou company. The sight of Cathay in Greek, looking like poetry, stimulated crosscurrents.

INTERVIEWER: Do you think that free verse is particularly an American form? I imagine that William Carlos Williams probably does, and thinks of the iambic as English.

POUND: I like Eliot's sentence: "No verse is *libre* for the man who wants to do a good job." I think the best free verse comes from an attempt to get back to quantitative meter.

I suppose it may be *un-English* without being specifically *American.* I remember Cocteau playing drums in a jazz band as if it were a very difficult mathematical problem.

I'll tell you a thing that I think *is* an American form, and that is the Jamesian parenthesis. You realize that the person you are talking to hasn't got the different steps, and you go back over them. In fact the Jamesian parenthesis has immensely increased now. That I think is something that is definitely American. The struggle that one has when one meets another man who has had a lot of experience to find the point where the two experiences touch, so that he really knows what you are talking about.

INTERVIEWER: Your work includes a great range of experience, as well as of form. What do you think is the greatest quality a poet can have? Is it formal, or is it a quality of thinking?

POUND: I don't know that you can put the needed qualities in hierarchic order, but he must have a continuous curiosity, which of course does not make him a writer, but if he hasn't got that he will wither. And the question of doing anything about it depends on a persistent energy. A man like Agassiz is never bored, never tired. The transit from the reception of stimuli to the recording, to the correlation, that is what takes the whole energy of a lifetime.

INTERVIEWER: Do you think that the modern world has changed the ways in which poetry can be written?

POUND: There is a lot of competition that never was there before. Take the serious side of Disney, the Confucian side of Disney. It's in having taken an ethos, as he does in *Perri,* that squirrel film, where you have the values of courage and tenderness asserted in a way that everybody can understand. You have got an absolute genius there. You have got a greater correlation of nature than you have had since the time of Alexander the Great. Alexander gave orders to the fishermen that if they found out anything about fish that was interesting, a specific thing, they were to tell Aristotle. And with that correlation you got ichthyology to the scientific point where it stayed for two thousand years. And now one has got with the camera an *enormous* correlation of particulars. That capacity for making contact is a tremendous challenge to literature. It throws up the question of what needs to be done and what is superfluous.

INTERVIEWER: Maybe it's an opportunity, too. When you

were a young man in particular, and even through the *Cantos,* you changed your poetic style again and again. You have never been content to stick anywhere. Were you consciously looking to extend your style? Does the artist *need* to keep moving?

POUND: I think the artist *has* to keep moving. You are trying to render life in a way that won't bore people and you are trying to put down what you see.

INTERVIEWER: I wonder what you think of contemporary movements. I haven't seen remarks of yours about poets more recent than Cummings, except for Bunting and Zukovsky. Other things have occupied you, I suppose.

POUND: One can't read everything. I was trying to find out a number of historic facts, and you can't see out of the back of your head. I do not think there is any record of a man being able to criticize the people that come after him. It is a sheer question of the amount of reading one man can do.

I don't know whether it is his own or whether it is a gem that he collected, but at any rate one of the things Frost said in London in 19—whenever it was—1912, was this: "Summary of prayer: 'Oh God, pay attention to *me.*' " And that is the approach of younger writers—not to divinity exactly!—and in general one has to limit one's reading to younger poets who are recommended by at least one other younger poet, as a sponsor. Of course a routine of that kind could lead to conspiracy, but at any rate . . .

As far as criticizing younger people, one has not the time to make a *comparative* estimate. People one is learning from, one does measure one against the other. I see a stirring now, but . . . For *general* conditions there is undoubtedly a *liveliness.* And Cal [Robert] Lowell is very good.

INTERVIEWER: You have given advice to the young all your life. Do you have anything special to say to them now?

POUND: To improve their curiosity and not to fake. But that is not enough. The mere registering of bellyache and the mere dumping of the ashcan is not enough. In fact the University of Pennsylvania student *Punchbowl* used to have as its motto, "Any damn fool can be spontaneous."

INTERVIEWER: You once wrote that you had four useful hints from living literary predecessors, who were Thomas Hardy, William Butler Yeats, Ford Madox Ford, and Robert Bridges. What were these things?

POUND: Bridges' was the simplest. Bridges' was a warning against homophones. Hardy's was the degree to which he would concentrate on the subject matter, not on the manner. Ford's in general was the *freshness* of language. And Yeats you say was the fourth? Well, Yeats by 1908 had written simple lyrics in which there were no departures from the natural order of words.

INTERVIEWER: You were secretary to Yeats in 1913 and 1914. What sort of thing did you do for him?

POUND: Mostly reading aloud. Doughty's *Dawn in Britain,* and so on. And wrangling, you see. The Irish like contradiction. He tried to learn fencing at forty-five, which was amusing. He would thrash around with the foils like a whale. He sometimes gave the impression of being even a worse idiot than I am.

INTERVIEWER: There is an academic controversy about your influence on Yeats. Did you work over his poetry with him? Did you cut any of his poems in the way you cut *The Waste Land?*

POUND: I don't think I can remember anything like that. I am sure I objected to particular expressions. Once out at Rapallo I tried for God's sake to prevent him from printing a thing. I told him it was rubbish. All he did was print it with a preface saying that I *said* it was rubbish.

I remember when Tagore had taken to doodling on the edge of his proofs, and they told him it was art. There was a show of it in Paris. "Is this art?" Nobody was very keen on these doodlings, but of course so many people lied to him.

As far as the change in Yeats goes, I think that Ford Madox Ford might have some credit. Yeats never would have taken advice from Ford, but I think that Fordie helped him, via me, in trying to get towards a natural way of writing.

INTERVIEWER: Did anyone ever help you with your work as extensively as you have helped others? I mean by criticism or cutting.

POUND: Apart from Fordie, rolling on the floor undecorously and holding his head in his hands, and groaning on one occasion, I don't think anybody helped me through my manuscripts. Ford's stuff appeared too loose then, but he led the fight against tertiary archaisms.

INTERVIEWER: You have been closely associated with visual artists—Gaudier-Brzeska and Wyndham Lewis in the vorticist movement, and later Picabia, Picasso, and Brancusi. Has this had anything to do with you as a writer?

POUND: I don't believe so. One looked at paintings in galleries and one might have found out something. "The Game of Chess" poems shows the effect of modern abstract art, but vorticism from my angle was a renewal of the sense of construction. Color went dead and Manet and the impressionists revived it. Then what I would call the sense of form was blurred, and vorticism, as distinct from cubism, was an attempt to revive the sense of form—the form you had in Piero della Francesca's *De Prospettive Pingendi,* his treatise on the proportions and composition. I got started on the idea of comparative forms before I left America. A fellow named Poole did a book on composition. I did have *some* things in my head when I got to London, and I *had* heard of Catullus before I heard about modern French poetry. There's a bit of biography that might be rectified.

INTERVIEWER: I have wondered about your literary activities in America before you came to Europe. When did you first come over, by the way?

POUND: In 1898. At the age of twelve. With my great aunt.

INTERVIEWER: Were you reading French poetry then?

POUND: No, I suppose I was reading Grey's "Elegy in a

Country Churchyard" or something. No, I wasn't reading French poetry. I was starting Latin next year.

INTERVIEWER: You entered college at fifteen, I believe?

POUND: I did it to get out of drill at Military Academy.

INTERVIEWER: How did you get started being a poet?

POUND: My grandfather on one side used to correspond with the local bank president in verse. My grandmother on the other side and her brothers used verse back and forth in their letters. It was taken for granted that anyone would write it.

INTERVIEWER: Did you learn anything in your university studies which helped you as a poet? I think you were a student for seven or eight years.

POUND: Only six. Well, six years and four months. I was writing all the time, especially as a graduate student. I started in freshman year studying Layamon's *Brut* and Latin. I got into college on my Latin; it was the only reason they *did* take me in. I did have the idea, at fifteen, of making a general survey. Of course whether I was or wasn't a poet was a matter for the gods to decide, but at least it was up to me to find out what had been done.

INTERVIEWER: You taught for four months only, as I remember. But you know that now the poets in America are mostly teachers. Do you have any ideas on the connection of teaching in the university with writing poetry?

POUND: It is the economic factor. A man's got to get in his rent somehow.

INTERVIEWER: How did you manage all the years in Europe?

POUND: Oh, God. A miracle of God. My income gained from October 1914 to October 1915 was £42.10.0. That figure is clearly engraved on my memory. . . .

I was never too good a hand at writing for the magazines. I once did a satirical article for *Vogue,* I think it was. On a painter whom I did not admire. They thought I had got just the right tone and then Verhaeren died and they asked me to do a note on Verhaeren. And I went down and said, "You want a nice bright snappy obituary notice of the gloomiest man in Europe."

"What, gloomy cuss, was he?"

"Yes," I said. "He wrote about peasants."

"Peasants or pheasants?"

"Peasants."

"Oh, I don't think we ought to touch it."

That is the way I crippled my earning capacity by not knowing enough to keep quiet.

INTERVIEWER: I read somewhere—I think you wrote it—that you once tried to write a novel. Did that get anywhere?

POUND: It got, fortunately, into the fireplace at Langham Place. I think there were two attempts, before I had any idea whatever of what a novel ought to be.

INTERVIEWER: Did they have anything to do with "Hugh Selwyn Mauberley"?

POUND: These were long before "Mauberley." "Mauberley" was later, but it *was* the definite attempt to get the novel cut down to the size of verse. It really is "Contacts and Life." Wadsworth seemed to think "Propertius" difficult because it was about Rome, so one applied the same thing to the contemporary outside.

INTERVIEWER: You said it was Ford who helped you toward a natural language, didn't you? Let's get back to London again.

POUND: One was hunting for a simple and natural language, and Ford was ten years older, and accelerated the process toward it. It was a continual discussion of that sort of thing. Ford knew the best of the people who were there before him, you see, and he had nobody to play with until Wyndham and I and my generation came along. He was definitely in opposition to the dialect, let us say, of Lionel Johnson and Oxford.

INTERVIEWER: You were for two or three decades at least in contact with all of the leading writers in English of the day and a lot of the painters, sculptors, and musicians. Of all these people, who were the most stimulating to you as an artist?

POUND: I saw most of Ford and Gaudier, I suppose. I should think that the people that I have written about were the most important to me. There isn't much revision to make there.

I may have limited my work, and limited the interest in it, by concentrating on the particular intelligence of particular people, instead of looking at the complete character and personality of my friends. Wyndham Lewis always claimed that I never *saw* people because I never noticed how wicked they were, what S.O.B.'s they were. I wasn't the least interested in the vices of my friends, but in their intelligence.

INTERVIEWER: Was James a kind of a standard for you in London?

POUND: When he died one felt there was no one to ask about anything. Up to then one felt someone knew. After I was sixty-five I had great difficulty in realizing that I was older than James had been when I met him.

INTERVIEWER: Did you know Remy de Gourmont personally? You've mentioned him frequently.

POUND: Only by letter. There was one letter, which Jean de Gourmont also considered important, where he said, *"Franchement d'écrire ce qu'on pense, seul plaisir d'un écrivain."*

INTERVIEWER: It is amazing that you could come to Europe and quickly associate yourself with the best living writers. Had you been aware of any of the poets writing in America before you left? Was Robinson anything to you?

POUND: Aiken tried to sell me Robinson and I didn't fall. This was in London too. I then dragged it out of him that there was a guy at Harvard doing funny stuff. Mr. Eliot turned up a year or so later.

No, I should say that about 1900, you had Carman and Hovey, Carwine and Vance Cheney. The impression then was that the American stuff wasn't *quite* as good as the English at any point. And you had Mosher's pirated editions of the English stuff. No, I went to London because I thought Yeats knew more about poetry than anybody else. I made my life in London by going to see Ford in the afternoons and Yeats in the evenings. By mentioning one to the other one could always start a discussion. That was the exercise. I went to study with Yeats and found that Ford disagreed with him. So then I kept on disagreeing with *them* for twenty years.

INTERVIEWER: In 1942, you wrote that you and Eliot disagreed by calling each other protestants. I wonder when you and Eliot diverged.

POUND: Oh, Eliot and I started diverging from the beginning. The fun of an intellectual friendship is that you diverge on something or other and agree on a few points. Eliot, having had the Christian patience of tolerance all his life and so forth, and working very hard, must have found me very trying. We started disagreeing about a number of things from the time we met. We also agreed on a few things and I suppose both of us must have been right about something or other.

INTERVIEWER: Well, was there a point at which poetically and intellectually you felt further apart than you had been?

POUND: There's the whole problem of the relation of Christianity to Confucianism, and there's the whole problem of the different brands of Christianity. There is the struggle for orthodoxy—Eliot for the Church, me gunning round for particular theologians. In one sense Eliot's curiosity would appear to have been focused on a smaller number of problems. Even that is too much to say. The actual outlook of the experimental generation was all a question of the private ethos.

INTERVIEWER: Do you think that as poets you felt a divergence on technical grounds, unrelated to your subject matter?

POUND: I should think the divergence was first a difference in subject matter. He has undoubtedly got a natural language. In the language in the plays, he seems to me to have made a very great contribution. And in being able to make contact with an extant milieu, and an extant state of comprehension.

INTERVIEWER: That reminds me of the two operas—*Villon* and *Cavalcanti*—which you wrote. How did you come to compose music?

POUND: One wanted the word *and* the tune. One wanted great poetry *sung,* and the technique of the English opera libretto was not satisfactory. One wanted, with the quality of the texts of Villon and of Cavalcanti, to get something more extended than the single lyric. That's all.

INTERVIEWER: I suppose your interest in words to be sung was especially stimulated by your study of Provence. Do you feel that the discovery of Provençal poetry was your greatest breakthrough? Or perhaps the Fenollosa manuscripts?

POUND: The Provençal began with a very early interest, so that it wasn't really a discovery. And the Fenollosa was a windfall and one struggled against one's ignorance. One had the inside knowledge of Fenollosa's notes and the ignorance of a five-year-old child.

INTERVIEWER: How did Mrs. Fenollosa happen to hit upon you?

POUND: Well, I met her at Sarojini Naidu's and she said that Fenollosa had been in opposition to all the profs and academes, and she had seen some of my stuff and said I was the only person who could finish up these notes as Ernest would have wanted them done. Fenollosa saw what needed to be done but he didn't have time to finish it.

INTERVIEWER: Let me change the subject now, and ask you some questions which are more biographical than literary. I have read that you were born in Hailey, Idaho, in 1885. I suppose it must have been pretty rough out there then?

POUND: I left at the age of eighteen months and I don't remember the roughness.

INTERVIEWER: You did not grow up in Hailey?

POUND: I did not grow up in Hailey.

INTERVIEWER: What was your family doing there when you were born?

POUND: Dad opened the Government Land Office out there. I grew up near Philadelphia. The suburbs of Philadelphia.

INTERVIEWER: The wild Indian from the West then was not . . . ?

POUND: The wild Indian from the West is apocryphal, and the assistant assayer of the mint was not one of the most noted bandits of the frontier.

INTERVIEWER: I believe it's *true* that your grandfather built a railroad. What was the story of that?

POUND: Well, he got the railroad into Chippewa Falls, and they ganged up on him and would not let him buy any rails. That's in the *Cantos.* He went up to the north of New York State and found some rails on an abandoned road up there, bought them and had them shipped out, and then used his credit with the lumberjacks to get the road going to Chippewa Falls. What one learns in the home one learns in a way one doesn't learn in school.

INTERVIEWER: Does your particular interest in coinage start from your father's work at the mint?

POUND: You can go on for a long time on that. The government offices were more informal then, though I don't know that any other kids got in and visited. Now the visitors are taken through glass tunnels and see things from a distance, but you could then be taken around in the smelting room and see the gold piled up in the safe. You were offered a large bag of gold and told you could have it if you could take it away with you. You couldn't lift it.

When the Democrats finally came back in, they recounted all the silver dollars, four million dollars in silver. All the bags had rotted in these enormous vaults, and they were heaving it into the counting machines with shovels bigger than coal shovels. This spectacle of coin being shoveled around like it was litter—these fellows naked to the waist shoveling it around in the gas flares—things like that strike your imagination.

Then there's the whole technique of making metallic money. First, the testing of the silver is much more tricky than testing gold. Gold is simple. It is weighed, then refined and weighed again. You can tell the grade of the ore by the relative weights. But the test for silver is a cloudy solution; the accuracy of the eye in measuring the thickness of the cloud is an aesthetic perception, like the critical sense. I like the idea of the *fineness* of the metal, and it moves by analogy to the habit of testing verbal manifestations. At that time, you see, gold bricks, and specimens of iron pyrites mistaken for gold, were brought up to Dad's office. You heard the talk about the last guy who brought a gold brick and it turned out to be fool's gold.

INTERVIEWER: I know you consider monetary reform the key to good government. I wonder by what process you moved from aesthetic problems toward governmental ones. Did the great war, which slaughtered so many of your friends, do the moving?

POUND: The great war came as a surprise, and certainly to see the English—these people who had never done anything—get hold of themselves, fight it, was immensely impressive. But as soon as it was over they went dead, and then one spent the next twenty years trying to prevent the Second War. I can't say exactly where my study of government started. I think the *New Age* office helped me to see the war not as a separate event but as part of a system, one war after another.

INTERVIEWER: One point of connection between literature and politics which you make in your writing interests me particularly. In the *A.B.C. of Reading* you say that good writers are those who keep the language efficient, and that this is their function. You disassociate this function from party. Can a man of the wrong party use language efficiently?

POUND: Yes. That's the whole trouble! A gun is just as good, no matter who shoots it.

INTERVIEWER: Can an instrument which is orderly be used

to create disorder? Suppose good language is used to forward bad government? Doesn't bad government make bad language?

POUND: Yes, but bad language is *bound* to make in addition bad government, whereas good language is *not* bound to make bad government. That again is clear Confucius: if the orders aren't clear they can't be carried out. Lloyd George's laws were such a mess, the lawyers never knew what they meant. And Talleyrand proclaimed that they changed the meaning of words between one conference and another. The means of communication breaks down, and that of course is what we are suffering now. We are enduring the drive to work on the subconscious without appealing to the reason. They repeat a trade name with the music a few times, and then repeat the music without it so that the music will give you the name. I think of the *assault.* We suffer from the use of language to conceal thought and to withhold all vital and direct answers. There is the definite use of propaganda, forensic lànguage, merely to conceal and mislead.

INTERVIEWER: Where do ignorance and innocence end and the chicanery begin?

POUND: There is natural ignorance and there is artificial ignorance. I should say at the present moment the artificial ignorance is about eighty-five per cent.

INTERVIEWER: What kind of action can you hope to take?

POUND: The only chance for victory over the brainwash is the right of every man to have his ideas judged one at a time. You never get clarity as long as you have these package words, as long as a word is used by twenty-five people in twenty-five different ways. That seems to me to be the first fight, if there is going to be any intellect left.

It is doubtful whether the individual soul is going to be allowed to survive at all. Now you get a Buddhist movement with everything *except* Confucius taken into it. An Indian Circe of negation and dissolution.

We are up against so many mysteries. There is the problem of benevolence, the point at which benevolence has ceased to be operative. Eliot says that they spend their time trying to imagine systems so perfect that nobody will have to be good. A lot of questions asked in that essay of Eliot's cannot be dodged, like the question of whether there need be any change from the Dantesquan scale of values or the Chaucerian scale of values. If so, how much? People who have lost reverence have lost a great deal. That was where I split with Tiffany Thayer. All these large words fall into clichés.

There is the mystery of the scattering, the fact that the people who presumably understand each other are geographically scattered. A man who fits in his milieu as Frost does, is to be considered a happy man.

Oh, the luck of a man like Mavrocordato, who is in touch with other scholars, so that there is somewhere where he can verify a point! Now for certain points where I want verification there is a fellow named Dazzi in Venice that I write to and he comes up with an answer, as it might be about the forged Donation of Constantine. But the advantages which were supposed to inhere in the university—where there are other people to *contrôl** opinion or to *contrôl* the data—were very great. It is crippling not to have had them. Of course I have been trying over a ten-year period to get any member of an American faculty to mention any other member of his same faculty, in his own department or outside it, whose intelligence he respects or with whom he will discuss serious matters. In one case the gentleman regretted that someone else had *left* the faculty.

I have been unable to get straight answers out of people on what appeared to me to be vital questions. That may have been due to my violence or obscurity with which I framed the questions. Often, I think, so-called obscurity is not obscurity in the language but in the other person's not being able to make out *why* you are saying a thing. For instance the attack on En-

* Pound indicates that he is using the French *contrôler:* "to verify, check information, a fact."

dymion was complicated because Gifford and company couldn't see why the deuce Keats was doing it.

Another struggle has been the struggle to keep the value of a local and particular character, of a particular culture in this awful maelstrom, this awful avalanche toward uniformity. The whole fight is for the conservation of the individual soul. The enemy is the suppression of history; against us is the bewildering propaganda and brianwash, luxury and violence. Sixty years ago, poetry was the poor man's art: a man off on the edge of the wilderness, or Frémont, going off with a Greek text in his pocket. A man who wanted the best could have it on a lonely farm. Then there was the cinema, and now television.

INTERVIEWER: The political action of yours that everybody remembers is your broadcasts from Italy during the war. When you gave these talks, were you conscious of breaking the American law?

POUND: No, I was completely surprised. You see I had that promise. I was given the freedom of the microphone twice a week. "He will not be asked to say anything contrary to his conscience or contrary to his duty as an American citizen." I thought that covered it.

INTERVIEWER: Doesn't the law of treason talk about "giving aid and comfort to the enemy," and isn't the enemy the country with whom we are at war?

POUND: I thought I was fighting for a constitutional point. I mean to say, I may have been completely nuts, but I certainly *felt* that it wasn't committing treason.

Wodehouse went on the air and the British asked him not to. Nobody asked me not to. There was no announcement until the collapse that the people who had spoken on the radio would be prosecuted.

Having worked for years to prevent war, and seeing the folly of Italy and America being at war—! I certainly wasn't telling the troops to revolt. I thought I was fighting an internal question of constitutional government. And if any man, any individual man, can say he has had a bad deal from me because of race, creed, or color, let him come out and state it with particulars. The *Guide to Kulchur* was dedicated to Basil Bunting and Louis Zukofsky, a Quaker and a Jew.

I don't know whether you think the Russians ought to be in Berlin or not. I don't know whether I was doing any good or not, whether I was doing any harm. Oh, I was probably offside. But the ruling in Boston was that there is no treason without treasonable intention.

What I was right about was the conservation of individual rights. If, when the executive or any other branch exceeds its legitimate powers, no one protests, you will lose all your liberties. My method of opposing tyranny was wrong over a thirty-year period; it had nothing to do with the Second World War in particular. If the individual, or heretic, gets hold of some essential truth, or sees some error in the system being practiced, he commits so many marginal errors himself that he is worn out before he can establish his point.

The world in twenty years has piled up hysteria—anxiety over a third war, bureaucratic tyranny, and hysteria from paper forms. The immense and undeniable loss of freedoms, as they were in 1900, is undeniable. We have seen the acceleration in efficiency of the tyrannizing factors. It's enough to keep a man worried. Wars are made to make debt. I suppose there's a possible out in space satellites and other ways of making debt.

INTERVIEWER: When you were arrested by the Americans, did you then expect to be convicted? To be hanged?

POUND: At first I puzzled over having missed a cog somewhere. I expected to turn myself in and to be asked about what I learned. I did and I wasn't. I know that I checked myself, on several occasions during the broadcasts, on reflecting that it was not up to me to do certain things, or to take service with a foreign country. Oh, it was paranoia to think one could argue against the usurpations, against the folks who got the war started to get America into it. Yet I hate the idea of obedience to something which is wrong.

Then later I was driven into the courtyard at Chiavari. They had been shooting them, and I thought I was finished then and there. Then finally a guy came in and said he was damned if he would hand me over to the Americans unless I wanted to be handed over to them.

INTERVIEWER: In 1942, when the war started for America, I understand you tried to leave Italy and come back to the United States. What were the circumstances of the refusal?

POUND: Those circumstances were by hearsay. I am a bit hazy in my head about a considerable period, and I think that . . . I know that I had a chance to get as far as Lisbon, and be cooped up there for the rest of the war.

INTERVIEWER: Why did you want to get back to the States at that time?

POUND: I wanted to get back during the election, before the election.

INTERVIEWER: The election was in 1940, wasn't it?

POUND: That would be 1940. I don't honestly remember what happened. My parents were too old to travel. They would have had to stay there in Rapallo. Dad retired there on his pension.

INTERVIEWER: During those years in the war in Italy did you write poetry? The *Pisan Cantos* were written when you were interned. What did you write during those years?

POUND: Arguments, arguments and arguments. Oh, I did some of the Confucius translation.

INTERVIEWER: How was it that you began to write poetry again only after you were interned? You didn't write any cantos at all during the war, did you?

POUND: Let's see—the Adams stuff came out just before the war shut off. No. There was *Oro e Lavoro.* I was writing economic stuff in Italian.

INTERVIEWER: Since your internment, you've published

three collections of *Cantos, Thrones* just recently. You must be near the end. Can you say what you are going to do in the remaining *Cantos?*

POUND: It is difficult to write a paradiso when all the superficial indications are that you ought to write an apocalypse. It is obviously much easier to find inhabitants for an inferno or even a purgatorio. I am trying to collect the record of the top flights of the mind. I might have done better to put Agassiz on top instead of Confucius.

INTERVIEWER: Are you more or less stuck?

POUND: Okay, I am stuck. The question is, am I dead, as Messrs. A.B.C. might wish? In case I conk out, this is provisionally what I have to do: I must clarify obscurities; I must make clearer definite ideas or dissociations. I must find a verbal formula to combat the rise of brutality—the principle of order versus the split atom. There was a man in the bug house, by the way, who insisted that the atom had never been split.

An epic is a poem containing history. The modern mind contains heteroclite elements. The past epos has succeeded when all or a great many of the answers were assumed, at least between author and audience, or a great mass of audience. The attempt in an experimental age is therefore rash. Do you know the story: "What are you drawing, Johnny?"

"God."

"But nobody knows what He looks like."

"They will when I get through!"

That confidence is no longer obtainable.

There *are* epic subjects. The struggle for individual rights is an epic subject, consecutive from jury trial in Athens to Anselm versus William Rufus, to the murder of Becket and to Coke and through John Adams.

Then the struggle appears to come up against a block. The nature of sovereignty is epic matter, though it may be a bit obscured by circumstance. Some of this *can* be traced, pointed; obviously it has to be condensed to get into the form. The nature of the individual, the heteroclite contents of contemporary consciousness. It's the fight for light versus subconsciousness; it demands obscurities and penumbras. A lot of contemporary writing avoids inconvenient areas of the subject.

I am writing to resist the view that Europe and civilization are going to Hell. If I am being "crucified for an idea"—that is, the coherent idea around which my muddles accumulated—it is probably the idea that European culture ought to survive, that the best qualities of it ought to survive along with whatever other cultures, in whatever universality. Against the propaganda of terror and the propaganda of luxury, have you a nice simple answer? One has worked on certain materials trying to establish bases and axes of reference. In writing so as to be understood, there is always the problem of rectification without giving up what is correct. There is the struggle not to sign on the dotted line for the opposition.

INTERVIEWER: Do the separate sections of the *Cantos,* now—the last three sections have appeared under separate names—mean that you are attacking particular problems in particular sections?

POUND: No. *Rock Drill* was intended to imply the necessary resistance in getting a certain main thesis across—hammering. I was not following the three divisions of the *Divine Comedy* exactly. One can't follow the Dantesquan cosmos in an age of experiment. But I have made the division between people dominated by emotion, people struggling upwards, and those who have some part of the divine vision. The thrones in Dante's *Paradiso* are for the spirits of the people who have been responsible for good government. The thrones in the *Cantos* are an attempt to move out from egoism and to establish some definition of an order possible or at any rate conceivable on earth. One is held up by the low percentage of reason which seems to operate in human affairs. *Thrones* concerns the states of mind of people responsible for something more than their personal conduct.

INTERVIEWER: Now that you come near the end, have you

made any plans for revising the *Cantos,* after you've finished?

POUND: I don't know. There's need of elaboration, of clarification, but I don't know that a comprehensive revision is in order. There is no doubt that the writing is too obscure as it stands, but I hope that the order of ascension in the Paradiso will be toward a greater limpidity. Of course there ought to be a corrected edition because of errors that have crept in.

INTERVIEWER: Let me change the subject again, if I may. In all those years in St. Elizabeth's, did you get a sense of contemporary America from your visitors?

POUND: The trouble with visitors is that you don't get enough of the opposition. I suffer from the cumulative isolation of not having had enough contact—fifteen years living more with ideas than with persons.

INTERVIEWER Do you have any plans for going back to the States? Do you want to?

POUND: I undoubtedly want to. But whether it is nostalgia for America that isn't there any more or not I don't know. This is a difference between an abstract Adams–Jefferson–Adams–Jackson America, and whatever is really going on. I undoubtedly have moments when I should like very much to live in America. There are these concrete difficulties against the general desire. Richmond is a beautiful city, but you can't live in it unless you drive an automobile. I'd like at least to spend a month or two a year in the U.S.

INTERVIEWER: You said the other day that as you grew older you felt more American all the time. How does this work?

POUND: It works. Exotics were necessary as an attempt at a foundation. One is transplanted and grows, and one is pulled up and taken back to what one has been transplanted from and it is no longer there. The contacts aren't there and I suppose one reverts to one's organic nature and finds it merciful. Have you ever read Andy White's memoirs? He's the fellow who founded Cornell University. That was the period of euphoria, when everybody thought that all the good things in America were going to function, before the decline, about 1900. White covers a period of history that goes back to Buchanan on one side. He alternated between being Ambassador to Russia and head of Cornell.

INTERVIEWER: Your return to Italy has been a disappointment, then?

POUND: Undoubtedly. Europe was a shock. The shock of no longer feeling oneself in the center of something is probably part of it. Then there is the incomprehension, Europe's incomprehension, of organic America. There are so many things which I, as an American, cannot say to a European with any hope of being understood. Somebody said that I am the last American living the tragedy of Europe.

Index

COPYRIGHT ACKNOWLEDGMENTS

Grateful acknowledgment is made for permission to reprint the following:

The poems of Dylan Thomas. Copyright 1939, 1946 by New Directions Publishing Corporation. Reprinted by permission of New Directions Publishing Corporation and J. M. Dent and Sons, Ltd., London, England.

Lines from "Personae" by Ezra Pound. Copyright 1926 by Ezra Pound. Reprinted by permission of New Directions Publishing Corporation.

Lines from "The Cantos" of Ezra Pound. Copyright 1934, copyright © 1959, 1968 by Ezra Pound. Reprinted by permission of New Directions Publishing Corporation and Faber and Faber Ltd., London, England.

Lines from "Gaudier-Brzeska" by Ezra Pound. All rights reserved. Copyright © 1970 by Ezra Pound. Reprinted by permission of New Directions Publishing Corporation.

Lines from "Lady Lazarus" in *Ariel* by Sylvia Plath. Copyright © 1963 by Ted Hughes. Used by permission of Harper & Row, Publishers, Inc.

Excerpt from "Anne Sexton: Light Up the Cave" by Denise Levertov. First appeared in *The Real Paper,* Boston, Massachusetts. Reprinted by permission of the author.

Lines from "Transformations" from *Collected Poems of Thomas Hardy.* Copyright 1925 by Macmillan Publishing Co., Inc. and reprinted by permission of Macmillan Publishing Co., Inc., the Macmillan Co. of Canada, Ltd., and Macmillan Press, Ltd., Hampshire, England.

Lines from "The Waste Land" by T. S. Eliot are reprinted by permission of Harcourt Brace Jovanovich, Inc.

Excerpt from article by Harry Levin which originally appeared in the Boston *Globe,* July 26, 1972, issue. Reprinted by permission.

Excerpt from letter by Philip Toynbee reprinted by permission of the author and the *New Statesman.*

Excerpt from *Writers at Work: The Paris Review Interviews,* Second Series, edited by George Plimpton. Copyright © 1963 by The Paris Review, Inc. Reprinted by permission of The Viking Press.

Excerpt from letter to Donald Hall from James Laughlin is published by courtesy of Mr. James Laughlin.

Lines from *The Poetry of Robert Frost* edited by Edward Connery Lathem. Copyright 1923, 1930, 1939, © 1969 by Holt, Rinehart and Winston. Copyright 1951, © 1958 by Robert Frost. Copyright © 1967 by Lesley Frost Ballantine. Reprinted by permission of Holt, Rinehart and Winston Publishers.

Hall, Donald, 1928-

Remembering poets

DATE